The Volleyball Coaching Bible

VOLUME II

American Volleyball Coaches Association

Cecile Reynaud, Editor

Human Kinetics

Library of Congress Cataloging-in-Publication Data

The volleyball coaching bible / Cecile Reynaud, editor.
   p. cm.
1. Volleyball—Coaching. I. Reynaud, Cecile, 1953-.
GV1015.5.C63 V65 2002
796.325—dc21

2002007964

ISBN: 978-1-4504-9198-3 (print)

The web addresses cited in this text were current as of March 2015, unless otherwise noted.

Acquisitions Editor: Justin Klug; **Developmental Editor:** Anne Hall; **Associate Managing Editor:** Nicole Moore; **Copyeditor:** Patsy Fortney; **Graphic Designer:** Julie L. Denzer; **Cover Designer:** Keith Blomberg; **Photograph (cover):** AP Photo/Nati Harnik; **Photo (interior):** © Human Kinetics, unless otherwise noted; **Photo Asset Manager:** Laura Fitch; **Visual Production Assistant:** Joyce Brumfield; **Photo Production Manager:** Jason Allen; **Art Manager:** Kelly Hendren; **Associate Art Manager:** Alan L. Wilborn; **Illustrations:** © Human Kinetics; **Printer:** United Graphics

Human Kinetics books are available at special discounts for bulk purchase. Special editions or book excerpts can also be created to specification. For details, contact the Special Sales Manager at Human Kinetics.

Printed in the United States of America   10 9 8 7 6 5 4 3 2 1

The paper in this book is certified under a sustainable forestry program.

Human Kinetics
Website: www.HumanKinetics.com

United States: Human Kinetics
P.O. Box 5076
Champaign, IL 61825-5076
800-747-4457
e-mail: humank@hkusa.com

Canada: Human Kinetics
475 Devonshire Road Unit 100
Windsor, ON N8Y 2L5
800-465-7301 (in Canada only)
e-mail: info@hkcanada.com

Europe: Human Kinetics
107 Bradford Road
Stanningley
Leeds LS28 6AT, United Kingdom
+44 (0) 113 255 5665
e-mail: hk@hkeurope.com

Australia: Human Kinetics
57A Price Avenue
Lower Mitcham, South Australia 5062
08 8372 0999
e-mail: info@hkaustralia.com

New Zealand: Human Kinetics
P.O. Box 80
Torrens Park, South Australia 5062
0800 222 062
e-mail: info@hknewzealand.com

E6283

The Volleyball Coaching Bible

VOLUME II

Contents

Key to Diagrams

D ——————— Digger
L ——————— Libero
LB ——————— Left-back player
LF ——————— Left-front player
MH ——————— Middle hitter
MB ——————— Middle-back player
MF ——————— Middle-front player
OH ——————— Outside hitter
Opp ——————— Opposite
RB ——————— Right-back player
RF ——————— Right-front player
RH ——————— Right-side hitter
S/H ——————— Setter/Hitter
⬤ ——————— Floor marker
●—————● ——————— Net
⟶ ——————— Movement arrow

PART ONE

COACHING PRIORITIES

1

Sharing the Passion

John Kessel

The sport of volleyball, invented in 1895 at a YMCA in Holyoke, Massachusetts has gone on to become one of the most popular sports in the world. The inventor, William G. Morgan, would likely not recognize the sport today as a result of the modifications that have been made in over 100 years since he put down his first rules. He would, however, likely be amazed at the level of athleticism of the hundreds of millions of players around the world, and the level of passion the sport's fans have for the game he created.

This sport-for-a-lifetime, which you have chosen to share with others, has an international federation (the International Volleyball Federation [FIVB]) with members from 220 nations, whose motto is simple: Keep the ball flying. No other sport in the world boasts as many nations in its international community. USA Volleyball, one of the most respected national federations in the world, played a big part in bringing the game to the Olympics and in its success in those Olympics over the last 30 years. Americans involved in volleyball who go abroad are seen as leaders in the sport who know most or all of the secrets of the game. Many people also assume that Americans involved in volleyball know Karch Kiraly, the three-time U.S. gold medalist who was voted the world's best player in the sport's first 100 years by the FIVB. In October 2014, Kiraly coached the U.S. women's national team to its first gold medal in world competition in 62 years.

We hope, in your passion for volleyball, that you share the secrets, insights, and skills that have made the United States one of just two nations to qualify for every Olympics for three decades. Only 12 nations make the Olympiad every four years, and 208 nations stay home—and for 16 years, the United States was a spectator nation, competing in Mexico in 1968 and then not again until Los Angeles in 1984.

As coaches, one of our jobs is to teach parents and players alike about the many challenges that are special to playing volleyball. It is a rebound game, but we cannot go to the store to buy new and improved rebounding implements—such as new, ever-larger tennis rackets or golf clubs. We compete using our own bodies. We are the only people in the gym who know where the lost badminton birdies and prom balloons are, because we spend the majority of our time looking up—which is why we have to know where the court lines are kinesthetically. Ours is the only sport in which repeated maximal contact (spiking the ball) is done unsupported in the air. Imagine how good baseball hitters would be if they had to jump maximally before swinging the bat.

Because we rotate our positions constantly, we need to be all-around players—good at all skills and great at one or two. What would baseball or football be if, after every score, the players had to rotate to new positions? Volleyball is a noncontact sport with a net no one may touch, even though it is right where most of the action takes place. Every contact is judged in volleyball (do refs take points away if a quarterback throws a wobbly pass or a shooter makes a basket with a spinning ball?). We are allowed only three contacts before the ball must go over the net, so true team players in volleyball work very hard to "better the ball," knowing that errors are just part of the game and that their job is simply to improve the next contact, not complain about it. What would basketball be if players had to shoot after the third contact? What would volleyball be if fouls were allowed? Understanding these challenges allows all involved to realize how amazing the game is when played at any level, but especially when serves and spikes are traveling over 100 kilometers an hour (62 mph).

Here is a pretty amazing fact about our game: With contact times ranging between 0.008 and 0.1 seconds, depending on the skill (from spiking to setting), the average international player touches the ball less than a total of 30 seconds in an entire Olympic competition. This means that the most important skill in our sport is not technical; it is reading the game between contacts, anticipating, judging, and timing.

PRIMARY VERSIONS OF VOLLEYBALL

The three primary versions of our sport are the indoor 6v6 game, the sand (or grass) 2v2 outdoor game, and ParaVolley, which includes the most popular version being played sitting on the floor over a much lower net and smaller court. One of the most popular versions is coed; tens of thousands of coed competitions in all three disciplines are held annually. Personally, my second most favorite way to compete is in reverse coed, in which the net is at women's height and males play in the back row only (serving, digging, and attacking). The rallies are magnificent, and players of both sexes get to compete at full speed together. Go out and organize a reverse coed event at your school or in your program, and see what I am talking about!

Teach your players these three words: *citius, altius, fortius,* the Olympic motto in Latin, which means "swifter, higher, stronger." The key is the *er* part of each word, because there can be only one *est:* Olympism is about individually growing to be the best you can be. Some consider this a growth mind-set, to help athletes know what they can and cannot control in our team game, and to work to be as good as they can be, day after day.

A SPORT FOR A LIFETIME

It is more than symbolic that this first chapter shares ideas on collaborating to grow this sport-for-a-lifetime that first was known as mintonette. The inventor of the game, Morgan, worked with his fellow YMCA staffers and those playing the game to both rename the game and change the rules. Throughout its history, however, it has remained a sport-for-a-lifetime. When I work with 13U female players, who are starting to play with the women's net height, I let them know that they will be hitting every third hit over nets at this height for the next 52 years. Do you know that USA Volleyball has a 75 and over age group national championship, in addition to an 11 and under division? At every age, players must hit every first and third ball over the net. Consider posting a sign in your gym that says: "Use of the Court without Use of the Net Is Prohibited." Posters allow you to share the passion (USA Volleyball and the FIVB provide free skill and motivation posters on their websites).

This next May and June, take the time to create Mother's and Father's Day doubles tournaments. Over a decade ago, Leon Fell, the tournament director of Vail King of the Mountain (a doubles volleyball event held since the early 1970s), let me add father/daughter and father/son divisions on Father's Day. Today, the event has 18, 16, 14, 12, and 10 and under age divisions. Over 100 teams compete in pool play and then elimination competitions beneath Colorado's majestic Gore Range. In other states, the same is happening on Mother's Day. There is nothing quite like partnering up in competition with your child, regardless of your skill level.

YOU WILL BE A BETTER PLAYER IF YOU COACH

One of the best ways to get better at volleyball is to teach the sport to others less experienced than you are. Seneca the Younger, the Roman philosopher, understood this when he said, "While we teach, we learn." Mentoring and coaching is safe to do at any age in volleyball. In Asia, where amazing levels of play occur at the elementary school level, older kids spend half their time teaching volleyball to younger kids after school while the head coach watches. All over the South Pacific, the spirit of 'ohana, meaning "family," results in young children playing the game with their aunts, uncles, and grandparents. In Honolulu, nine Olympians came out of one program, which has three sand courts, one of which is a baby court with a lowered net. There, the youth of the Outrigger Canoe Club start playing at a very young age and are watched and mentored by adults.

If you are a coach, you should be a good storyteller. You see, you do not coach volleyball; you coach people—and people remember and learn better from stories. A Jewish proverb notes, "What is truer than truth? The story." Your parents read you bedtime stories to teach you about life, not to impart facts. By working on your storytelling skills, you can better share your volleyball passion.

An experience I had teaching volleyball taught me much about the importance of passion in our game. In 1995 I was working the World Games for the Special Olympics, teaching an athlete clinic with U.S. national men's team player Bryan Ivie. We were on the commons of the University of New Haven and had a couple of nets set up alongside playing areas for a dozen other sports. Special Olympians from 125 nations attended the Games, and the idea was to experience new sports, not just ones they came to compete in.

Some 20 athletes arrived at the start, many of whom did not speak English, to learn volleyball. We gestured to them to stand and watch, and I stood near the net and tossed a ball to Bryan's forehead. He said one word, "Superman," and overhead passed the ball to me. I said "Superman" and set him well off the net. He jumped lightly and spiked the ball over the lower net. We repeated the sequence three times; then gestured to the athletes to get in small lines. We repeated the overhead pass/set/spike with them and kept showing and saying "Superman," chasing their passes down and setting balls for them to hit. In less than five minutes, Special Olympians who had never played volleyball before were passing and hitting. The most important thing began to happen about 10 minutes in, when we heard other sports' coaches yelling, "Get back here; we aren't done!" Athlete after athlete stopped shooting baskets, putting, and fishing, and like moths to a light, gathered to wait their turns to spike a volleyball. This is a lesson for all who love the game: let everyone spike early and often; it is fun!

> ***One of*** the secrets to helping newcomers love our sport is to stop teaching the forearm pass first. I wish coaches and teachers who start their clinics with the statement "Can't pass, can't hit" would see the pained faces of first-timers as they return to the back of the traditional line drill. When newbies' first experience with volleyball is to strike a hard ball off their forearms, they go home and say to their parents: "This sadomasochist came to school today—um, do you have any ice for my bruised arms? Do I have to go back?" Please, when you go out to help grow the game, teach hitting and overhead passing first; then torque serving (which is in players' control and has the torque action that allows even young players to send the ball over the net). Only once they are hooked should you share the very odd skill of eye-to-forearm contact and deflecting a ball off the arms to a teammate.

In volleyball, as in other sports, the coach who knows why will beat the coach who knows how—and the same goes for players. As Ralph Waldo Emerson once put it: "The man who knows how will always have a job. The man who knows why will always be his boss." A love for this sport lasts longer when it comes from within, not from the coach. Guide your players' discovery, but do not give them the answers. They will have a better volleyball IQ for it.

Simply speaking, the game teaches the game. You know this already from learning a sport far more dangerous than volleyball: bike riding. You did not have a bike riding coach, nor were you sent to bike riding summer camp. You did not learn by doing bike riding drills or progressions, and for those who say, "But what about training wheels?" two things come to mind. First, the majority of bike riders around the globe did not learn with training wheels. Second, research shows that using training wheels slows the learning of riding an actual bike considerably.

> ***Those whom*** you coach also need to know one important part of you: your coaching philosophy. It needs to be written, and it needs to reflect why you coach. Keep it simple, post it to your online bio, and stick to it.

VOLLEYBALL AROUND THE GLOBE

I have taught coaches, teachers, and players in volleyball clinics in over 50 nations. In many nations, people don't have volleyballs or nets, but somehow they find a way to play the game. Players build their own balls from wrapped banana leaves or soft-sided drink containers wrapped with sliced tire inner tube bands. They make antennae from fishing poles or bamboo. They have a passion for volleyball and come up with ways to make the game happen. In the end, the game will find a way. This section shows some of the remarkable ways kids have found a way to play volleyball all around the globe.

Playing 1v1 over a tree limb in the Cook Islands.
Photo courtesy of John Kessel

Cook Islands lunchtime competition.

Photo courtesy of John Kessel

Vanuatu kids playing 3v3 with a rope net and bamboo for their standards.

Photo courtesy of John Kessel

U.S. Air Force Academy's Arnold Hall with 16 ParaVolley courts set up with ribbon nets and chairs with 50-pound free weights on the seats for standards and blue painter's tape to line the courts.

Photo courtesy of John Kessel

Ten and under division of King of the Mountain Doubles tournament on grass in Vail, Colorado.

Photo courtesy of John Kessel

South Carolina Palmetto Region: 2v2 monarch of the court game, losers-become-the-net version.

Photo courtesy of John Kessel

Using a net from another great sport and playing 1v1 with a 70-gram First Touch fabric ball.

Photo courtesy of Chris Vadala USAV

Get more nets up: Rope ribbon band or four nets on one rope with swim noodles for low-cost antenna.

Photo courtesy of John Kessel

ADAPTING EXISTING FACILITIES

Volleyball is often played in facilities that are not set up for the game. There are some simple ways to adapt them for our sport. Gyms have six basketball hoops (aka volleyball accuracy training devices in which players must send the ball without banking it), but often only one volleyball net. By putting a ribbon, rope, net band, or smaller nets on one long rope down the middle of the net, anchoring to 11-foot vertical ropes or standards tied next to the wall, you can set up nets of any height. You get four to six smaller courts for small-sided games and can also teach badminton, tennis, and sitting volleyball, other great lifetime sports.

There are three things you can do to help grow the game of volleyball at lightning speed. The first is to simply use the preceding net system on only half the main gym. This gives other athletes a chance to see how much fun it is to play volleyball, especially spiking.

The second thing you can do is get permission to leave one net up in a gym all the time. Although this is easier in larger gyms, it can be done even in two-court facilities. The point is, when a basketball player asks to check out a ball to shoot some hoops, a staff member need only hand over a ball. When a volleyball player asks to play, the staff member may sigh heavily and say, "You'll have to give me 20 minutes to set up the net." The solution is to have one padded net system permanently set up, and half-court basketball played there if needed, or to have the hoopsters take the net system down and then put it back up when they are finished. Currently, volleyball people have to get the basketball system out of the way, set up the net, and then return the court to basketball readiness. To move away from this expectation while not alienating others, don't ask to have the whole gym set up for volleyball, just one court. It makes a big difference in growing the game for all players to move away from this expectation while not alienating others.

The third thing you can do to help grow the game is not to cut players—at any age. The challenge of creating programming that gives everyone a chance to play comes from the long-term athletic development (LTAD) models, the goal of which is to decide slowly, keeping as many athletes playing as long as possible. We also need to accommodate players, providing practice or game sessions at earlier or later times, as swimming and ice hockey programs do. Create open programs during open gym times. Set up more courts: smaller ones on regular indoor courts; courts in unused racquetball, squash, and tennis courts; multiple linked courts on grass fields; or courts in cafeteria spaces. Give volleyball a chance to be a player's favorite sport.

Volleyball is a late specialization sport, as compared to sports such as gymnastics. Many people believe that athletes need to specialize in a sport early in life to succeed at that sport in college or professionally. However, only about one percent of high school players get college scholarships in their sports, so the best reason for participating in any sport, volleyball included, is for the life lessons to be learned. Specializing early is fine, if a person loves a specific sport. It is also fine to experience many sports and come to love a sport later.

Take a look at the "Late bloomer" Wikipedia entry at www.wikipedia.org/wiki/Late_bloomer to see an amazing list of those who found something they loved later in life. The following quiz is a fun test to find out some lesser-known facts about some of our most famous athletes. Specific to sport, see if you can match the following athletes to their sport backgrounds. The answers appear at the bottom.

The word *coach* comes from the term "carriage," a vehicle used to carry valuable people from where they were to where they wanted to be. This definition is still true of coaches: the more you empower your players to compete on the court without you, the better everyone else will be, because in the end, the coach never plays. For younger players, the Brazilians have a great statement: Your first coach should be the game. Too often, adults get far too involved with younger players learning the game, rather than letting them just create and figure things out through play, not drills. After all, did you learn to play tag by doing tag drills?

Please also take the time to teach the history of our sport—from its best players and teams, to the way the sport has risen from a single game at a YMCA in the United States to being one of the most popular participation and fan sports in both the Olympics and the Paralympics. USA Volleyball has a section on the history of the sport on its website: www.teamusa.org/USA-Volleyball/About-Us/Historical. Indeed, this organization has a SportKit DVD that you can get for just the cost of shipping, which contains drill and skill videos, books, articles, posters, and many ideas for teachers and coaches. If interested, check out the Grassroots section of the USA Volleyball website.

Match Quiz

A. Michael Jordan	1. Played only basketball in college at Arizona
B. Larry Walker	2. Was only 5'11" as a senior in high school
C. Kenny Lofton	3. Was not recruited out of high school
D. Cynthia Cooper	4. Wanted to be a pro ice hockey goalie, but was cut
E. Scottie Pippen	5. Did not start playing ball until 14 years old
F. Sammy Sosa	6. Did not start playing ball until 16 years old
G. Mark McGwire	7. Was an outstanding goalkeeper in soccer
H. Hakeem Olajuwon	8. Was a top college basketball player at UCLA
I. John Stockton	9. Was cut from his high school hoops team at 16 years old
J. Jackie Joyner-Kersee	10. Eyesight as a child was 20/500
K. Chris Drury	11. Pitched in the Little League World Series
L. Tom Brady	12. Played pro basketball before winning an Olympic medal in another team sport
M. Mike Whitmarsh	13. Drafted 199th yet by his fourth season had two Super Bowl MVP awards
N. Bart Starr	14. Drafted in the 17th round yet won seven league titles

A-9, B-4, C-1, D-6, E-2, F-5, G-10, H-7, I-3, J-8, K-11, L-13, M-12, N-14

CONCLUSION

In closing, I offer some final thoughts. The first is to follow a key part of doctors' Hippocratic Oath: *Primum non nocere*—"First do no harm." Another is to never be a child's last coach, thus to judge your "coaching" record by how many players keep playing volleyball after you are done teaching them. We are teaching what is perhaps the ultimate team game, and we need to make sure not to let the pleasure of competition be overtaken by the pressure of competition. Volleyball is such a joy to play; players love the fight as a team to keep the ball off the floor on their side and put it down on the other side. In practice and competition, help your players understand the randomness of the game: in the hundreds of millions of matches played since the creation of the sport, 50 percent of the teams lost. Likewise, the athletes you coach will spend about 50 percent of their time competing at a level below their average. This is just a fact. Your job is to raise that average, even though your athletes will play below it half the time. Be their biggest supporter, win or lose.

It is also important to ask lots more questions, to guide players' discovery, and give them hints without a rule. This form of teaching is remembered far better than being told what to do. Remember, players don't care how much you know until they know how much you care.

Finally, make a point of catching your players doing things right. Most coaches only seem to give feedback or attention after a player errs and ignore the times a player gets it right.

In the end, if you have shared the beauty and excitement of volleyball that is in your heart, and focused on the mastery of the game over the outcome, you will have players who love the game as much as you do. Then, you can truly measure your success as a coach—which is by never being a player's last coach.

2

Defining Expectations

Charlie Sullivan

Defining expectations is very important for any group attempting to work together to achieve the highest level possible. When all members are on the same page about what is expected, achieving goals is easier. For a leader not to communicate expectations is not fair. Whenever I bring my three children under the age of eight into a store, or when we go to church, I say, "OK, kids, here are the expectations." I do the same with my team. Expectations clarify for everyone what constitutes best behavior and give a leader credibility when a player does not achieve them. Identifying the expectations of being a team member in our program, and not assuming that everyone knows those expectations, is very important.

RELATIONSHIPS

The first expectation of our volleyball program at Springfield College in Massachusetts is that we work hard on developing relationships. For a team to play a championship level of volleyball, the players must get along and be able to work together. This may sound like a description of team cohesion, but there is more to it than that. This chapter will help you and your athletes develop great relationships that will help you all perform at your best. This has been the foundation of our program and any success we have had.

Coaches identify early on that the highest level of a relationship with their players is trust. The best way to develop trust is to communicate well and often. Therefore, early in every season, we identify times for our players to communicate with each other.

We tell our players that 75 percent of communication occurs through body language. We show them their body language on video and, without hearing their words, identify what they are communicating to other players. We also explain that they can probably know what someone is thinking or feeling by looking in their eyes—and that they should communicate with their eyes and look their teammates in the eyes. When I am talking to a player who is facing away from me, I sometimes reposition my body so we are facing each other and can see each other's eyes.

If I have to give a player instructions during a time-out in the fifth set of a national championship match at 13-13, I want 100 percent trust between me and that player. Maybe our scouting report had our zone 2 (right-side) blocker staying in tight versus the opponent's rotation 1. For the entire match, I might have reiterated to our zone 2 blocker to stay tight versus rotation 1, but now I want this blocker out wide. Without trust, if I give this player this instruction, he might doubt what I am saying and think I am insane. However, if the player trusts me, he might, without any hesitation, get into a spread-ready position and play the rally to the best of his ability. Without a trusting relationship, players cannot reach their potential.

What that player does not know and does not need to know at the time of the new instruction is that we saw the opponent substitute in a player who hit a great high ball in a previous match, and we anticipate that the setter will set him again. We want to make sure that our zone 2 blocker is in a good spot. It is best at that time to say, simply, "Hey, get wide and front that high ball." Ideally, the player will perform without hesitation, and we can trust that he is going to be in a good spot. This is why our coaching staff identifies trust as the highest level of a relationship.

Following is a list of communication expectations that our team developed for the 2014 season:

Team Trust

The highest level of a relationship is *trust*.

The best way to get there is *communication*.

Opportune times to communicate are during and between rallies.

Your list

Setter communication with hitters and reverse

Discuss block assignments before play

Call for set three times

Call for high ball sets in transition

Communicate front-row setter

Front row and back row discussing if they are taking line, seam, or cross

Back row talking about what defense they are in

Who has second contact on setter dig

Discussing hitter or server tendencies

Third blocker on three-man block calling three

Serve receivers discussing seam pre-serve

Calling "in" or "out" for serves

Calling "up" when player digs a ball

Calling "I got it"

Compliment and encourage—stay positive

How to communicate

Huddle between rallies—all in, 100%

Positive body language

Positive communication with one another

Talking before, during, and after plays

Tone can affect communication

Not getting upset when a mistake occurs or a teammate is performing well. Pick up your teammate for the next rally.

Communicate through effort and work ethic

Make a play

Negative criticism is not acceptable

Drill to Foster Team Communication

This drill works on communication and trust. Three serve receivers are on the court with a setter, and a few players serve into that group of four. The players receive a serve and run an audible offense. Of the three players who receive the serve, the person who passes the ball is required to hit a back-row attack. Of the two remaining players, the one farther left on the court runs a quick attack or a fast tempo in the middle of the net, and the one farther right runs an attack on either antenna. The players who are farther right and left vary depending on which of the three players passes the ball. You can vary the responsibilities to modify the drill. The player who passes could be on a pin, the one farther left could be back row, and the one farther right could be the quick attack. All this takes place in a split second. The setter must listen to the play sets that players are calling and make a great set.

This drill is usually total chaos at first, but as players improve their communication during the season, it gets smoother. We use it to observe our progress during the season and to admire how our relationships have grown, especially during our championship month of April!

EXPECTATIONS DEFINED

After teaching players to communicate, the next step in getting everyone in the program on the same page is to share a list of expectations with the players. In recent years the list has grown to include social media expectations to reflect the current generation. If a problem arises during a season and I realize that I did not communicate how disappointed I was in that action, I add it to my expectations list for the following season. Our list of expectations includes some seemingly mundane things such as the expectation that all players on the men's volleyball team say hello to all faculty members when they see them on campus. This is an old policy at Springfield College that we want to continue. Following are our players' expectations for the 2014 season. You will have your own list of expectations that pertains to your program, but this can serve as a model.

Overall Rules to Live By

Do not do anything that will represent yourself, your family, Springfield College, and the Men's Volleyball team in a negative fashion.

Discipline is doing the right thing in the best possible manner at the correct time, and that is not such a bad thing.

You might be thinking that if you have expectations, you will need consequences. For a variety of reasons, I do not agree. I state in my expectations that failure to comply with any of them will require a meeting with the head coach, at which time disciplinary decisions will be made. We work hard to recruit players who are not only great volleyball players, but also great people. We explain that we trust that they will make the right decisions and give them our trust until they give us a reason not to trust them. Therefore, we do not anticipate any of our players having trouble with our expectations list. We let them know the expectations during the recruiting process, and if they do not think they can live up to them, we probably will not have them in our program. With that said, we handle discipline issues on a case-by-case basis because every situation is unique and we do not want to be boxed into taking actions we are not sure will be best based on the situation.

TEAM HANDBOOK

The next step we take in defining expectations and communicating all facets of the program to our players is publishing an annual team handbook. My favorite section of the handbook is "Defining a Springfield College Volleyball Player," which explains how to act to be a great player in our program. I love this section because it is an open invitation to greatness. I love it more when players take us up on the offer and choose what to put in the list. A couple of examples of what it takes to be a great player would be "attends all classes and completes all homework assignments" or "sits in the front row of all his or her classes." I highly recommend a similar list for your players.

Our team handbook includes my coaching philosophy, because my decisions are based on it. If a team's philosophy is to run a quick offense to the pins, then the setter should not need to ask what tempo to set the ball at from the attack line.

Springfield College Men's Volleyball Player Expectations

1. Players are expected to be knowledgeable and abide by all alcohol and drug policies as stated in the student handbook.

2. Players are expected to be knowledgeable and abide by the rights and responsibility section of the student handbook under resident life.

3. Players are expected to never use the excuse of "I did not know" in reference to the consequences of discipline determined by the Dean of Students office as a result of their violation.

4. Players are expected not to get written up, and Coach Sullivan does not condone the use of drugs and alcohol.

5. Players are expected to represent themselves, their families, and the SC Men's Volleyball program in an exceptional manner in everything they do including competition, classes, behavior in the dorms, working women's matches, and off-campus events.

6. Players are expected to attend all classes and meet with professors in advance to make up classes that will be missed due to away matches.

7. Players are expected not to post inappropriate photos on any Facebook or online personal page that they have. Springfield College Dean of Students has the right to take disciplinary action based on photos on students' personal web pages.

8. Players must be at the first practice in January and after spring break.

9. First-year players must have a completed grade chart and present it to Coach Sullivan every two weeks.

10. Players are expected to aid in the recruiting process by entertaining recruits during visits to campus.

11. Players are responsible for checking their email daily to receive important communication from the head coach.

12. When players are communicating through social media, it is expected that any message will not represent the program in a negative manner.

13. Players are responsible for contributing positively to team cohesion in an attempt to facilitate the program performance at its highest potential.

14. At Springfield College athletic events, team members are expected to represent themselves, their families, and the college by cheering for SC athletes only.

15. Volleyball players are expected to greet faculty members on campus.

16. Players are expected not to go on "spring break trips" in March.

17. Failure to comply with these policies will result in a meeting with the head coach. Discipline decisions will be made by the head coach.

The answer is implicit in the team's philosophy. The same is true of my coaching philosophy. The players should know how I will react based on my philosophy and how I approach coaching.

I was moved to write my coaching philosophy by one of the greatest coaches in men's volleyball history, Tom Hay, who coached the men's and women's teams at Springfield College. He was instrumental in developing the EIVA men's conference on the East Coast and is enshrined in the EIVA Hall of Fame. Unfortunately, Coach Hay passed in my second year of being the head coach at Springfield College. At his wake, among photos and memorabilia, Coach's family had posted his coaching philosophy. Not only was it remarkable in content, but it also made me wonder how I could expect to make daily coaching decisions without a standard as to the reason why? As Coach Hay did for so many people, he inspired me to build better relationships, to communicate more effectively, to define expectations more clearly, and to be a better coach. Thanks, Coach!

PLAYER EVALUATIONS

We want to be clear to our players how they are going to be evaluated in our program. Our team handbook includes all the categories in each position on which players will be evaluated, as well as general qualities such as respect, communication, and work ethic. These lists include subjective and objective categories. Again, if the players know our expectations and how they will be evaluated, they can choose to work hard in those categories. We have a spreadsheet that we share with the players before the season begins. Every position has the same set of eight subjective evaluation categories, so that all players are evaluated equally. Each position then has a set of objective evaluation categories that pertain to the position. The players are rated 1, 2, or 3 in each category.

We use our evaluation forms to ignite some great communications and build trusting relationships. We have the players fill out the forms rating their own performances in each category. Then, as the head coach, I rate each player. Sometimes I rate the players with my entire coaching staff, or the player and each coach rate the player in all the categories separately. However you choose to do it, the great moment is when players compare their completed forms to yours. That can stimulate some great conversations and literally get everyone on the same page. A player might have rated himself a 1 in serve receive, and I might have rated him a 2. He may believe that he performs the serve receive at a high level, and he learns that we think a bit differently. In evaluations, we listen to the player's perspective, give our own views, and leave the meeting on the same page with the next steps outlined for working to achieve the player's potential.

These meetings can be quick if we are all on the same page, or they can be a bit longer if we need to work out some confusion or define expectations more clearly. Sometimes we have the whole team go through the evaluation process together; players who are struggling or need more communication go through the process individually.

We also use the evaluation form to get a statistical comparison between two players. If two setters are battling it out for a starting position and it is very close, the coaches may meet and give each player a rating in each category and then compare them. Coaches can also take into consideration one category that might be more significant than another. For the setter position, for example, one setter may serve and block better than the other, but the other setter may win every drill in practice. A variety of issues may need to be taken into consideration. We find the evaluation form to be great for both defining expectations and communicating.

POSITIONAL MEETINGS

Positional meetings are yet another way to communicate with players. We plan these meetings for every two weeks, but weekly meetings are most effective. A positional meeting is a great time for communicating to everyone in the position and the individual players as well. We first go over things that are going well in the position and then move on to any problems and the things we need to improve to play championship-level volleyball.

The last thing we do in a positional meeting is give each player a ranking in the position. It is not an easy conversation sometimes, but it is a good one. If there are four guys in a position, we say very directly, "You are number one, you are the second-ranked player, you are the third, and you are the fourth." Then we give our reasons for ranking them this way and explain what each player needs to do to move up in the ranking as well as things he needs to do to maintain his current position. These meetings get everyone on the same page and help players accept their roles. The players who are lower in rank know what they have to do to move up and do not feel hopeless. We also give the players who are lower in rank an opportunity to come to practice early to work on some fundamentals to improve their performances. This keeps everyone engaged in the program, everyone knows his role, and the quality of our relationships improves. Things always feel better after these meetings.

Sometimes you just need a quick conversation with a player. This can take place before practice while players are warming up. Taking time to check in with a player, ask how his classes are going, or tell him something you liked about his performance in practice yesterday is valuable. In our program we can always talk about the statistics because we take statistics in every practice and e-mail them to the players every night. The players have a chance to see the statistics along with the coaching staff and get feedback about their performances.

STATISTICS

Ultimately, the bottom line in any program is the product, the numbers, effectiveness in competitions—in other words, the results. That's the reality. Websites give results after matches. Society is product driven. When my six-year-old daughter gets out of the car in her neon orange soccer uniform, my neighbor, who is the nicest person in the world, inevitably asks a terrible question, "Did you win?" Really, is that what these youth sport performers should be worried about? There are so many variables that go into a youth soccer game, and I am not sure the reliable measure of my daughter's performance is a win or loss. Nonetheless, this is the world we live in, so we must learn to excel in this world.

Three Objectives of Statistics

The three objectives we have when using statistics are as follows:

As an indicator of the level at which we are performing. Statistical goals are in the team handbook, so all players should know the statistical level at which we need to perform for each skill. If these vary by position, then the players in the position need to know the differences for their position. Therefore, we can look at the statistics per skill and per position and know what we need to work on and what is going well.

As a goal. If we achieve established levels of performance, our chances of winning volleyball matches increase substantially. Therefore, we use statistics to see where we stand vis a vis our goals. The more we achieve these goals, the closer we are to playing championship-level volleyball.

As motivation to work hard to achieve them and as motivation to compete against other players. Players know that if they are playing well, their chances of playing more increase. When we rank players statistically, we are communicating very clearly that we value those who can compete and win in our program. Players need to learn to compete in practice so that they are prepared for competition.

Process

We preach the process in our program at Springfield College, although you may not believe that we are process oriented if you looked at our preparation. Even though we use statistics a lot, we want our players to focus on the process more than the product. However, we confront them with a lot of product (i.e., statistics) to help them practice ignoring this distraction. If they work daily on eliminating the distraction of the statistical product, then they are more equipped to do so on the most important days of the year, match days. Our players see their statistics daily after practice. Some days we rank players in comparison to the other players in their position, both in terms of skills and overall. This is a lot of product for players to deal with. In reality, the players who do the best are those who can focus on the process, their self-talk, or a simple fundamental skill, and let their errors pass them by. These are the players who finish statistically higher. Although it is not easy, when our players focus on the process, our team competes better.

The best example of focusing on the process is that of a player in our program who graduated in 2007 who I will call "Joe." In his junior season, Joe had started as an outside hitter on our national championship team. In his senior year, Joe got beaten out by a freshman. No longer on the starting team, Joe practiced with the second team daily and became totally immersed in the process and all the behaviors and thoughts he needed for playing at his best. He became more focused, he got better, and we noticed that statistically he was competing better and better all the time. We qualified as one of the four teams in the national championship, and in the few games prior to those matches, Joe came off the bench and was a spark in helping our team play better. In the semifinal match, we were struggling a bit, and here came superman. He ran in from the bench, subbed in, and immediately added a process orientation to our team that eliminated the distraction of playing for goals. This helped our team bring the level of play up. We fortunately won that match, and on the morning of the national championship match, it was a surprise to no one that Joe was our starting outside hitter. Joe had become the master of process orientation and focus and was able to eliminate the distraction of this national championship product that other players had fallen victim to. Joe's performance is still vivid in my mind. I mostly remember the strategies he developed to focus on process rather than product in his daily practice.

CONCLUSION

Building trusting relationships results in consistent behavior, as well as a great team personality. With this foundation, our players are on their way to achieving their potential and achieving our goal of playing what we call championship-level volleyball. What fun!

Our team works all season long on communicating and building relationships, and expectations are continually defined. Without this foundation, our opportunities for success diminish.

3

Developing a Positive Team Culture

Becky Schmidt

Think back to a time when you worked hard, had fun, learned a lot, and achieved at a high level. What characterized that environment? What characterized the relationships you had with your peers? Your leader? Seldom do people look back and recall these times as easy, but they also don't describe them as negative. A balance exists on teams that reach their potential—between challenge and skill, criticism and encouragement, trust and accountability, fun and focus, as well as between team and individual. How you, as a coach, facilitate the balance of these factors, both in your relationships with your athletes and in the way they relate to each other and the environment, is where the art of coaching is found.

The aspects of your program on which you have some influence are all based on relationships. The effectiveness of the drills you choose or the tactics you employ is based, in part, on the strength of your relationships with your players. The selflessness and team focus of your players are influenced, in part, by their relationships with each other. Their ability to be engaged in the moment and focus on the task at hand is facilitated, in part, by their relationships with their training and competitive environment. Although these relationships are sometimes difficult to control, they are certainly open to being influenced by the head coach.

BALANCE OF CHALLENGE AND SKILL

You may remember a time competing, as a player or as a coach, when you got lost in the moment. Time was transformed, your movement felt effortless, your focus was precise, and your performance was exemplary. In short, the experience was perfect, and somewhat elusive. We might remember these moments so clearly because they don't happen that often. Important research was conducted by Mihaly Csikszentmihalyi in the late 20th century to investigate why these "flow" experiences happen and how they can happen more often. An important factor in their occurrence is the balance between the challenge presented by the context of the game or training environment and the skill level of the athletes involved. If the opponent or drill is too challenging for the participant based on skill level, frustration is likely to prevent a good performance. Likewise, if the contest or drill is too easy or simple for a team, boredom will prevent the athletes from having motivation to achieve optimal performance. The key is to manipulate the competitive and training environments to keep the balance of challenge and skill appropriate to maintain maximal motivation.

Coach–Player

As the coach, you have control over the drills you build into practice, the level of performance you demand, the way you structure groups and teams, and the level of competition in the nonleague portion of your schedule. The first task in an effort to achieve balance between challenge and skill is to evaluate your talent. At what skills do the players on your team demonstrate proficiency, and where are they weak? At what point do the skills at which they are proficient begin to break down? Evaluating these factors will help you find the sweet spot in training where athletes will experience enough challenge to feel pushed but also enough success to remain confident.

Another factor contributing to the balance of challenge and skill is the way athletes and coaches interpret failure. After all, the negativity that comes with frustration is rooted in the perception that failure is a bad thing. One of the common characteristics of training programs that elicit the most success from their performers is that failure is not something to be feared. In fact, failure is appreciated because it means that participants are willing to risk and to push themselves outside of their comfort zones to improve. People who fear failure attempt only the things they can already do. The player who fears failure and can attack very well crosscourt will focus only on her crosscourt attack, limiting the opportunity to develop her line shot. If you, as a coach, focus on failure (by either calling attention to it or punishing it), then you will end up fostering a mind-set that prevents risk taking and limits growth. Table 3.1 provides examples of how to manipulate the training and competitive environments to create a balance of challenge and skill to encourage peak performance.

Player–Player

A positive team climate is not just dependent on the relationships between the players and coaches: it is one in which the players have a positive influence on each other. But how can players influence the balance between challenge and skill for each other? The answer comes in the way the team is grouped and how team members take responsibility for each other. At Hope College in Michigan, where I coach, I often structure scrimmage teams so that the top front-row players are attacking against the top back-row players. This makes it so that players who need more developmental work in the back row are digging balls against a front row

TABLE 3.1   Training to Encourage Peak Performance

To reduce challenge		To increase challenge
• Slow down the drill. • Have a specific focus that is under the athlete's control. • Decrease the standard.	Skill development	• Speed up the drill. • Increase the number of stimuli. • Increase the standard.
• Control the rally to focus on only specific tactical criteria. • Reward winning the rally regardless of tactics. • Reduce environmental distractions.	Tactical execution	• Create a more gamelike environment. • Reward tactical execution. • Add environmental distractions.
• Create homogeneous groups. • Create a smaller team.	Team building	• Increase the diversity of personality types and backgrounds. • Increase team size.
• Reduce the competitive level. • Evaluate performance on a singular focus that is within the team's control (i.e., effort).	Competitive performance	• Play up into a more competitive age bracket or division. • Evaluate performance on multiple or more complicated factors.

that is also working on developing skills. Both groups are playing with and against teammates in ways that are developmentally appropriate.

On occasion, ignoring developmental level when grouping players can be incredibly positive. I worked with a volleyball club that would do position-specific practice with players from every age group on the same court by position. Experienced and talented 18-year-olds were grouped with 14-year-old novices. The challenge–skill balance was maintained because the experienced players were tasked with being good models of fundamental techniques for the younger players and with providing peer instruction. The younger players were encouraged to focus on the process (technique) rather than the result.

Player–Environment

Another way that we try to promote a balance of challenge and skill is to make sure that our players understand the big picture of our training. We use a whiteboard at practice to share our practice plan, the focus points and goals of each drill, and where our players are supposed to go. This helps players identify how the skills developed early in practice will prepare them for performance in the scrimmages later on. It identifies coaching cues and focus points that our staff will be verbalizing during the drills. The whiteboard also helps us track our performance in drills over time, which facilitates setting appropriate goals and standards. For instance, we do a crosscourt ball-control exchange drill in which players try to take a specific number of aggressive swings in five minutes. We keep the highest scores in that drill in the corner of our whiteboard as a reminder of the standard and players' past achievements.

BALANCE OF CRITICISM AND ENCOURAGEMENT

A positive team climate is one in which athletes improve their ability and learn more about their potential. The feedback they receive from their coaches, each other, and the environment contributes to both of these objectives. Telling players what they do well, although positive, does not help them maximize their skills. Focusing on the negative, for most athletes, results in frustration and decreased self-confidence. Again, the coach's task is to find a balance between the two as well as provide multiple sources of feedback.

Coach-Player

In my experience, athletes desire two types of feedback from their coaches:

- ◆ To be acknowledged when they do something well
- ◆ To be told specifically how to improve when they fail

At Hope College we want our coaches working hard to provide both types of feedback. We want to acknowledge and celebrate when our athletes succeed, both in result and process. I went through a phase in my coaching when I felt as though telling players "great pass" after getting the ball to target was redundant. They could see that the pass was perfect and didn't need me to tell them. I found that my athletes appreciated my praising their passes (or any other obvious demonstrations of skill) because pleasing me was important to them. This is further demonstrated in how often my players ask, "Coach, did you see that?" when they achieve success at something they have been working on. The athlete knows that she was successful, but she wants to share that success with me.

In addition to praising successful execution, we also want to praise successful process. Specific feedback on techniques that improve athletes' chances of success or attempts that are outside their comfort zones are worthy of encouragement. It helps to know exactly what your players are working to improve, so that you can give appropriate feedback when you see them make progress. Write down their goals or objectives, as well as the areas in which you would like to see them improve, and carry it with you during practice. Sharing those goals with your assistant coaches will keep will keep them engaged and help them know where they can make a contribution.

When I realized that praising both success and progress toward goals was valued by my players, I also realized that I could be much more specific than just saying, "Great pass." We don't have a lot of time to convey a lot of information, so we use specific cues to convey exactly what led to the success. During one afternoon of our preseason, we spend a couple of hours in volley-school (an idea taken from the U.S. national team program), in which we explain all of the coaching cues our staff uses and exactly what each word means. This cuts down on needing to use whole sentences to explain the specifics of what the athlete did well or poorly; we need only one or two words that are well understood. We use words such as *balance*, *square*, *plant*, and *press* to convey specific aspects of skills quickly. You can use instructional feedback with motivational feedback to let your athletes know specifically what led to their positive results. Have a manager track the type of feedback you provide to see whether you are as positive, specific, and motivational as you can be.

The Positive Coaching Alliance (www.positivecoach.org) uses the phrase *emotional gas tanks* to convey athlete's emotional health. Praise, instruction, opportunity, and positive body language add to the emotional gas tank of an athlete. Criticism, punishment, and decreased opportunity result in emotional gas tank withdrawals. Keeping an eye on the emotional gas tank of each player on the team (how often you have made additions and how often you have made withdrawals) will help you predict how they will respond to the feedback. This is not to say that you should never make a withdrawal. Sometimes it is important to be critical, to uphold a standard, or to let athletes know that their behavior, attitude, or effort is unacceptable. However, in those situations, unless significant investments have been made, their motivation or self-confidence may diminish.

Player–Player

Players sometimes receive feedback from teammates more easily than from coaches. Such feedback can feel less threatening and also increase trust between teammates who are competing for the same position. We have developed a culture in which peer feedback is an important part of our program. The foundation is a lack of hierarchy within our team. For instance, we do not want our seniors to believe that they are any more important than our freshmen, or for sophomores to believe that they have any less value than juniors. We encourage our freshmen to give advice to seniors when they see an opportunity, and we ask our seniors to take the advice that they get from anyone with an outsider's perspective regardless of year.

In our program, the first 15 to 20 seconds of time-outs involve players getting into position groups so that the players on the bench can tell the players on the floor what they are seeing. This also gives the coaches a few seconds to meet and put together a cohesive, concise message for the entire team. For drill work in practice situations, we break up the team into smaller groups; while one group is performing the drill, another is positioned to give feedback. When we are working on blocking, one player says yes or no to communicate whether the middle closes the block, another player along the net says yes or no regarding the blocker's hands getting over the net, and another player identifies whether the block is timed correctly with the attack. The goal for the blockers, regardless of the result of the block, is to get three yeses from the players giving feedback. How can you strategically position your players who are not involved in drill so that they can provide valuable feedback to the players in the drill?

In a drill we call hot seat, which is a 6v6 scrimmage, one player is designated as the only one who can score a kill. One of our players did so well in that drill that a teammate bought a little red stool and wrote *hot seat* on it and put it in her teammate's locker to call attention to her great performance. When another teammate had a strong practice the next day, the first recipient of the hot seat passed it to her. Now, the little red stool moves from locker to locker as the previous recipient tries to identify the teammate who had the most impressive practice of the day. Such peer recognition goes a long way to build a team culture of encouragement, success, and positivity.

Player–Environment

Coaches can use video to provide important feedback in a way that builds motivation and confidence and increases effort. Many athletes are visual learners and benefit from seeing themselves perform. Technological advances have made access to video information very easy. We use an iPad app called BaM Video Delay to create a live delay on an iPad attached to a tripod. The delay is perfectly timed so that an athlete can perform a repetition in a drill, exit the drill, and watch her execution while a teammate performs the same drill on camera. The visual feedback allows players to see what they are doing correctly and incorrectly while also giving them the opportunity to experiment with a variety of techniques.

Videos of match play can also show players successful and problematic behaviors. Take advantage of available camera angles to focus on specific aspects of the game. For instance, if you can film only from the center line, focus on block penetration or the distance of the set off the net. When filming from behind the court, focus on blocking footwork and set distance. Be sure to focus on both positives and things to work on. Recently, as we were getting ready to watch a film of our serve-receive patterns from a match we had lost, I chose to show only the clips we had won. Seeing themselves succeed gave the players confidence in their ability to excel in their next match. Although this strategy worked in this situation, it shouldn't be the norm; it is important for teams to understand the reality of failure and to learn from those opportunities rather than disregard them.

BALANCE OF TRUST AND ACCOUNTABILITY

A positive team climate is one in which there is trust among coaches, players, and the administration. In the brilliant leadership fable *The Five Dysfunctions of a Team*, Patrick Lencioni states: "Great teams do not hold back with one another. They are unafraid to air their dirty laundry. They admit their mistakes, their weaknesses, and their concerns without fear of reprisal" (2002, p. 44). When trust is developed among all members of the program (including parents in high school programs), an environment is created that allows everyone to take risks that help them reach their potential. When trust is held in high esteem, accountability to the standards is more likely to happen because coaches and players do not fear losing the relationship. This section focuses on developing trust between coaches and players, but I believe that trust is important to cultivate with administrators, staff, and parents as well. Trust is developed by doing two things: being clear in your expectations and being a good listener.

Coach–Player

We do a number of things to develop trust between our coaches and players, but it starts with hard work. None of our players second-guess the importance we place on the success we are trying to achieve because they know how hard we work. This work ethic is demonstrated through the level of detail in our practice plans and scouting reports, the organization of team trips, and the support we show to our athletes off the volleyball court (e.g., we keep a calendar of all our players' exams and research paper due dates so that we can check in to see how their classes are going).

Our work ethic extends to the relationships we build with our players. Each member of the coaching staff reaches out to players individually. Although, as head coach, I need to develop a relationship with each player, some players may resonate with another member of the coaching staff on a more personal level. We have tried to make sure our coaching staff is diverse in personality so that every player will have at least one member of the staff with whom she feels a connection.

We ask our players for input on drill suggestions through our weekly goal sheets and provide written feedback on those sheets about the progress we see them making. We ask our players (especially our leaders) to share their opinions on a variety of decisions we make. This is because we believe that players don't necessarily need to have their way, but they need to feel heard. In the end, my team knows that I make the final decision and that the decision is based on my experience and long-term vision for the program's success.

Player–Player

As a coach, I am around my team for approximately two hours a day during the season. Teammates, on the other hand, are around each other in that same time frame as well as in some classes, in dorms and apartments, in the locker room, and during treatments and in the weight room. In short, they are around each other much more than I am. Developing a program in which trust and accountability are developed among players extends a positive team climate to the areas outside of the gym walls and the presence of a coach.

We have a team meeting in the third week of every season in which every player shares the role she sees herself playing. The meeting then opens up and all members of the team share what they appreciate about their teammates as well as what they need more of from them. It took a few years for this conversation to be as honest as it needs to be, so don't get too frustrated if during the first couple of years nothing is shared or it becomes a "love fest" without any real substance. Once something has been brought up, whether good or bad, acknowledge it and continue to reinforce that everyone is a part of the team to help each other reach their potential.

On our team we have an accountability program in which we pair each underclassman with an upperclassman (we call them sisters). These partners pair up with each other in the weight room, eat meals and room together on road trips (at least the first one), provide notes or gifts of encouragement to each other on match days, and look out for each other. When one of my players seems to be having a rough day, I ask her directly if everything is OK. Typically, I get an answer such as, "Oh yeah, Coach… everything is fine," but with incongruent body language, intonation, and tone. This tells me that I still have work to do to develop that player's trust in me. In these situations, I go to the player's sister to see if she knows what is going on. I don't ask that player to break confidence with me unless she thinks the issue is not a big deal to share (stressful week versus problems with her boyfriend), but I do make sure that the player is getting the support and love she needs. I then talk to the captains to make sure they are looking out for the player. The same process happens when I need more from a player. Her sister on the team (and the captains) has a role in providing encouragement and accountability.

The most important criterion for pairing accountability partners is to pair older players with younger players, but then it comes down to personality. Don't put complete opposites together, but don't put those who are extremely similar together either. They shouldn't already be close friends (or best friends if your team is small), but they should have something about their personality in common. In this way, they can use their common trait to encourage each other and hold each other accountable in the areas in which they may be weak.

Player–Environment

The most important aspect of trust between players and their environment is safety. In no way can players give maximal effort if they fear for their safety. Prophylactic ankle bracing, pads on the poles and a free-zone clear of obstacles, proper instruction and coaching in the weight room, and ample water and rest breaks help to meet the most basic needs of your players so that they feel safe in their environment.

Environment goes beyond space and equipment. Coaches who do not trust their administrators might choose to play it safe and not take the risks that result in realizing their teams' potential. Trust applies to other staff as well, such as athletic trainers, strength and conditioning coaches, and teachers. Look for ways to inform these groups and seek their opinions on decisions that they will have responsibility in implementing.

We do not have a strength and conditioning coach (other than me and my assistants), but I meet with our athletic trainers to see if there are any program-wide chronic injuries that can be reduced through off-season training. I respect their opinion, and, in turn, they have increased trust in the way we work together to develop our athletes. In his video *Team Toughness Trojan Style* (Championship Productions, 2009), Mike Voight shares how Mick Haley (head coach at the University of Southern California) refers to the entire team of coaches, nutritionists, administrators, and athletic trainers as the performance team and actively seeks their support and insight into helping realize the team's potential. Who is on your performance team, and how can you cultivate trust so that they feel valued, respected, and influential in your program? Do parents belong on your performance team?

Parents are important. In the lives of millennial athletes, parents are typically seen as close friends, and they have a much more open relationship with their children than in any previous generation. This is both good and bad. Youth seek the counsel of more experienced adults on important issues, but today's parents often struggle with using tough love and withholding praise that is not earned. If parents don't trust the coach, they will likely undermine the coach's efforts in the minivan on the way home from practice, in the stands with other parents, or around the dinner table. This issue is just as important for the college coach as for the high school and middle school coach. If the college coach doesn't establish trust with parents, the parents will not send their children to that college. If a high school or middle school coach does not establish trust with parents, the athletic director will receive calls from disgruntled parents (another reason to have the AD on your performance team). Establish clear boundaries between you and parents to empower their children and teach them self-reliance, but keep parents informed of what is going on in the program—especially when you see their son or daughter growing or making a contribution. You might be surprised at how powerful a short note or e-mail can be for keeping parents on your side even when you are practicing some tough love with their children—they will probably be relieved that it is you doing it and not them.

BALANCE OF FUN AND FOCUS

Positive environments are those that stimulate the senses and get teams' competitive juices flowing. Sometimes, however, overstimulation can decrease an athlete's ability to focus on the task at hand. Demonstrating consistency and understanding, valuing your players for the fun and focus they bring to the court, and handling the training and competitive environments well can help your players navigate this balance.

Coach–Player

A coach's first job is to identify the ways the team has fun. Sport psychology research tells us that we experience pleasure in sport participation mainly from the stimulation of the game itself, the feeling of accomplishing a difficult goal, and the enjoyment of learning a new task. Because these things resonate with your athletes differently, it is important that you use all three to provide enjoyment for everyone. Simply asking the question, "What do you love about the game of volleyball?" should give you a better understanding of the type of enjoyment that results in maximal motivation.

It is important to acknowledge (and I do this with my team) that I find the driven pursuit of winning to be the way I define having fun. Although this may be a different definition than my team might use, it speaks to a bias that I hold for behaviors that I encourage and those that I don't. Head coaches need a clear understanding of where to set the standard that determines when focus is lost. However, they also must know when too much detailed focus is preventing players from enjoying their participation and reducing the effort they put into the process.

The LA Lakers and Chicago Bulls, coached under Phil Jackson, were known for the triangle offense and the incredible talent that comprised their NBA championship teams. Often, Jackson would allow his players to use their talents in a free-form offense, but all it took was a whistle from him and they would return to running the detail-dependent triangle offense. Just as Jackson knew when to allow his players to play and when to have them perform, you too must know where to strike the balance. It is important to remain consistent in this understanding. Don't leave your players guessing when it is OK to loosen up and when they need to buckle down. It is also important that you not let your mood drive where you hold these standards. Being consistent will result in your players having the exact mind-set that you want from them.

We have taken a lesson from the way the U.S. women's national team breaks up practice to clearly define the learning objectives. During the training block that I observed, part of the practice was spent in a doubles tournament with the coaches keeping track of the winning and losing records of each team. Part of the time was spent in "school" (e.g., attacking school, passing school, blocking school), in which the athletes had a detailed focus on skills they were trying to develop, received precise feedback from coaches, and had no penalties for failure because the intent of the session was to develop a skill in which they were not yet proficient. The last part of the practice involved modified scrimmage and team play, in which there was more to focus on, but there were consequences for the team that lost or didn't meet the standard. We have tried to bring a similar structure to our gym so that the athletes know what is expected of them at every phase of practice.

On occasion, we like to make having fun a higher priority than developing volleyball skills. It breaks up the monotony during a long season, develops relationships among teammates, and brings a sense of perspective to the athletes (and the coaches). We play some warm-up games that have very little to do with volleyball. One of the favorites with my team is volleyball soccer, in which two teams are divided on a basketball court (no net) trying to use volleyball skills to advance the ball and score a goal (attacking the ball against a mat under the basketball hoop). The game is out of control, but it is high energy and involves lots of laughing. Although such a game might last only 5 to 15 minutes, once or twice a season we run a pyramid practice that consists entirely of playing games. It starts with volleyball tennis (1v1 with one contact), and all players keep track of their wins. After 10 minutes (there's usually a lot of standing around so we don't do this game for very long) the players arrange themselves on a line corresponding to the number of wins they achieved. We then pair the player with the most wins with the player with the fewest wins for a doubles tournament. We then move to triples, quads, fives, and finally sixes. Each time, the players get reassigned to teams based on their personal win total throughout the day. The focus of this session is learning how to compete and find ways to win while having a lot of fun.

Player–Player

We try to recruit players who demonstrate a balance of fun and focus in the way they practice and compete. We like to see them smile, joke around with their teammates (when the moment is right), keep their heads held high, and stand tall with confidence. We look at how our recruits interact with their parents and coaches, how much they complain or pout, and whether their body language indicates disengagement. We watch recruits as they are line judging to see whether they are focused and respecting the game even when not playing. As a college coach, I have the opportunity to select my players, but I understand that high school and middle school coaches have less control. In that case, consider keeping a player on your team who might not add a lot of skill, but who brings gregariousness that helps others have more fun. To continue finding the balance, empower one of your introverted players to be a leader and hold the line on the level of focus expected.

Player–Environment

A stimulating environment will help your players experience pleasure and have fun in your gym. We have worked hard to build a fan base at Hope College so that our matches are well attended and spirited. Resources on how to develop a loyal fan base are readily available, but it is important to acknowledge that playing in front of a packed house is more fun than playing in an empty gym. We are blessed with two gyms in which to hold our matches. One seats 700 fans, and the other seats 3,500. When we are expecting fewer than 1,000 fans at a match, we play in the smaller gym because it feels crowded, loud, and intense. For matches in which when we expect 1,000 or more fans, we move into our arena because playing in front of 1,000 fans is fun no matter the size of the gym! Do you have a way to create a more intimate competitive environment to help your athletes feel the simulation provided by the crowd?

On a visit to a Michigan State men's basketball practice, I was impressed with how often head coach Tom Izzo used music during practice to create a more stimulating practice environment. I purchased a portable speaker with an iPod docking station to pull out to practice (and take on our bus) so that we can have music playing while we warm up and during specific drills (doubles and triples play). We turn it off when a little more focus is required, a subtle hint to buckle down and get to work. I see my team smiling, dancing, acting more energetic, and having more fun during some of the more basic parts of practice than I remember and regret that it took me 13 years to embrace using music in practice.

BALANCE OF TEAM AND INDIVIDUAL

"For the strength of the pack is the wolf, and the strength of the wolf is the pack." This line from Rudyard Kipling's poem "The Law for the Wolves" helps to explain the responsibility a team has to each individual and the responsibility each individual has to the team. You can't achieve success without a focus on each player working hard to become the best she is capable of becoming, but you must also understand that what the team achieves together is what really matters. How you go about getting your athletes to give their best for the success of the team depends on the voice you provide your players, how team roles are defined and appreciated, how players view the diversity of their talents, and how often they are reminded of the power in their collective strength.

Coach–Player

As I mentioned before, we ask for our athletes for their opinions on many team issues. They know that our team is not a democracy and that the final decision on all things is mine, but I do value their opinions and want them to feel as though they have a voice. I have seen my athletes take greater responsibility for themselves and their program when they believe that their opinions are valued. It is for this reason that I also try to use *we* language as often as possible: "We need to be on time, we need to be responsible for communicating with our professors when missing class, we are capable of working harder." Using *we* makes leadership feel less like a top-down approach and more of a "we are all in this together" style. I coach my team leaders to use the same language when interacting with their teammates.

As head coach, I also need to be clear in the way I define and appreciate players' roles. I have noticed that my athletes begin to lose motivation, focus, and enthusiasm when they do not understand their role on the team or when that role is not appreciated. We have meetings with players to talk about the contribution we see them making to the team as well as the unique skills and abilities they bring. We also discuss the roles that need to be filled on the team and encourage them to apply their skills to the needs of the team. This is less of an issue for the athletes in the starting lineup because they typically feel that their role is important and appreciated. Finding ways to encourage the reserve players, for whom appreciation is less obvious, is more challenging.

Be sure to acknowledge your players' improvement (even if it doesn't change their role), invest in their life outside of volleyball, and celebrate their successes in front of the team. You can argue that feeling appreciated is not necessary for giving maximal effort, but the fact is that not many coaches served in a reserve role when they played. A little empathy goes a long way in helping an athlete find her value on a team.

Player–Player

The most valuable exercise we do at Hope College is helping players understand their value and that of the team using the DiSC Behavioral Assessment. The DiSC is just one of many personality/behavioral assessments that describe how people solve problems and work differently. It is beyond the scope of this chapter to cover the details of the profiles contained in the DiSC, but the reason this exercise has been so helpful is that it shows everyone on the team that she has a unique view of the world and how that diversity makes us stronger. It reveals that everyone on the team has specific gifts that are useful in different situations. It also reveals that everyone has blind spots and must rely on those who are different from her when appropriate. For instance, when my team is struggling to perform a complicated drill, some on the team will want to stop and analyze the situation while others will want to keep running it and figure it out as they go. There is value to both perspectives, and having a session in which those differences are identified and discussed helps our team empathize with and ultimately have greater respect for their teammates. Many of these assessments are reliable and valid psychometric instruments and should be administered by a trained professional. Check with your counseling or career services office to find someone who is experienced with the instrument to lead a workshop with your team.

Player–Environment

Most people acknowledge that valuing the team over the self is an important life lesson learned through team sport participation. Most also acknowledge that this is difficult to put into practice all the time, and at some point, our selfish natures take over. Consider ways that your competitive and training environment inspires and reminds team members to achieve their potential while also committing to the values and goals of the team. You might want to put an inspirational quote on the back of your practice T-shirts or on the wall of your locker room or gym. We have a team picture of every conference championship team on a wall in our locker room over the pictures of every all-American or all-conference players because we want our team to focus on what the team can achieve. However, because we also want our players to be inspired individually, we place a card in every player's locker with the name of the graduated senior who wore that number in the past (asterisks behind her name indicate the number of times she earned all-conference recognition). There is one card in each player's locker with the name of all the players wearing that jersey in the past (as many as 10 players are on that card).

If you choose to post newspaper articles, stats, or other visuals with an individual focus, make sure all team members are represented. Posting an article of a reserve player's comeback following an injury would be a great balance to the article featuring your team's setter. I made the mistake once of leaving out a key substitute when a reporter asked to do a story on our attackers. The player took the unintended snub in stride, but I missed a significant opportunity to show her how important she was to the success of our team. If you post team stats, be sure to also provide access to practice stats so that players other than starters can monitor their progress.

CONCLUSION

A positive team climate results in athletes who work hard, have a love of the game, improve in their skill and ability to work as a team, and have the opportunity to reach their potential. The primary way coaches influence these factors is through the relationships they foster. Find ways to invest in your players every day. Provide opportunities for them to have a voice in their experience. Build a training environment in which they feel free to take risks and to learn from their failure without fearing it. Be vulnerable and know that you will make mistakes as a coach—when you do, follow the advice you give your athletes: learn from it and move on.

4

Growth Mindset

Jamie Morrison

Hugh McCutcheon, former head coach of the U.S. men's and women's national volleyball teams, once told me, "As coaches, we are two things: salesmen and change agents." The following words describe everything you do in your profession. Your first job as a coach in any sport is to get your athletes to dedicate themselves to your systems, techniques, culture, and all other aspects of your program. Once you have buy-in, your second job is to create change. Look to improve behavior and make your athletes better people, better students, and better teammates. Look to change the way your athletes' bodies move to perform the fundamentals of the game at a higher level. You are a teacher, and the volleyball court is your classroom.

A large part of your job as a teacher is to create the best possible environment for promoting learning among athletes. Let's explore the idea of a growth mindset, its benefits to learning, and some ways to develop a growth mindset in your athletes as well as your coaches. The goal is to gain the knowledge and tools so that you can give your athletes the best chance to develop and thrive.

CREATING A CULTURE OF GROWTH

Humans are wired to survive in a world of challenges. The natural reaction to danger is to tense up, flee, or defend yourself. What has evolved is the ability to use the rational parts of the brain to make plans, use tools, and respond rationally to situations in the environment. To create a growth mindset, you have to train your brain to think in drastically different ways. It is a difficult task, but as a coach you can develop it within yourself and then develop it in your athletes.

Admit You Aren't Good Enough

The first step of developing a growth mindset is realizing that you will never be perfect. Even people who are considered experts in their fields will fail at times. The best inventors fail countless times before they have success. The best surgeons fail and lose patients. The best volleyball players fail in the biggest moments in a match.

The growth mindset starts with you as a coach. The best coaches have their teams believe that they (the coaches) will make mistakes, but at the same time their athletes have full belief and confidence in every decision that the coaches make. This comes from developing a deep trust with each athlete—a trust that will convince them that each decision is the best they can make for the team.

Realign Your Thoughts

Remember Hugh McCutcheon said that coaches are salesmen and change agents. Not only do you have to change the way your athletes respond to the opponent's tipping, but you also have to guide athletes to new and productive thoughts that mold their mindset.

FIFTH-GRADERS AND LEARNING

In *Mindset: The New Psychology of Success* (2007), Carol Dweck outlines a series of experiments done over 10 years on 400 fifth-graders. Her experiments shed light on how perception of ability to learn can influence the decisions you make, your view of failure, and your ability to learn. Students were divided into two testing groups and put through a series of four tests.

Test 1

Students were given a simple nonverbal IQ test. Upon receiving their high test scores, group 1 was praised for their intelligence that resulted in a high test score. The students in group 2 were praised for the effort that they put in to get high scores.

Test 2

All students were given a choice of the next test they would take. These were their choices:

- Harder version: Students were told that this was an opportunity to challenge themselves and grow.
- Easier version: Students were told that this test would be similar to the first test and they would perform similarly.

The results differed dramatically between the two groups. In the group praised for their intelligence, 67 percent of students chose the easier version of the next test. Conversely, in the group given praise for their effort, 92 percent of students chose to challenge themselves with the more difficult test that followed.

What You Can Learn From These Tests

While your athletes are going through the easiest phases of learning, find times to give praise for the work going into improving. At some point in the learning process, things will get difficult. The foundation that you put down early in your season when things are easier will give your athletes the fuel they need when the learning process becomes more difficult.

Your goal as a coach should be to get athletes addicted to improving. You can do this by explaining the learning process, praise them when they are making the right mistakes, (such as serving out at the end line instead of serving in the net) then find ways to correct them and learn.

Video can also be a great tool for showing improvement. Give your athletes growth homework (a small change for them to focus on during a week), and use video to show them their improvement as the week goes on. A good rule is to show one clip of them doing something right and one clip of an improvement they need to make.

If you simply praise athletes for their successes, they will look for safe avenues to success in the future and will avoid trying new things and risking what is usually required for learning something new. Find places in your training to give praise for the work going into making change, and find ways to get your athletes engulfed in the process of making change.

Test 3

All of the students were given a test with impossible questions. As before, the two groups of students handled the challenges differently. The group praised for their intelligence was much quicker to get frustrated and give up on the test. The group that was praised for effort worked harder on the questions, stuck with the test for a longer time, and actually enjoyed the challenge as they were going through it.

What You Can Learn From This Test

Positive reinforcement is the strongest tool you have in making changes in physical and psychological behavior. Athletes will begin to create an identity early in their development.

There will be those who are praised for their talent—the kids who are told that they are gifted with talent. This kind of mindset is referred to as fixed. These fixed-mindset athletes will begin to identify with their talent that was granted to them and not earned. When difficult situations that threaten that identity present themselves, these athletes will avoid them. They view these challenges as a threat to who they are and what they are praised for. They will make excuses for not taking part in difficult drills in practice. When injured, they will not put in the work to get back on the court. They might even shrink in big moments in matches.

In these situations, athletes avoid the situation not because of the situation itself; they avoid the situation because of how they might be viewed if they fail. They shrink away from big moments not because of fear of the moment but because of the fear of what their teammates will think of them, what their parents will think of them, or what their coaches will think of them.

There is another group of athletes: one that was praised not for who they are now but for how they got there. This mindset is referred to as growth. These growth-mindset athletes are praised for and are held accountable for the work they put in and the improvement they made because of that work. Their coaches don't hold them accountable for mistakes but rather encourage mistakes and offer opportunities to learn from them. From early in their career, these athletes are not called gifted or believe that anything was given to them. They know that they have worked hard for everything that made them what they are. When these athletes are presented with difficult situations, how do you think they view it? If you have done your job well, they view these as opportunities to improve. They know that growth requires work and look forward to that work. Table 4.1 outlines some of the characteristics of fixed- and growth-mindset athletes' behaviors and beliefs.

Behavioral changes are the hardest to make both as a coach and as a player. To develop a growth mindset in your team, you must make this a priority. On the first day of practice, this ideal must be a building block that your team's culture and success will be built on. Tom Black, the assistant coach for the U.S. women's national volleyball team and head volleyball coach at Loyola Marymount University, shared the following guiding principles from the book *Mindset* and expectations of athletes on the first day in the gym.

1. Value process, dedication, growth, and learning, not genius, talent, height, or vertical jump.
2. Don't expect that you've arrived here fully formed. You've arrived here ready to learn.
3. Stretch beyond your comfort zone and take reasonable risks. Do not do the thing you're good at over and over.
4. Value and reward process. Reward taking on big but reasonable challenges and pursuing them doggedly. Reward teamwork.

Establish what your team will be about and create an expectation for that starting on the first day of practice.

TABLE 4.1 Feelings and Behaviors of Fixed and Growth Mindsets

| Fixed mindset | | Coaching points | Growth mindset | |
Behavior	Feeling		Feeling	Behavior
	Something is given to me	Talent	Something that I earn	
Aloof; listening but not processing	A threat: you are saying I'm not good?	Feedback	An opportunity: being given another way to get better	Engaged: asking questions and getting involved
Complaining, going through the motions	Something that people who aren't good enough do	Hard work	The only way to improve	Accepting and honest about workload
Upset and defensive	Signs of weakness	Mistakes	Opportunities to learn	Contemplative
Complaining and acting as a victim	Focused on the past and focused on the problem	Setbacks	Forward thinking and solution based	Finding solutions and acting on them
Tight and mechanical	What will people think of me if I mess up?	Pressure	Process	Loose and free
Deflecting blame to others or making excuses	What will other people think of me?	Failure	What do I need to get better at?	Accountable and forward- and solution-based thinking
Celebrating and content with place	I've made it	Success	What could I have done better?	Analyzes successes as thoroughly as failures

CONSISTENCY OF YOUR MESSAGE

It is easy to say something but more difficult to live it every day. If you want to make difficult change in your athletes, you need to do many things.

Repeat Your Message

Identify the things that are truly important to you and what traits you want your team to embody. Once you have done this, constantly revisit the things that you find important to both prove their importance and provoke thoughts about those topics.

Live It

If you ask your athletes to make difficult changes, you need to make those changes as well for multiple reasons. First, you need to provide a model of behavior for athletes to follow. The best model they can have is a player on your team. If you have someone who models this mindset, don't directly point it out. It is usually obvious to your athletes, so let them discover it on their own. Outline the characteristics of a growth mindset presented earlier in this chapter.

Second, if you ask athletes to do something difficult, they will be much more likely to try harder to make this change if they see you putting in the effort. A study in 1967 by Dr. Albert Mehrabian showed that up to 93 percent of what people say is communicated through tone and body language. To give feedback in a way that athletes feel safe enough to make mistakes, you can't display frustration with your body language or portray a tone of disappointment using your voice. You have to truly believe that mistakes are part of the learning process. You have to be convinced that every one of your athletes can make the changes you need them to make.

Give Examples

One of the greatest teaching tools in volleyball is to give examples. You can do this by showing the passers video of the best passer in the world or video of themselves doing it right. Do the same thing to encourage a growth mindset. When you come across a book or an example of someone displaying characteristics of this mindset in other sports or business, share the examples with your athletes. Every one of your athletes might resonate with a different story, and you never know when you are going to get that "aha" moment.

POWER OF PRAISE

The most powerful tool you have in making change is praise. Countless studies prove that giving someone praise after doing something is the most powerful thing you can do to encourage the repetition of behaviors or actions. However, as you learned from Carol Dweck's research, *what* you praise is extremely important. Table 4.2 provides some examples of the type of praise you should avoid and what you can look for to praise.

TABLE 4.2 Giving Praise

Avoid praising	Instead, praise this
Being gifted	Improvement in a skill or behavior
Results: simply getting a kill or dig	Process: effort put in to make a change
Wins	Specific process in the match or improvement

PROCESS-BASED FEEDBACK

There is a common misconception that positive coaching revolves around constantly telling your athletes what they are doing right and never addressing the things that they are doing wrong. Positive coaching is based on focusing a person's energy on what they can be rather than what they are now.

Julio Velasco, one of the greatest international volleyball coaches of our generation, says, "Have a movie in your head of what your team is realistically capable of looking like. Once you have a clear vision, point your athletes toward one specific change you can make and one change your team can make to get closer to that movie."

John Wooden is the greatest coach that the sporting world has seen. He led his UCLA basketball teams to 10 national championships in 12 years, 7 of those consecutive. One of Wooden's former players summed this up perfectly when asked about the feedback he received from his coach:

> **As a** former student who committed many errors during practice and therefore having been the recipient of plenty of corrections, it was the "information" I received during the correction that I needed most. Having received it, I could then make the adjustments and changes needed. It was the information that promoted change. Had the majority of Coach Wooden's corrective strategies been positive ("Good job") or negative ("No, that's not the way"), I would have been left with an evaluation, not a solution. Also, corrections in the form of information did not address, or attack me as a person. New information was aimed at the act, rather than the actor.
>
> ~Gallimore and Tharp 2004

When coaching, focus on moving athletes one small step at a time toward the vision you have for your team. Never attack the person; rather, address the action or decision and how the athlete can improve it the next time the opportunity arises. If you can create a culture of growth and continually give your athletes specific attainable goals, teaching becomes easy.

You should also have a vision of what your athletes' mindset should be. To make a shift to a growth mindset, ask your athletes to make specific changes in their thoughts and give them feedback just as you would give them on any skill taught in the game.

SOLUTION-BASED THOUGHT

It is easy to dwell on problems, hang on to the past, and complain about circumstances. You have to teach yourself to understand the problem but then turn your focus from the problem to the solution. If your program doesn't have the financial resources of your competitor's program, instead of using this as an excuse, focus your attention on finding a way to make a small improvement.

Once you can lead by example, you need to teach your athletes to do the same. You should put them in difficult situations in practice and in life and then give them the feedback they need when their minds start wandering to the problem rather than the solution.

PITFALL OF PERFECTION

As you have discovered, the first step to developing a growth mindset is accepting that you will never attain perfection. The goal should be to get as close to it as you can. You are simply trying to make small improvements in all aspects of life to get closer to that goal. As soon as you accept that you will never be perfect, you will begin to reduce the pressure that you put on yourself to be a finished product today and engross yourself in the small steps that you need to take to improve.

Your goal in coaching is to be good over long periods. You do not need to be perfect or even great for an extended time. In no sport is perfection expected. In volleyball, you are amazing if you kill the ball 60 percent of the time. In baseball, you are considered elite if you get a hit 35 percent of the time. Present teams with two overriding goals on the volleyball court:

1. Be good for as long a period as you can. If you drift away from good, find ways to get back there quickly.
2. Be a better version of your team every time you step on the court.

THE POWER OF MISTAKES

Mistakes are the most important component in the learning process. If you are not making mistakes, you are not pushing yourself beyond your boundaries. The most difficult task in creating a growth mindset is getting your athletes to believe this concept.

Encourage your athletes to make mistakes in practice. Second, accept mistakes as they happen and give feedback so that they don't happen again or as often. I commonly see young coaches modeling the behavior of older coaches by simply giving negative feedback for a behavior without giving any explanation of what the athletes should be doing. Let your athletes feel free to push their boundaries with mistakes, and give them guidance when they do make mistakes.

To accelerate the growth of athletes' abilities and personality, you must foster these beliefs:

- You are not born with inherent gifts or abilities other than your physical attributes (height or jumping ability).
- You are not a perfect version of yourself and never will be.
- The amount of work that you put in will dictate what you are able to do or be.

If you can do this, you will create a group of people who aren't concerned with what the outside world thinks of them. Because of this, you develop a team that stands up to pressure in matches because their only concern is improving from who they were in the previous match. You create a group that wants to work hard because they know they will see results.

CONCLUSION

Ironically, in some ways developing a growth mindset requires a growth mindset to begin with. You were not born with the gift of a growth mindset. You were born with the reflex to protect yourself when you make a mistake or defend yourself when someone tells you that you're wrong. You will never be perfect at personifying a growth mindset. You will have times when things get difficult and you will question your faith that the work you do will lead you where you want to be. However, if you work really hard, both with your teams and with your staff, you can create a mindset that will help you be the best you can be in all aspects of life.

REFERENCES

Dweck, C. (2007). *Mindset: The new psychology of success*. New York: Ballantine Books.

Gallimore, R., & Tharp, R. (2004). What a coach can teach a teacher, 1975-2004: Reflections and reanalysis of John Wooden's teaching practices. *The Sport Psychologist*, 18(2): 119-137.

Mehrabian, A., & Ferris, S.R. (1967). Inference of attitudes from nonverbal communication in two channels. *Journal of Consulting Psychology*, 31(3): 248–252.

PROGRAM BUILDING AND MANAGEMENT

5

Building a Winning High School Program

Randy Dagostino

When I started coaching girls' volleyball at Berkeley Preparatory School in Tampa, Florida, in 1983, it was the perfect time to get passionate about this sport in this part of the state and the country. Let's just say that volleyball was very much different than it is today. That year I also started the first girls' volleyball club in Florida, the Tampa Bay Juniors Volleyball Club (TBJVC).

I guess you can say that I was one of the early pioneers of this sport, at least in the Southeastern United States. What I knew from the very beginning was that I loved the sport and had a good idea of what it was supposed to look like when played well. This vision was all in my head because I had never played volleyball, other than taking two classes at the University of Illinois at Chicago and playing in a couple of beach volleyball tournaments after relocating to the Tampa Bay area.

My desire to become more knowledgeable really intensified after my first high school season. The motivator often in my early career was a very hard, close loss to our arch rival in the district final, only to have this rival go on to win its third consecutive state championship.

At the conclusion of my first season, I wanted to continue with the sport so much that I started the TBJVC. It was a challenge because when you are the first at anything, it is difficult to find others to compete against. We had no peers to play against locally or, for that matter, in Florida. So our competition was against college teams that were in their spring season, which was legal at that time. This was actually a very good situation for us because the college teams prepared us well for the end of our first season. We went to five college spring tournaments throughout the state before finally ending our first club season by attending the AAU national championship in Benet, Illinois.

Upon returning to Florida, I knew that I wanted to do as much as possible with this sport, and so I completely immersed myself in it.

COACH HAS TO BE THE HARDEST WORKER

If you expect your athletes and their families to make sacrifices, you have to show that you are willing to work harder than your players and the rest of your staff. When I became the head volleyball coach, I was also the athletic director, the head boys' baseball coach, and a physical education teacher at Berkeley Prep School. I wore all of those hats for three more years, but I decided in 1986 that changes had to take place because I wanted to do more with volleyball. That school year I stepped down from being the athletic director and also the head baseball coach. My degree was in physical education, so I continued as a physical education teacher and the girls' volleyball coach. Because my contract with Berkeley required me to coach another sport, I became the girls' basketball coach so I could leave the spring season open for club volleyball.

The transition from being the head of athletics to focusing on learning as much as I could about coaching volleyball was now complete. My passion to learn took on many forms, including working at volleyball camps, attending coaching clinics and USA Volleyball training sessions, going to the American Volleyball Coaches Association (AVCA) convention, and traveling to as many out-of-state club tournaments as I could with my teams. How did this make our Berkeley program better? First, many of the Berkeley volleyball players mixed in with other players from the Tampa Bay Area and became part of this journey with me. They traveled to those club tournaments, and early on we took our lumps. Together we saw what we could be doing with this game, which motivated all of us to do more. Second, because I am a visual learner, I would sit for hours and watch other teams play in these events, with notepad in hand.

Attending these events made me a better and more knowledgeable coach. I felt more confident in teaching this sport to my teams. It was not uncommon for teams connected with TBJVC to travel to three out-of-state tournaments per season in those early years, whereas the other clubs that were popping up in Florida did not leave the state. Soon three out-of-state tournaments became five, and we were having success at both the high school and the club level; many teams and athletes qualified for national championships, and many players were recruited to play in college. The pattern had formed and the system was in place to perpetuate itself over and over again. My school/club volleyball year appeared to never end, which was a process that would continue for more than 30 years.

DON'T EVER COACH TO BE UNDEFEATED

In the late 1980s, I decided that if our club success was due to our demanding schedule and increased training, why not do the same with our high school program? From 1988 to 1993, Berkeley Prep did not lose a volleyball match in Florida; we also won six straight state championships, but we never had an undefeated season. Our losses occurred when our team traveled out of state to very strong competitive high school tournaments, first in Chicago, then in Las Vegas, on to Santa Barbara, and then back to Chicago over the years. The Berkeley volleyball team still competes in out-of-state tournaments such as these today. Our high school record from 1983 to 2011, when I retired as the head girls' volleyball coach, was 836 to 161. That record includes 15 state championships and over 100 girls receiving scholarships to play in college, but not one undefeated season. As soon as I would start to feel that my team was the best, I would remember that although I had these feelings before, I had still never finished with an undefeated season. So there was still room for improvement.

ATHLETIC CONDITIONING = SPEED, WEIGHT, AND JUMP TRAINING

At the same time that Berkeley Prep had established itself as the high school volleyball power in Florida, I sensed that other clubs and schools were recognizing the value of more demanding schedules and more training hours. At this time hiring personal trainers was the new craze. Many of the athletes from Berkeley were signing up with these trainers who cost money and also took up study time. I approached my Berkeley Prep department chairperson and convinced her that, with our physical education background, we could do very similar forms of training right here at Berkeley. I suggested that many students would sign up for a conditioning class for physical education credits. Athletic Conditioning became a class offering in our physical education curriculum, and it still exists today. I taught this class for 20 years, and many volleyball players took it for two or three years.

To prepare to offer this class, I convinced my school to send me for some training. I attended the Olympic Training Center in Colorado Springs, where I watched, again with notepad in hand, how athletes in many sports (e.g., volleyball, basketball, weightlifting) were doing physical training. I read books on speed training and jump training. Athletic Conditioning at Berkeley was a yearlong class that did not have a sport exemption option, meaning that if you were in season you could not opt out of it to get a study hall. I stressed that for the athletes to really benefit from this form of training, they had to do it both during the season and in the off-season. I am convinced that our volleyball players developed an advantage over our opponents because they were stronger, quicker, and fitter, and could jump higher, because of their dedication to our Athletic Conditioning class. Now many programs work a training component into the overall development of their teams. We were one of the first, but certainly have much company now.

WHOLE-PART-WHOLE

As I have said, I am a visual learner. What that means is that I can see someone perform a skill and understand what doing that skill perfectly should look like. To take that a step further, I believe that many of the movements and body angles in volleyball are found in other sports that I grew up playing. After practice, my volleyball players would often feel that not only did they learn something new about volleyball, but also their golf swing, baseball swing, tennis serve, or basketball defense posture had also improved.

Volleyball is a game of repetition. Many of the skills are awkward and foreign to most of us. In our early development, we don't play games that require us to rebound the ball off various body parts, as in volleyball. Most of the games we play when we are young involve the skills of catching, throwing, or hitting a ball with an object. In volleyball the skills of passing, serving, hitting, digging, setting, and blocking are all rebound skills. We never have complete control (holding the ball) as we do in other sports, except when serving. Even though volleyball skills are different, they can be learned pretty quickly, as can the basic tenets of the game with the whole-part-whole method. My goal as a coach was always to create a training environment that maximized playing the game.

Because each player needs many repetitions of these skills to gain the necessary control to play volleyball the right way, my number one challenge was to make sure this took place in our practices. When players understand that making three contacts is the key to success, and practice performing these three contacts, they are working on gaining an advantage until they can win the rally. An ideal setting for that to happen was in our mini volleyball practices. Here is a description:

- Mini volleyball is played on a much smaller court (44 by 17 feet). A normal-size gym is big enough to have two official-size practice courts running the opposite direction to the main competition court; that gym is big enough for six of these mini courts.
- Each court has a point value. Court 1 is worth 1 point, court 2 is worth 2 points, and so on, up to 6 points for court 6.
- Two players are on each side of a court. They play 2v2 but with a different scoring system. If a pair wins a rally using only one or two contacts, the team earns 1 point. However, if a pair performs three contacts, which directly leads to winning the rally, then 5 points are awarded. This is called a 5-point rally.
- Each competitive game is timed (three to five minutes). At the conclusion of the game, the winning teams rotate to the next-highest-valued court, and the losers rotate to the next-lowest-valued court. For example, the pair that won on court 5 would get 5 points for that victory and rotate up to court 6. The loser on court 5 would rotate down to court 4 and receive no points for the loss. Each team adds up its points, and at the end of this lesson, the pair with the highest number of court points wins.

Following are the benefits of mini-volleyball lessons:

- Every player performs a maximum number of contacts because, with only two players per team, everyone is forced to play the ball in every rally.
- Using a 5-point rally scoring system encourages the players to use 3 contacts, which consistently shows them how to earn an advantage over their opponent.

- On a smaller court, players have to play with more ball control; otherwise, the ball often goes out of bounds.
- Most important, all of these contacts and all of this controlled play teaches players the game of volleyball in a competitive setting. Their focus is not on any particular skill such as passing, but rather on the sequence of skills needed for playing the game the right way.

When athletes were playing mini-volleyball games, I would shout one-word or short-phrase instructions to make a point to an athlete or the group as a whole, without interfering with the flow of the games. This is an example of the whole-part-whole method of teaching.

NEVER PUT LIMITS ON YOUR PLAYERS

I will never understand why coaches believe it is their responsibility to tell an athlete "You will never be able to achieve that goal." Throughout history people have accomplished unbelievable things, and one of the reasons is that they had a passion for what they did that defied all odds. When I hear that an athlete has been told that he will never perform at a certain level, the first thing I think of is the U.S. men's hockey team at the 1980 Winter Olympics—the Miracle on Ice—to remind myself that these types of coaches are wrong.

I will take this a step further and say that such coaches have no business leading others. Being a coach means trying to figure out a way to help athletes accomplish never-before-achieved levels of success. That is what good to great teachers and coaches were put on this earth to do. When a connection is made between a coach and an athlete over a shared goal, then both rise to their best. I can honestly say that I have been fortunate on many occasions to be part of this process, and it is the most enjoyable part of being a coach.

TEAM CHEMISTRY = ROLES OF IMPORTANCE

I have had the good fortune over a lot of years of coaching this sport to see many successful coaches interact with their teams in many different ways. Some are very quiet and command the attention of their players because they have to listen carefully just to hear the message. Others are very loud and somewhat intimidating, at least to the casual onlooker, but this seems to work for their teams. Some coaches have the patience of a saint and, during a match, use everything that occurs as a teachable moment, almost to the point of letting the match get away from them. Others have a quick hook, meaning that they substitute players out for what appears to be the first miscue or error (especially to these players' parents). The most successful coaches know their teams so well that the buttons they push on the sidelines and the timing of their messages are completely familiar to their players.

Knowing your team well and forming bonds to create a good team is something to focus on constantly. In any given year, a coach may have a group of talented players who are superior to most of the opponents they may face. That coach is going to win a lot of matches with such a gifted group. However, in order to beat the toughest opponents the *individual* players will have to fulfill a specific *team* role.

I have said for a long time that I would rather have a collection of players who have good ability and are good learners than one or two amazing players who need to carry the team. My reasoning is quite simple. When a team has a few stars, what happens if one of those stars has an off game? Or what if the team plays against such a well-coached team that the stars are limited in what they can produce? I think the answer is pretty clear: this team loses.

The team that has a collection of good players who fulfill their roles ends up being pretty tough to beat. The key is a coach who can manage the egos and get across to the team that if each player takes care of her part of the game, they will win a lot.

This concept goes hand in hand with the idea of a coach not putting limits on players. The coach is responsible for identifying the attributes each player brings to the team and then devising a plan, with these talents, to put a successful team in motion. It would be very easy from the outset for a coach to dwell on the short-comings of a team or certain players. Another concept entirely is to embrace the challenge of "coaching this team up" to new levels of success. The secret is to let players consistently know, in every practice and every set played, what they must do to fulfill their roles so that the team will succeed. The following player story is an example.

I am presently coaching a boys' 18s team. From the outset I knew that the setter on this team is the best and most knowledgeable player I have ever coached. He is a born leader and the engine that would make any team go. He is also very good at disguising his sets and, because of that, would create many one-on-one situations for his pin attackers. In the first practice of our season, within the first 10 minutes, I walked up to our 6-foot, 5-inch left-handed opposite, whom I did not know, and said, "You will be our terminating attacker on this team." I could tell by the expression on his face that no one had ever said something of that importance about his contribution to a team before. I backed it up by saying, "In free-ball situations, I do not want you to worry about playing any ball." Continuing, I said, "You are to transition off the court and get ready to terminate the ball, because you know our setter is going to create the best possibility for that to happen." At the same time, I announced to the team that this would be our strategy.

Now I needed to make sure everyone else bought into this change. I told our middles that on this play they would now retreat to zone 2, a place where well-coached teams like to send free balls. Our middles were going to have to get better at playing this short ball high enough, most likely with their hands to our setter, to keep themselves as options for free-ball plays. They would also then attack, moving back in front of our setter to draw more attention away from our opposite. At the same time, I told our libero that he should now have a clear view of the free ball coming to our side of the court, and I knew that he had the speed and the talent to cover the space on our side of the court. I told him that his goal was to be mobile and vocal enough to play the majority of the free balls. Certainly, our outside and middle-back players were ready to cover their spots on the court. At this point in our season, after going to two very competitive national qualifying tournaments, it is clear that my assessment was dead on. Our setter is creating a ton of one-on-one situations for our pin attackers, and because of that, our opposite is clearly our leading terminating attacker.

I could continue with examples here, but the point is that, as a coach, you must recognize the differences in your players—physical attributes, mental maturity, and game experience. Then you must coach to each player's strengths to find the best way for them to contribute to the team. This means that you may need to tell players in the same position, such as outside hitters, to each focus on something different.

The game of volleyball is built around errors, so as you recognize the strengths of your nonstarters, you can create a learning atmosphere in which they can contribute when the starters are not performing at their peak. Your goal should be to convince each player that a positive contribution, in any form, affects the team's success and is therefore critical to the team as a whole. Much like the sixth player in basketball or the utility player in baseball, players who can come off the bench and make an immediate positive impact in multiple positions are valuable to any team.

On the best teams I have coached, I have also had players take on what may appear to be more limited roles, but I know that they have felt the importance of their contributions. Developing a defensive specialist who can enter the game and make positive plays because he believes he has great instincts for the game, or a serving specialist who knows that her serve is critical to begin a rally in a position of advantage is a crucial coaching skill. Creating these roles can generate a special chemistry among athletes who have never played together before because they are made to feel that they are all important to the team's success and they understand the scope of their contributions.

FOCUS OUTWARD

If you have coached this great sport for a while, you understand the frustration that happens for everyone, from coach to players, when the pressure of the game gets the best of a team, or some players. This typically happens when a particular skill, such as passing, starts to break down. Players may have been passing very well in matches, and then all of a sudden they hit a mental wall. This Achilles' heel can lead to the total shutdown of the rest of their game. What do you do?

You might immediately make some moves, with the hope that this player will snap out of it. Here are some examples:

- ◆ Provide words of encouragement or a technical correction.
- ◆ Alter the serve-receive pattern. At the same time, encourage your libero, if he is not the player who is having trouble, to cover more space.

- Call a time-out, provided you have any left. Based on what you know about your player, you can either address the issue directly or skirt around what is happening and hope the brief time off the floor does the trick.
- The last choice is to substitute for the affected player, no matter how much your team relies on her.

What I have learned over the years is to help players reach the point of being competitive with every touch on the ball. They should want every ball they play to be perfect, knowing that this is impossible. How does this help? As I mentioned in the section Team Chemistry = Roles of Importance, all players have to know what they are responsible for in order to ensure that their team performs at its best. If passing is a skill a player is responsible for, she must go after it as best she can. If she starts to break down with this skill, she should let her team know *outwardly* that she is not going to tank. Here are some ways she could do this:

- Go to the team captain and announce, "I am still with you."
- Pat another team member on the back with words of encouragement if that player made an error.
- Remind the team that when the opponent was last in this rotation, they ran a certain play.
- Tell the setter that on the next good pass, she wants the ball, reminding the setter she is still ready to hit and that part of her game is not affected.

The preceding are outward signs to the rest of the team that the player is going to fight through this. Consider starters, who contribute in a variety of ways. If one of their skills starts to suffer, the rest of their game needs to remain competitive. Without shouting it aloud, they can demonstrate an outward focus by expressing to their teammates that they are going to be there for them, even if the skill takes a while to come back.

If an athlete chooses to crumble, or anytime an athlete starts to show signs of losing his edge, that athlete and I are going to have a heart to heart about selfishness. Athletes who want everything to come easily don't allow the best part of becoming a competitor to really take hold: learning about themselves.

HELP PLAYERS GET RECRUITED

If your program attracts athletes who have the potential to be recruited to play in college, you must explain to them and their parents at the outset of your season the fine line between being a member of a team and improving their chances of being recruited. Their focus must be on their performance for the team. Your job is to make them see the correlation between being a strong team player and getting recruited. If their focus is on being a strong team player, it helps the recruiting process: college coaches will take notice.

Your high school team's needs are likely to be different from those of a club team your players may play on. A player on your high school team with physical or skill attributes that help your team may not be used the same way on a club team. Thus, a one-on-one discussion with the athlete and a follow-up discussion with the parents about how you anticipate using the player are important. You must put the betterment of the team first, which you need to express to players and their parents. The goal is to improve every player's total game, which improves the team's performance, which in the end should improve the chances for every worthy player to be recruited.

Players and parents need to understand that college coaches know their jobs, and they need to let them do them and trust that they know how to get the information they need to evaluate players fairly. The majority of the recruiting process takes place during the club season. If a coach whom a player and parents have contacted is courtside watching your team, chances are that he is watching the player in question and also other players. Players must understand that their normal capabilities and skills, executed in the way they always execute them, are what these coaches want to see. They must focus on playing the game the way they know how, within the team strategy, and let college coaches do their job of evaluating.

Finally, as a coach, you must accept that where an athlete plays after high school is a family decision and not yours. As much as you want to believe that you know which college program would be best for an athlete, the parents and the athlete should make this decision without undue influence by you. Their future should not be about your placing another notch on your resume.

There are a number of things you can do to help families in the recruiting process. The first is to have a general meeting with all athletes who arc of the appropriate age to cover the basics and let them know what you are willing to do. Also, meetings with individual players and their parents are needed for helping to develop a plan for each athlete. Following are topics to include in a general recruiting meeting for all athletes of the appropriate age:

- The role you are willing to play in the process, such as calling college coaches, e-mailing, helping them create a skills video, and having periodic family meetings.
- Basic NCAA rules about what contact is and is not allowed depending on the athlete's age (you can find these on the NCAA website). This is an important area that parents need to understand. You may also have athletes recruited to junior colleges (NJCAA) or NAIA schools who will need to understand those recruiting and eligibility rules, which are different from NCAA Division I, II, and III rules.
- The importance of maintaining good grades and keeping their class selection on track to meet NCAA Eligibility Center requirements.
- Recruiting sources, services, and seminars that may be available.

- A list of important websites to browse.
- A list of questions to be answered, or homework, before their individual meetings.

Homework questions for athletes to answer before their individual meetings:

1. What type of school are you looking for?
   a. Campus size, student body size, public or private
   b. Location: rural or urban, weather preferences, distance from home, ease to get to
2. What schools that fit that description have volleyball programs?
3. What area of study are you looking for, and what schools have that discipline?
4. What type of financial assistance do you need, if any?
5. What is your academic status, and how does that match each school's requirement?

Next, schedule meetings with individual players and their parents to review their answers to the homework questions. Make sure you thoroughly understand the desires of the athletes and their parents, because they can differ. Encourage athletes to write letters to each school they are interested in to introduce themselves and provide some basic personal information, as well as their upcoming playing schedule. Encourage them to more fully research each school and its coaching staff and maybe even plan visits to the campus on their own. Make sure they understand the NCAA rules about unofficial visits. Once families and athletes have narrowed their selection of colleges, request a list so that you can start the process of contacting college coaches to speak on behalf of the athletes.

Stay in touch with college coaches to see what positions they are looking for in a particular year of recruiting. Always let the families know what you have found out, positively or negatively, when it pertains to the athletes.

In the end, don't forget to ask one important question of the players: Is this a school you would want to attend even if your volleyball career ended? That should get them thinking.

WORK WITH PARENTS

I have learned that the best way to work with the parents of my players is to communicate with them regularly via e-mail. It is a practice of mine to write a recap of every match or tournament to share my thoughts with the parents. In these recaps, win or lose, my focus is on *team growth* and *improvement*. I specifically mention certain players' contributions in a match and how that helped our team maintain focus. I keep a record to make sure that over a period of time I touch on every player on our team. I also send an individual e-mail to the parents of an athlete who had a special practice, letting them know how much I appreciated their son's or daughter's efforts that day and how, as a result of that performance, our team became better.

Parents are always welcome at my practices. Depending on your confidence level and style of coaching, this is either going to be a good or bad choice. All of my practices have one central theme, which helps us work together to become the best we can be. I want the parents to hear often that the most important thing is our team. What I have learned is that if you are a hardworking coach who is organized and runs a fair practice that involves everyone, having the parents see that increases their respect for you. It helps alleviate most misconceptions that parents can adopt because they just don't know. You will find that this open style of coaching combined with communication will prevent a lot of confrontations and create a positive relationship with parents as a whole. It makes them feel part of the process, and they buy in to your team-first mentality. I also want my parents to be involved with anything they feel comfortable doing, such as calling lines, taking tickets, score keeping, providing pregame meals, helping with food schedules when we are traveling, and assisting with any jobs connected with running a tournament.

I make a big deal about the help I have received from the parents over the course of the season at our annual team banquet, which is held near or at the end of our season. Again, the focus of my presentation is how much we were able to accomplish together, along with the help and support of the parents. Although this is a forum for speaking about every player individually, and I do, the bigger message is how each of these players helped us improve as a team. Just as their children buy in to the team-first concept, parents do too after *reading* about it in e-mails, *seeing* it at practices and matches, and *hearing* it at functions such as a banquet.

CONCLUSION

In closing, being a coach has been the second most rewarding experience I have had in my life, trailing only after being a father and husband. Even though this was my job, it never felt that way. Being able to wrap so many of my personal life experiences around volleyball, including travel, meeting and working with people, and being able to share that with my family, has been most fulfilling. In looking back, there was never a special recipe or secret to creating a winning program. The passion I experienced as a collegiate athlete and has been part of my life all along is what led me to success. Like anything in life, if you have a passion for what you do, you will always strive to learn the most you can and be successful. That passion is contagious to others you are around—especially the athletes you coach.

6

Building a Successful College Program

Todd Lowery

As I reflect on my 11th season as a coach, I feel blessed by the opportunities I have been given. I feel fortunate that along the way I have had so many great players, peers, and friends who have guided me through the building of two collegiate programs that on the surface seem to share many characteristics, although the underlying challenges were vastly different. When given the opportunity to share what goes into building a successful college program, I reflected on the sources of my ideas. Some of them I accidentally discovered in my early years of coaching, and some I borrowed from players, coaches, and, most important, people I believed were just winners at the game of life.

I was hired for my first job as a head coach only seven weeks before the start of the fall season. The university had recently eliminated all of its athletic teams except two. I was straight out of graduate school and far from qualified to be a head coach. Looking back, I realize that I was probably the only one willing to accept the position. I had spent two years as a graduate assistant prior to that, which did little to prepare me for the duties of a head coach. My exposure to volleyball was limited to about three years at that time, but growing up as a multisport athlete and being part of a team was something I felt comfortable with.

As I entered the gym to face a group of young women who for certain knew more about the game than I did, one of only three returning players on a squad of eight approached me. She said, "We are like any other team. We are a reflection of whatever you are." It was in that first 10 seconds of coaching that I realized I had all the tools I needed to be a successful college coach. Don't get me wrong—when I look back on many things I did in those early years, I wonder how the program survived much less thrived.

As years have passed and my coaching career has evolved, so has my definition of success. As a young coach, I thought success was measured only by wins and losses, and to an extent any athletic team is measured by what happens on the court. However, different levels of college volleyball programs have different goals.

I discovered that the goals that had nothing to do with wins and losses led to the success we achieved on the court. Success for our program now means graduating quality young women who through our program have gained valuable tools to be winners in the real world. Every program comes with unique expectations, but improving and guiding the lives of young adults to better themselves both mentally and physical is a measure of success that spans any level of college volleyball.

ADMINISTRATION

A key contributor to any program's success is administrative support, which can come in many shapes and forms.

Staff

Somebody once told me that a great head coach is like a turtle on top of a fence post. You know they had some help getting up there. This is a true statement in sport as well. So many people play a role in the success of a program aside from the obvious people such as the head coach and assistant coaches. Just as in business, there are the college volleyball programs that have plenty of money for a full staff, and then there are the rest of us.

So what are the keys to building a great program whether you have the funding for two assistant coaches and a director of operations or you don't? First of all, if you are fortunate enough to have one full-time assistant, this is a very important hire for your program. Before selecting an assistant coach, you must do an honest assessment of yourself. What are your strengths, or what do you do really well, and what are your weaknesses, or what areas do you really need help with?

Once you are comfortable acknowledging your weaknesses, you can begin to identify candidates who will add to your program instead of just giving you more of what you already have. Once you have chosen your assistant, don't be afraid to let him do what you brought him there to do. If you are not a great recruiter and you hired a great recruiter, let him run with it. If you hired somebody to train players in a certain position, let her train them. New coaches, especially young ones, often believe that they need to be in charge of everything. What ends up happening is that they do everything in an average way instead of focusing on a couple of areas and doing them great and letting their assistants focus on a couple of areas that they can do great.

Surrounding yourself with staff members who share your philosophy ensures that the message is consistent throughout the program. With that said, a similar philosophy is not the same as similar personality. When I look at many of the great coaching staffs out there, often the members of the team have very different personalities. Every year, new and unique athletes will enter your program, and the more resources or the greater the diversity of thought you have to connect with them, the better your team will be. Being creative with volunteers, student assistants, and managers can be very beneficial for teams with limited resources.

Often, these people bring great value to the program at little cost. Make sure they feel part of the program, which fosters buy-in and motivates them to contribute for reasons other than monetary gain.

Managing Staff

When I first started coaching, I was an "if you want something done right you have to do it yourself" type of coach. I still feel this way with certain aspects of our program, but I have learned to delegate some responsibilities to others. Luckily, I have had some really good assistant coaches who have contributed greatly to my program over the years. The first several years I was a head coach, though, I had no assistance, not even a student assistant, and I found myself run down by midseason. From having to break down film to washing uniforms on the road, it was simply too much for one person to handle. I finally took on a student assistant to whom I could shift some of the simple day-to-day tasks. When I got my first full-time assistant, we sat down and decided what her strengths were, and I allowed myself to give her a lot of control in those areas. By this time I was in my fifth season as head coach, and the help could not have come at a better time. I had spent five years trying to do everything, and it was starting to take its toll: I was starting to lose my passion for the game. Adding a great assistant allowed me to refocus on the game and everything became much easier and much more enjoyable again.

I have recently had my first experience dealing with multiple assistant coaches. I now know that more is not always better. It takes significant time to oversee the duties of several coaches and manage multiple personalities. As your coaching staff grows, it becomes even more important to look at personalities and coaching philosophies to get all of your staff members working toward a common goal. Your staff is basically a team within the team; you need to manage them much the way you do your players.

Hiring New Staff

Former players can be great assistants, and we all have athletes come through our programs who have what it takes to contribute as coaches. The good thing about hiring former players is that after four years in the program, they know your work ethic and what you expect. The major drawback of hiring former players is that they are probably a lot like you. Diversity on the staff is important because it brings new perspectives and new ideas. To diversify my staff, I have hired former players of teams whose coaches I know and respect.

Always keep an eye out for people who can help your program. Working at clinics and camps allows you to see and interact with a lot of coaches in a short amount of time. When I'm recruiting, I like to watch the coaches of the athletes I'm recruiting. If a player has everything I'm looking for, then the person coaching that player must be doing something right. Your next great assistant coach can be anywhere, so keep your eyes open. Even if you do not currently have a position open on your staff, you should be identifying who you might like to bring on if a position comes open.

One Voice

Having one voice as a coaching staff is very important. The people on your coaching staff, much like your players, need to clearly understand what you expect of them and what their roles are. Giving your staff members the respect they deserve is key. If you listen to any of the great coaches in any sport, you never hear them say "I" in anything the team or the staff accomplishes. They always give credit to their staff by saying "we." If you do not give credit to staff members, one of two things will happen: they will not be around for very long, or they will not support you. Support and respect are two-way streets: you must give them if you expect to get them. I give my assistants a great deal of space to speak in practice, in matches, and in public. I have a lot of confidence in the staff I have hired. If I don't trust them enough to speak at any time, then I have failed in doing my job of communicating what we are trying to accomplish.

Our staff meets and plans practice together every day. As a result, when we walk into the gym we all know exactly what we want to accomplish that day, what drills our players will perform, and what coaching cues we will use to accomplish our goals. Having a great staff requires hard work. You need to put a lot of time and effort into developing them; if you do, they will move on and become successful head coaches.

RECRUITING

Recruiting may be the most important factor in the success of any program. As coaches, we may believe that we are great teachers of the game and can develop talent, but getting the right recruits is so much more than just procuring great talent. I was lucky to recruit four freshmen in my first season who ended up having a huge impact on our program. That first season I did not have much time to plan recruiting or go after a certain type of athlete. I simply took the best players available. However, that first recruiting class opened my eyes to so much more than just recruiting athletic talent.

When I set out to develop a recruiting philosophy earlier in my career, I was at a small private school in South Dakota with a below-average scholarship budget. I quickly realized that a traditional method of recruiting was not going to work. We had limited resources to travel to club tournaments out of state, and at that time club volleyball was almost nonexistent in South Dakota. Our student body was somewhere around 400 students. Approximately 150 of them were traditional-aged students, and of those, about 90 were international students. Because we experienced great success with the international players on our roster, we chose to focus on this niche.

The Right Fit

Recruiting should start with identifying what sets your school apart from all other schools. Find out what attracts the general student population to your school. Is it location, a certain academic program, or, as in our case, a great history of recruiting students from around the world? I am reminded of my older sister's recruiting experience. She was a much better athlete than I and actually had people fighting for her to attend their schools. At an early age she was set on becoming a chemical engineer, and all the schools that were interested in her that were not known for science and engineering had no chance of signing her. This taught me about the importance of fit when recruiting students to an institution.

You must find student-athletes who are going to fit into your community and be happy while also improving as volleyball players. Unhappy players, more often than not, underachieve. Make sure you know your institution and area as much as you know your team and what type of personalities are going to fit with your group of athletes.

Over the years I have put more effort into recruiting athletes who will fit with our team than in recruiting the best talent out there. We have won championships when we did not have the most talented group, but did have the right chemistry; and we have lost championships when we were far more talented, but struggled with personality issues on the team.

Academics

Another area I have focused on during the recruiting processes is academics. In my experience, the students who are the most successful in the classroom are also the most successful on the court. I have learned that high scores on SAT and ACT tests don't automatically translate into good grades in college. Looking at high school grade point averages seems to be a much better indicator of how students will do in college. I would say that 95 percent of all the students I have coached received almost the exact level of success in college that they did in high school. College grades have little to do with how smart students are and much more to do with how dedicated they are to their studies. Dedication in the classroom is much more difficult to achieve than dedication on the court. Volleyball is the fun part of most student-athletes' day. If they work to succeed in the classroom, they are most likely to work to succeed in the gym. This is why academic success has become a key component when we are evaluating potential recruits.

TEAM CULTURE

When you take into account the number of hours freshmen are going to spend with each other over the course of the next four years, it probably adds up to more than they will spend with any other person in their lives during this time—more than boyfriends or girlfriends, family members, and friends. This is why we strive to create a family culture on our team. Our players practice together, take classes together, travel together, live together, eat together, and pretty much do everything else together as well. As with any group of people that spends that much time together, they are going to get on each other's nerves and there are going to be disagreements, lots of laughs, and some tears. Creating a family culture helps us get through many challenges.

When I was a small child, I was picked on daily by my two older sisters. I also very distinctly remember my sisters' reactions when somebody outside of our family picked on me. They would walk across hot coals barefooted to come to my rescue. The thing about creating a culture of family on a team is that at the end of the day, no matter what has happened, team members are always willing to forgive each other. When the sun comes up the next morning, it will be the start of a new day; whatever happened yesterday can be left behind, and the team can get back to work. Of course, it is not always easy, but we have seen that a family feeling helps us get through the hard times.

We have also created a culture of winning and excellence on our team. When freshmen come into our program, they often don't understand the mentality of our upperclassmen or why they do what they do on a day-to-day basis. For example our athletes are always ready 15 minutes before we start. This way, if somebody is running late for some reason it does not affect our time together on the court. When you create the expectation of excellence, students tend to rise to that level. We expect it in everything we do. We are not just focused on being excellent on the court; we strive for excellence in everything we do. We teach our student-athletes to do the right thing even when nobody is watching.

Team Captains

Team captains play an integral role in the chemistry of a team. We use our captains as go-betweens who connect the coaching staff and the entire team. I'm not sure there is a magic formula for choosing team captains, but of course, you want them to be people with great leadership qualities. They also have to be players the team responds well to or who have personal power on the team. My experience has shown that it is best to have two captains. We always pick one who is very organized and detail oriented (and if she is a leader on the court, even better). Our second captain is an on-court leader either through example or by default.

Great leaders or student-athletes in your program who emerge as leaders on the court do not do so by their own conscious effort or by being told to step up as leaders. They are simply athletes whom all the other players on the team gravitate toward or look to when they need guidance. Some years it is clear who to choose for captains, and other years it has been a very difficult decision. We always try to balance the personalities of the two captains. If we have one person who gets straight to the point, we look to balance her with someone more fun-loving with an easygoing personality.

Our team captains have a great deal of responsibility in our program. They are the ones we contact when we need to get a message out to the entire team. They are the ones who make sure we look like a team when we show up for practice, when we travel, and during all other team activities. Having good team captains ensures that the culture of the team and the expectations of our program are passed along to all incoming players each year.

I have never allowed our team to pick our captains. It is my philosophy that we need team captains to be mediators between the team and the coaching staff. Not everybody is capable of doing this. Sometimes the best athlete or the most well-liked player is not good at accomplishing the tasks that a captain needs to accomplish. It is important to have the person we want in that position.

Player Meetings

I try to minimize individual meetings with players. We have them at the beginning of the season, at midseason, and after the season, and then we have them at the end of spring semester. Of course, individual meetings do occur as situations arise, but for the most part, we handle our problems as a team. I do meet with the two captains more often—probably once every couple of weeks—because there are always team dynamics going on that coaches do not see. It is important to be aware of those issues, and good captains keep us in the loop.

Team Rules

We have a very clear set of rules and standards for our team. We are very clear about what we expect, what is acceptable and unacceptable, and what the consequences are. Everybody on our team knows what will happen if our team rules or expectations are not met. There is no gray area when it comes to enforcing rules, or breaking the rules, for that matter. If the rule is to be on time, 1 minute late is the same as 15 minutes late. The most important thing I tell coaches is that whatever rules you place on your team, you have to be willing to enforce them with your best player on the day of the biggest match, and you must enforce them all the time regardless of the player or the situation. Consistency is key.

CONCLUSION

I have been very fortunate to have recruited very talented players. This has been coupled with the ability to get a handful of great players to buy in to the vision I have for my team. By no means do I have a magic formula for success, but we have been able to get a lot of really good players to work together and give everything they have for the team's success.

I feel fortunate to have been able to coach college volleyball for the past 15 years. Although the memories of the specific wins and losses fade over time, the impact that we as coaches get to have on student athletes are memories that last forever. Every coach and program measures success in different ways, but for me to see former players that are now bank managers, physical therapists, business owners, and even head volleyball coaches, is the greatest reward that a coach can have.

7

Starting a Sand Volleyball Program

Danalee Bragado-Corso

Beach volleyball has been played throughout the world for almost a century. It has become the most sought-after ticket and most viewed event at the Olympics and is now the newest NCAA championship sport. This progression is in line with the prolific success the United States has had at the Olympic Games, along with the booming expansion into junior clubs in recent years.

Because most universities are not located near beaches, the name *sand volleyball* has been used for programs around the country. It is often used interchangeably with the term beach volleyball, depending on where the sport is played. Getting sand volleyball into the collegiate ranks was an arduous road. With much support from the AVCA and despite the controversy that always comes with change, sand volleyball was approved to become an NCAA emergent sport beginning in the 2010-2011 academic year. The sport had 10 years to garner 40 committed programs for two consecutive years, after which it would become a NCAA-sponsored championship sport. Collegiate sand volleyball is the fastest sport to go through the emergent process; it established itself as an NCAA championship sport within only five years. With the additions of programs at California State University at Northridge, the University of Oregon, and Louisiana State University, sand volleyball had the 40 sponsored programs needed in the 2014-2015 season. The 2016-2017 season is slated to be sand volleyball's first year as an official NCAA championship sport.

ADVANTAGES OF A SAND PROGRAM

Riding the great success the United States has had both on the World Pro Tour and at the Olympic Games, beach volleyball has become one of the fastest-growing sports in the country. According to the 2013 Sports & Fitness Industry Association's Topline Participation Report, there has been an 80 percent growth in the participation of females ages 13 to 25 since 2007. Young aspiring volleyball players follow in the footsteps of their athletic idols; for a great majority of these athletes, Misty May-Treanor and Kerri Walsh Jennings have blazed a path toward beach volleyball success.

Indoor volleyball athletes are attracted to sand volleyball because of the fun factor, social atmosphere, and laid-back attitude associated with the beach lifestyle (figure 7.1). Some top-tier indoor volleyball athletes have played it and want to continue at the collegiate level. It is in the best interest of top-notch college programs to offer sand volleyball to attract these blue-chip indoor players. Additionally, most coaches enjoy the option of having their indoor players cross-train in the sand. If done properly, training for the sand game can greatly increase the fitness levels of indoor players and give them a new and interesting way to train.

Although indoor volleyball has become very specialized, beach volleyball is not, which means that sand athletes get to use all the skills of the game, which greatly increases their volleyball IQ as well as their enjoyment. The number of ball touches one player receives in a two-hour sand volleyball practice is enormous compared to an indoor practice. Sand volleyball athletes must be complete players mastering all the skills of volleyball to be good. Just walking in the sand is a difficult task, let alone sprinting, jumping, stabilizing, and changing direction. At Florida State University, our indoor athletes gained a significant increase in their vertical jump by joining the sand team. Most athletes see their overall cardiovascular fitness

FIGURE 7.1 Recreational action in the sand.

improve as well as their ability to push through tougher physical scenarios after training in the sand. Thus, sand volleyball also provides a break from the norm and a novel mental and physical outlet for athletes.

Sand volleyball also offers the opportunity for female athletes to get involved with collegiate athletics. At present, the only sand collegiate opportunities for men are at the junior college level in southern California. Title IX is always an important topic, and sand volleyball is an excellent option for providing much-needed playing opportunities for aspiring female athletes. Also, compared to other collegiate sports, it is quite inexpensive to run. As in track and field, schools may double count (i.e., count indoor athletes for both indoor and sand volleyball teams). However, in the long run, indoor athletes should not be the primary resource for filling a sand volleyball roster because the two versions of the sport are distinct. Collegiate sand volleyball should provide more opportunities for more female athletes as well as college scholarships for more young women.

SAND VOLLEYBALL BUDGET

New sand volleyball programs need to purchase some basics, many of which are one-time costs. The first decision is where the team will train and host events. Court space can be rented from city parks, beaches, churches, or schools. Typically, these groups charge a small flat fee to reserve the courts or a percentage of the gross receipts, or both. It is important to have the proper insurance through the university or other programs such as USA Volleyball or the Amateur Athletic Union (AAU). Check with the appropriate organization about the specific insurance needs for your program.

If you are building your own court or facility, it is important to do it the right way. Plenty of information about building courts is available on various websites. Following are a few that will walk you through the process:

www.avca.org/sand/facilities

www.volleyballusa.com/College-Volleyball-Court-Construction.html

www.volleyballmag.com/articles/43020-building-a-regulation-sand-volleyball-court

www.volleyballmag.com/articles/112-court-cents-build-your-own-sand-volleyball-court

Sand

Sand is the biggest expense. It is important to use quality sand with no rocks and minimal clay to limit the "dust" effect of the top 6 inches. Below that, you could use a less expensive, larger-grain sand that may include tiny rocks as a bed because it drains better than high-quality, fine sand. Another level below that will be gravel, landscape cloth, and French drains. Your site should also include showers, multiple electrical outlets, and lights if possible.

Net Systems

Good-quality net equipment systems include the standards (poles), padding, net, antennae, and the referee stand. Several companies make this equipment, including Volleyball USA and Sports Imports. You will also need to purchase court lines (for boundaries) and possibly court enclosures to keep volleyballs from rolling too far from the courts.

Balls

Volleyballs are your next consideration. Programs need about 16 to 20 outdoor volleyballs per court to run an efficient practice. Sand volleyballs last only three or four years before they get heavy and worn, unlike indoor balls, which last much longer. Because each brand of sand volleyball is unique, it is important to purchase the brand that your athletes will be using in competition throughout the year.

Uniforms

Uniforms typically consist of an athletic-style bikini or a sport bra and spandex bottoms. Uniform styles will most likely be determined by the sport governing body that oversees the conference your team is competing in and will be included in the rules. Sand socks are a necessity for hot as well as very cold weather. Sunglasses are necessary, and a hat or visor is highly recommended. The sunglasses need to fit properly and provide UV protection. Many types are available; try to make the best choice for your athletes. If you are in a cold climate, tights and an athletic long-sleeved shirt are also a necessity. A thermal sleeveless vest that zips up is extremely useful as well. At practice, athletes should have a towel to stretch on and to use to brush sand off themselves. Each athlete should also have a court bag to put all these items in.

Staff

A sand volleyball team should have an 8-to-1 player-to-coach ratio. Eight players play on a single court. If you are in a college program and the coach is given a head coach title, there may be a minimal salary for that coach. If the indoor volleyball assistant coach is also assisting with the sand team, that person can retain the assistant coach title. However, it is a lot of work to coach two teams with separate schedules, budgets, scholarships, and so on.

Extra Program Costs

Scholarship cost is another budget issue to consider when adding a sand volleyball program. Refer to current NCAA rules regarding the number of scholarships that can be offered and whether players with sand volleyball scholarships can play on the indoor team, and vice versa.

Another budget consideration is travel costs to events, which includes hotel rooms, transportation, food, and other costs. Home matches have certain expenses as well, such as officials, hospitality, and other miscellaneous expenses. A home event checklist is provided later in the chapter in the section Match Event Management.

RECRUITING PLAYERS

Because sand volleyball has only recently grown to include girls 18 and under, the number of skilled sand players is not as large as that of accomplished indoor volleyball players. With time and good training, some collegiate indoor players are having quick success converting to the sand game, but experience and time are definitely needed for them to fully understand the game.

USA Beach Volleyball has quickly developed its junior program, and many of their top players have been recruited as sand scholarship athletes. Additionally, indoor players that have all-around skill, but may be considered too small to be recruited for top schools for indoor volleyball, have successfully converted to sand volleyball athletes. However, these players may lack experience, which is critical to the success of a sand player, so they will need to play a lot of events to see whether they can handle the rigors and elements of the sand game and find enjoyment in the environment.

A number of national junior beach volleyball programs abroad have highly skilled athletes who are making their way to U.S. colleges to play sand volleyball. The best places in the United States to recruit strong players are USA Volleyball High Performance Championships and national invitational events such as the USA Volleyball Junior National Championship and the AAU Junior Olympics, in which you must win a bid to compete. A few collegiate combines are other places that coaches recruit sand players. The states of California and Florida host many junior beach volleyball events in the summer, in which many strong players are competing. Additionally, high school sand volleyball is growing quickly; Arizona was the first state to officially adopt the sport into its high school programs. Southern California and certain counties in Florida have also adopted the sport for high school girls as well, and it is growing quickly. Additionally, many seasonal and year-round sand volleyball clubs are developing around the country, but mainly in the hotbeds of indoor volleyball, which include regions such as Texas and the Midwest.

COACHING STAFF

Initially, for programs working with limited funding, staff and athlete roles may be filled by existing and interested indoor volleyball coaches and athletes. As stated earlier, the number of experienced beach players and coaches is still growing, but they will be scooped up by top programs offering scholarships, a high-level, experienced beach volleyball coaching staff, and other opportunities.

A fully staffed collegiate beach volleyball program would consist of three coaches: Full-time head coach, full-time or part-time assistant coach, and volunteer assistant coach. A minimum of 14 athletes is a good roster size. Only 10 players compete at a time, but unfortunately, athletes may get injured, and you should always have enough players to compete. If you are thinking of relying on the indoor team for players, remember that indoor coaches may not mandate that their athletes play on the beach team, so you may not end up with enough players to fill the roster.

Coaching Fundamentals

When player development begins, the primary focus should be on having fun with the learning process. Many polished indoor athletes are easily frustrated when they find themselves struggling in the sand at first. They may have trouble with ball control, the environment, and developing their sand legs. Our research has shown that, initially, outside hitters experience a drop in their vertical jump from 2 to 3 inches, and middle blockers may lose 6 to 8 inches on their vertical jumps. This can obviously greatly affect their timing as hitters on the sand. Initially, all athletes experience a 2- to 4-inch loss in vertical jump. Indoor athletes need time to adjust their game and develop their sand legs. It takes a minimum of five weeks to be comfortable in the sand. As a coaching staff, you must educate yourselves to defend against initial player frustration. Invest in beach volleyball–specific coaching and training DVDs, books, and Internet resources to ensure that your athletes are seeing that their newly acquired skills are leading them to success in the sand. The AVCA (American Volleyball Coaches Association) is a great resource for educational material on coaching beach volleyball: www.championshipproductions.com/cgi-bin/champ/c/Volleyball/Sand-Sand-Volleyball-2421.html. USA Volleyball also provides BCAP (Beach Coaching Accreditation Program) certification for coaches: www.usav.org/USA-Volleyball.

If you have a sand program with full-time sand players, training should be periodized and segmented to provide a proper progression throughout the preseason, in-season, and summer. If you are new to the beach game, you need to educate yourself. Listen to what your athletes are saying about their energy levels, and get in the sand yourself to gain a well-rounded understanding of what they are going through. Because of the physical load of working in the sand (i.e., it is much harder to work out in sand than it is on a solid surface), it is very easy to overtrain. Although double days are common in indoor volleyball practice, in the sand they are inappropriate and highly discouraged.

Coaching During Competition

The beach game comes with its own separate and developing guidelines for competition. Teams play duals, and the winner is the team that has won the majority of five *flighted* matches. *Flighted* means that teams are ranked according to skill level, as in collegiate tennis, in which the top-skilled team is the number one doubles team. Currently, many high schools use three flighted matches instead of five.

Coaches coming to the sand from the indoor game may face a tough transition in terms of coaching during competition. In the sand game, coaches have limited opportunities to provide feedback. They may speak directly to their athletes only during time-outs, during side switches, and between sets. Teams switch sides of the court on multiples of seven (e.g., 3-4, 7-7, 10-11), and during which the coach may walk along the side of the court and offer strategic or adjustment-oriented feedback. In no way should this interaction slow or stall the match. During play, the coach may instruct an athlete to call for a time-out. Teams have one time-out plus a technical time-out when the scores combine to equal 21. Outside of that, any communications should consist of vague encouragement and support.

Sand volleyball provides a unique coaching experience because coaches are not tied to one match (doubles team). The first match you start watching could be a blowout. You may leave that match and go to one featuring a dog fight, tight scores, and back-and-forth action. A coaching staff can go through the gamut of coaching skills within one dual, which can be exciting and keep the game fresh and alive. Only three collegiate coaches per team are allowed to participate during an event, and multiple matches could be going at the same time. Therefore, athletes must be self-sufficient and able coach themselves through a match, unlike in the indoor game, in which a coach is always present and may provide constant feedback and direction through every point.

FACILITY DESIGN

Because a dual consists of five matches, it is ideal to have a five-court facility with additional surrounding space to comfortably accommodate up to four competing teams and staff (figure 7.2). This allows for maximal use of time and formatting during competition as well as during practice.

A minimum of three courts is recommended because any fewer can really drag out the dual competition. The format for a three-court location should involve only two matches counting toward the overall dual in the first wave with perhaps an exhibition match on the third court. The second wave would consist of the final three matches to complete the dual competition. This is done so that the dual is not already determined after the completion of the first wave of matches, which could result in a 3-0 scenario, thereby making the next

FIGURE 7.2 Typical sand facility.
Courtesy of Arron Saltz

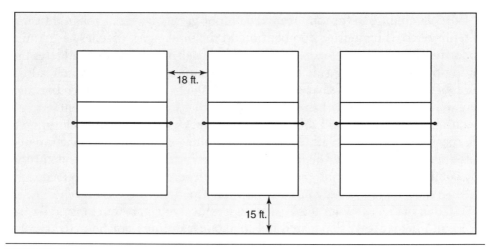

FIGURE 7.3 Example of a typical three-court facility.

two matches inconsequential. Most schools play flights 4 and 5 first and leave the more exciting matchups for the second wave of matches.

Site development should allow for ample space between courts (see figure 7.3). Collegiate requirements are 18 feet from sideline to sideline, which provides adequate space for safety and play of the ball without interfering with adjacent courts. There should also be plenty of room behind the end line for safety, jump serving, and real-time playing of the ball. Fifteen feet of clear space from the back line is ideal for reasons previously mentioned.

A daily maintenance regimen is needed for keeping the courts level and preventing them from getting bowled out. We use baseball infield rakes because they are lightweight and move a good amount of sand. Proper technique is to start pulling sand approximately 3 feet outside the edge of the court and toward the middle. As you pull the sand in, keep the rake level and allow the sand to fall, filling in divots as you go. You will end up with a small mound in the center of the court. Push the sand around the court and smooth as you go. Make sure to check the height of the net periodically to give you a consistent sense of the levelness of the court. Then run the rake around the perimeter of the court beneath the boundary lines for a finishing touch. Raking an entire court takes anywhere from 20 to 40 minutes, a minimum of twice a week.

As discussed in the budget section, many resources are available to help you build a sand court facility, which is relatively inexpensive and requires very little maintenance if it is drained properly.

TEAM COHESION AND PLAYER DEVELOPMENT

Collegiate sand volleyball is unique in that the program includes athletes from two disciplines with differing skill sets. Early on, most programs fill their rosters with indoor athletes who may have limited sand volleyball experience. Some programs have the funding to establish a sand-only team, but they may lean on the indoor program to complete it.

The sand coach's primary objective with indoor volleyball athletes is to make the sport an enjoyable experience because they are in their non-traditional season and participating on the sand team is optional. Their indoor coaches may strongly suggest that they play, but they should be under no obligation to participate on the sand volleyball team. Sand coaches must also develop strong team chemistry while they are folding in indoor players with the sand players they have been coaching during the fall semester, while the indoor team has been a separate team. Indoor athletes join the sand team at the beginning of the spring semester after they have finished their indoor season.

Indoor athletes need to get their sand legs initially and should probably not participate in scoring or competitive games at the beginning of their training in the sand. Losing in drills early on may cause disillusionment with the progress of their sand skill development and may discourage them to the point of quitting. This could have devastating effects beyond the athlete; it may also affect future prospects. Bringing indoor players in slowly can be done with simple noncompetitive ball-control and hitting exercises. This develops a base of confidence that adds to the excitement of learning a new skill set in a game they love.

RULES: DIFFERENCES AND SIMILARITIES

There are many rule differences between sand and indoor volleyball, some well-known, others not so much. Make sure to become familiar with the particular rules used in the organization governing the competition for your program. Following are some of the main rule differences:

- In sand volleyball the best two out of three sets wins a match for both men and women, as opposed to indoor volleyball's best three out of five. The first two sets are played to 21 points; the third set, to 15. All sets have no cap, which means that they must be won by a minimum of 2 points.
- The court dimensions for sand volleyball are 8 by 8 meters; those for indoor volleyball are 9 by 9 meters.
- Beach teams switch sides of the court during each set on multiples of 7 for sets to 21 points, and on multiples of 5 for sets to 15 points. The only time indoor teams switch sides during the play of a set is in the fifth set, where they switch sides when one team reaches a total of eight points.
- The collegiate sand game consists of duals of flighted play, which feature five matches of doubles. Indoor plays one team made up of their best six-person team of the moment.
- The touch off the block counts as one of the three contacts in sand volleyball.
- There is no center line in the sand game; players may go underneath the net as long as they do not contact or impede an opposing player. There are strict centerline limitations in the indoor game.

- ◆ The rules on hand setting are much tighter in sand than in indoor volleyball.
- ◆ Sand coaches are limited to communicating with players only during side switches, between sets, and during time-outs. The indoor coach may speak liberally to his or her team at any and all points of the match.
- ◆ Open-handed tipping is not allowed in the sand game; it is allowed in the indoor game.
- ◆ In the sand game, when a player is intentionally overhand setting over the net, the ball must cross the net directly to where the setter is facing; this can be either in front or directly behind. There are no such limitations in the indoor game on overhand setting the ball.
- ◆ The ball pressure for the sand game is 2.8 to 3.2 psi; for the indoor game it is 4.3 to 4.6 psi.
- ◆ Appropriate music can be played during the competition in sand volleyball. Music is not allowed while the ball is in play during indoor volleyball.

This list is not comprehensive, but it provides a quick look at some of the rule differences between the sand game and the indoor game. As the sport develops at the collegiate level, the rules may change slightly to achieve the fairest atmosphere to ensure success in the sport.

YEAR-ROUND TRAINING

In the overall development of our program, our greatest commodity is our athletes. They need special attention year-round to continually improve both on and off the court and to avoid injury. At Florida State University we provide our athletes with year-round lifting and conditioning programs. Our athletes train the way professionals do, except that we have them for only eight months a year. Thus, when they leave our program, they are well equipped to continue and build on their successes.

In our conditioning program, we focus on Olympic lifts and upper-body development because the sport demands a high level of power endurance and strength. To ensure safety, make sure your athletes are familiar with proper lifting techniques. Have a certified strength coach work with your athletes, or get certified yourself so that you are familiar with the best techniques and safe lifts. We incorporate all forms of resistance training from body weight to barbells, cable machines to sand bags. We periodize our lifts by using heavier cycles in the fall and lightening the load heading into the spring and in-season. In addition to resistance training, our athletes work through an extensive periodized track program to build explosive speed and endurance.

A preseason strength/power routine consists of three lifting sessions per week. We have our athletes perform an active warm-up prior to lifting, and the lift session might look something like this:

- Back squat: 3 or 4 sets of 6-10 reps
- Clean (hang clean or power clean): 2 or 3 sets of 3-6 reps
- Chest press: 3 or 4 sets of 6-10 reps
- Seated cable row: 3 or 4 sets of 8-10 reps
- Front squat to power jerk: 2 or 3 sets of 3 or 4 reps
- Front and lateral raise: 2 or 3 sets of 8-10 reps
- Lateral band walk: 2 or 3 sets of 10-12 reps
- Alternating biceps curl: 2 or 3 sets of 8-10 reps
- Variety of abdominal and core work: 3-5 exercises

An in-season routine might look like this:

- Hang clean to power jerk: 2 or 3 sets of 3 reps
- Power clean pull: 2 or 3 sets of 2 or 3 reps
- Back squat: 2 or 3 sets of 3-5 reps
- Chin-up: 2 or 3 sets of 3-6 reps
- Bench press: 2 sets of 6-10 reps
- TRX row: 2 sets of 6-10 reps
- Standing dumbbell (DB) military press: 2 sets of 8-10 reps
- Standing DB biceps curl: 2 sets of 8-10 reps
- Variety of abdominal and core work: 3-5 exercises

We also incorporate a multi-week plyometric program into our training. This comes after our athletes have laid a foundation of strength and power to maximize the effectiveness of plyometric training. We incorporate body weight exercises, plyometric box drills, medicine ball throws, stairs, hurdles, and cone work.

We have recently increased the use of foam rolling (SMR, or self-myofascial release) prior to practices as well as multipoint shoulder warm-ups with the use of bands. The primary reason for the increased use of foam rollers is to improve overall flexibility, prevent injuries, and increase functional movement. Band work has always been part of our program, but we have increased it by including it as a part of the daily prepractice warm-up routine to maintain the health of, and prevent injury to, athletes' shoulders.

For additional injury prevention, weekly yoga sessions are part of the program we use all year round. The focus is stretching rather than isometric holds and strength, which is already addressed in various forms. Taking a 10- to 15-minute ice bath several times a week is a requirement to promote recovery as the load on a sand volleyball player taxes every muscle in a very different way than the indoor game does. As always, we work closely with our athletic training staff on athlete recovery and rehabilitation.

MATCH EVENT MANAGEMENT

Running a sand volleyball event with all the logistics may seem hectic, especially if your background is indoor volleyball. From proper formatting to staffing with volunteers and hiring referees, there are a lot of moving parts.

It is important to have a competition manager (or director of operations) who is not the coach. This person's job is to delegate and manage all primary responsibilities such as assigning volunteers, managing score sheet collection, and making sure lunch has been ordered and is arriving on time. The manager must also coordinate with the officials and make sure hotel accommodations are in place, check with the assigning officials' coordinator to make sure the proper number of officials have been planned for, and be ready to manage an inclement weather plan. The manager must plan to have the facility set up two hours prior to the event, and make sure tents and the sound system are set up according to the schematic drawn up by the facilities staff. The courts must be raked, and tables, chairs, and umbrellas need to be set up. The marketing staff should arrive an hour prior to the start of the event. They will have confirmed the hiring of a knowledgeable announcer and a singer for the national anthem, and have appropriate music playing before the teams arrive and during the competition. They also need to be adaptable and ready for all the little things that pop up throughout the day that may interfere with the smooth running of the event. See figure 7.4 for a schematic drawing of our match-day event setup.

Following are the requirements for a basic home event:

- Two to five sand courts or more
- Net system: court boundary lines, nets, pole pads, antennae, and a referee stand
- Six to eight balls per court for the warm-up, three or four game balls per court for the match
- Table and chairs and portable scoreboard at the end of each court
- Four chairs and two umbrellas per court for the athletes and coaches to use prior to the start of and during the match and time-outs
- Separate tents for each school and for referees, medical staff, marketing staff, and volunteer staff
- Chairs or benches for each tent
- Sound system, microphone, and speakers for music prior to and during the event, for the announcer and marketing announcements
- Extra cups, water bottles, and coolers of water and ice for general use
- Extra scoring sheets for referees
- Marketing table displaying booster information, season schedule, and the event program
- Concession area for spectators
- Restrooms for event staff, players, and spectators

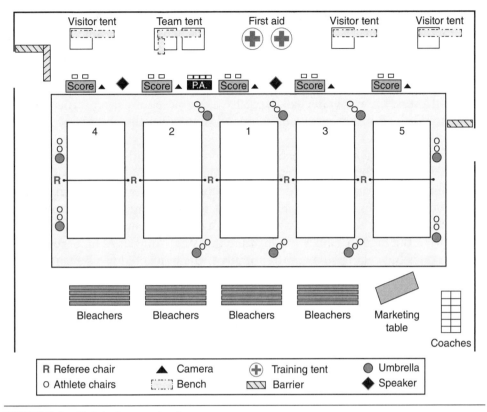

FIGURE 7.4 Match-day event setup.

Coaching at-home events can be difficult at times; you may feel as though you are putting out fires throughout the day. It is imperative that you have a well-organized staff whose members understand their roles and execute them professionally. As a head coach, you train not only your athletes, but also your support staff, which may be ever-changing. Make sure to have plans for inclement weather because protocols, ball management, and court management may change. Sand volleyball *will be played* in heavy rain and strong wind unless there is a threat of lightning (most athletic training departments have some type of lightning-detection equipment) or if the wind is so strong that the site is compromised. Play does not stop for extreme conditions that are deemed safe for being outdoors. Obviously, this also means that practice and training take place on rainy, cold, and windy days.

One major priority for event planning is to make sure the format provides enough play for all teams, which should include exhibition matches for the alternate players who don't receive many opportunities to play live matches. A match can last anywhere from 25 to 75 minutes. We have experimented with a variety of formats combining dual play and a flighted pair's tournament with teams 1 and 2 in one bracket and teams 3, 4, and 5 in another bracket. We have found much success with this format because all teams receive a minimum of three matches the first day (considering a four-school competition) and a minimum of two full matches the second day with many different matchups for the teams that make it to the finals. A five-court facility with four participating schools can finish a round-robin of dual play the first day usually in about 6 hours and a flighted pairs bracketed event the second day in about 8 hours. Bracket play would not necessarily be a true double elimination because there would be consolation matches for the early losers. In sand volleyball, typically, a double-elimination format reverts to single elimination during the final four to keep down the number of matches played per day.

The number of courts at the site, and the maximal and minimal number of matches played per team are the primary deciding factors in format development. Three full matches per day should be the maximum because more than that can be dangerous to athletes. The ideal number of matches per day is one. In reality, one match is unrealistic within the collegiate/high school/amateur setting, however, as you need the biggest bang for your time invested. You can reduce match play for top teams by making some of the rounds of the bracketed pair's event one set to 28 points.

CONCLUSION

These are amazing times in the sport of volleyball. With the addition of sand volleyball at the collegiate level, the opportunities for current and future athletes and coaches are tremendous. It has been a long and arduous road for the AVCA and for the first colleges that jumped on board to make sand volleyball the fastest-growing emergent sport in NCAA history. The sport will likely continue to grow exponentially because it has a strong television presence, it is an exciting spectator sport, it is relatively inexpensive to start up and maintain, and because of the continued need for universities to make steps toward being Title IX compliant.

In 2010 I was fortunate to be the first full-time head sand volleyball coach at the collegiate level and have been privileged to witness all the other programs being added. Although the sport itself has been around for some time recreationally, professionally, and in the Olympics, its acceptance into the collegiate ranks will truly catapult it throughout the country in all climates and for all ages. I have spent my career working specifically in beach volleyball. I am very blessed and grateful for the opportunity to work in sand volleyball at the college level and to see the sport I love grow so much.

8

Running a Successful Volleyball Camp

Chris Catanach

During my first year of coaching, some 30 years ago, I had the opportunity to raise money for my fledgling volleyball program by renting our gym for a volleyball camp hosted by a high-profile athlete. This camp was a sellout because of the status of the athlete and the big-name staff members listed on the brochure. The camp was marketed by a company out of California (which I was in touch with almost daily), and I was excited to be the point person for the University of Tampa. My role in the camp was to set up the courts, unlock the doors each day, and be a liaison for housing and food service. My daily conversations with representatives of the marketing company gave me a false sense of how organized this camp would be.

Within minutes of the staff arrival, I realized that there was no camp plan. Although the campers registered prior to arrival, they were not assigned room-mates, and there was no supervisory staff and no plan for directing the campers to and from sessions. There was no camp schedule and no group or staff assignments. The camper-to-staff ratio was about twelve to one, and the staff members were not interested in working very hard. By the end of the first session, I was no longer just a liaison; I was directing the camp from behind the scenes. At the end of the camp, the father of the celebrity athlete offered me the opportunity to run the camp in the future and keep the proceeds but pay his daughter $3,000 to make an appearance. As a result of my experience with this camp, I realized that, although a "celebrity athlete" or coach may help with attendance, the real success of a camp comes from providing an organized, fun experience at a reasonable price. I could do better than this. I decided that even if I drew only 50 kids in the first year, I could make a small profit and begin building the camp. As a result of hard work, organization, attention to detail, a desire to provide a great value, and a commitment to service, I have been fortunate to draw large numbers for each of our camps.

CAMP PHILOSOPHY

My philosophy on camps is simple: Make the camp experience all about the camper and not what is easiest or most convenient for the staff. You will know you have provided a great camp experience when a departing camper is thanking you for having her, raving about how much fun she had with her roommates, telling mom how great the food was, excited about playing volleyball again, and tired because your staff worked her so hard. If you did your job right, your campers will sign up early next summer, and they will bring their friends.

This chapter pertains mostly to three- or four-day resident and commuter camps. The three key facets to focus on to create a successful summer camp experience are organization and administration, volleyball training sessions, and the residential experience (food and housing). The order of importance is not the same for all campers. Elite-level campers may critique the curriculum or group assignments more than the food and housing, whereas beginners may gauge their experience based on food or housing rather than training sessions. Sometimes you can do everything right and a camper will have a bad experience because she could not get past her displeasure regarding her group assignment. Nevertheless, you should consider each camper your only customer and make it your daily goal to ensure that all facets of the camp are as good as they can be for everyone.

ORGANIZATION AND ADMINISTRATION

Organization is the key to running a successful camp. Planning should start well in advance of the actual camp date. Putting in the preparation time well before the first whistle blows will enable your camp to run smoothly. There are many things that go into the organization and administration of a successful camp. You must organize your business, secure facilities and staff, determine your pricing strategy, develop the camp schedule, and register campers. Below I will touch upon the topics I think are the most important.

Creating Your Business

The first order of business in establishing a camp is creating your company and incorporating it. The S Corp and the LLC are two of the best options for simple corporations. Consult with your accountant about what type of corporation would work best for your business. Both can be created online at a reasonable cost.

The reasons for incorporating are numerous. Most important is the reduction of liability because your business involves minors. We live in a lawsuit-happy country, and your good friend, the lawyer, will not hesitate to sue you, your camp insurance, the owner of the facility you are renting, the maker of the volleyballs and nets, or anyone else who is deemed to have deep pockets. Having your own business also allows you to make more timely purchases and pay staff without going through extensive paperwork at a university. Keeping good records of income and expenses is critical. Incorporating is also important for tax purposes. Again, consult an accountant to learn the benefits of the various types of corporations.

Identifying Costs and Developing a Budget

Determine your per camper cost by adding the expenses you will incur from all of the categories presented below. I create a budget for each category so that I can better manage the expenses incurred during the camp. For example, if my budget for staff salaries is $50 per camper, I will then make decisions about the number of extra staff I am willing to hire and how much I am willing to pay each staff member.

Facility Fees

Your university may have a per-camper fee for facility use or a lump sum fee per day. Schedule your camp to maximize this cost. If you pay a daily facility fee, then plan to have at least two sessions on both the first and last days to optimize your use of the facility. Don't forget to include sales tax in your rental fee budget. If you are charged a per-camper fee (for each camp), it is quite easy to put that amount into the budget.

Insurance

Most insurance companies will sell you a liability policy that requires you to purchase a secondary medical policy. A number of companies underwrite sports camp insurance policies. Coaches in your athletic department should be able to suggest companies with whom they have had good relationships. Premiums for liability and medical coverage for staff and campers will cost about 75 cents per day for residential campers and 55 cents per day for nonresidential, or commuter, campers. In addition to the liability and medical policies, your university may also require a sexual abuse policy that will add 25 cents per day.

All camp insurance companies require a minimal payment to write the policy. For example, if you have only 50 kids attending camp, the minimal fee for the policy may exceed the per-day figures noted earlier.

Food

One of the most important relationships to develop when running a camp is your relationship with your food service provider. You may be able to negotiate a price based on volume because providers' prices are based on volume and they should be willing to pass the savings on to you. Small colleges and universities that do not have huge summer school attendance usually are willing to bargain with camp programs because their food service providers need summer revenue to pay their salaried staff. When creating the schedule for the camp, avoid having a meal as the first activity on the first day because this adds a significant amount to your per-camper costs. Include staff food costs as well as sales tax in your per-camper budget.

Housing

When computing your housing costs, do not forget to budget for not only the campers, but also the staff. Once again, sales tax will come into play. Some states require the lessor to charge the local hotel tax rate for dorm rentals. It is also a good idea to gather all of the coaches who run camps on your campus and meet with the residence-life staff, or whoever assigns summer housing. Impress upon them your need for the use of air-conditioned and updated buildings.

At private universities, admissions directors can be a tremendous help in convincing the administration to provide the best the school has to offer in terms of housing and other facilities. The positive marketing for the university facilities is worth thousands. Every camper or parent who is impressed with your residence halls will tell at least five other friends, and word will spread. If you are offered better dorms for a higher price, it is probably worth the additional cost.

Staff Salaries

Hire your camp staff as contract labor because they provide a service to the camp for a short period of time. Create a contract identifying all areas of service, their employment status as contractors, salaries, duties, and policies on abuse. You should provide a brief sexual abuse training session with the staff prior to having them sign their contracts. When determining compensation for employees, take a look at what the competition is paying. The coach-to-camper ratio is up to you, but a ratio of one coach for every eight campers generally provides each camper with plenty of one-on-one interaction. Avoid the common mistake of hiring more staff than you need; this is best done by hiring as you receive registrations and deposits.

When determining what you will pay your assistant coaches for working the camps, I recommend an incentive plan. Paying your assistant(s) a predetermined amount per camper gives them an incentive to help grow the camps. They become invested in the success of every facet of the camp. This form of payment also creates a per-camper salary cost and helps you avoid overspending.

Background Checks and Fingerprinting

Many states require live scan fingerprinting of any people hired to work with children under the age of 18 during a summer or vacation period. The cost of a live scan is anywhere from $30 to $50 per person. Most states accept affidavits from the school system verifying that a teacher or coach employed by the school system has been screened within the past five years. For any staff members who cannot provide affidavits, arrange for screening locally, or require them to go to a testing agency near their homes to be screened. You should reimburse them for this expense in their first paycheck. Make sure to start this important process early because it may take a few weeks for processing.

Supplies

When budgeting for supplies and equipment, consider supplies you will need to run a quality operation outside of the gym as well. In addition to balls, ball carts, and floor tape, consider stocking up on paper for manuals and handouts, water cups, pens for staff, computer support supplies, certificates for camp awards, and training room supplies. If you run a camp over the weekend and maintenance personnel will not be around, stock up on paper towels, toilet paper, and large trash bags. Have your staff be responsible for keeping the areas clean and trash picked up.

Computer Software

A multitude of companies create websites, provide credit card services, and import registrations to a database. Most services provide access to the database so that you can assign groups or housing. The costs for these services range from around $3 per camper to as much as $7 per camper. These companies also charge you credit card use fees, but they ask you to build them into your camp price. A cheaper solution is to purchase database software such as FileMaker. For a $300 investment, you can accomplish everything the camp data companies offer in their services for multiple years. This is a much more economical option for camps that service more than 100 campers.

Camp Gifts

The most common camp gift is a T-shirt. If you shop around, you should be able to purchase a white T-shirt with a two-color design for under $5 each, or a colored T-shirt with a two-color design for under $6. The T-shirt pricing is based on volume, so the more you buy, the cheaper the price will be. Other camp gift ideas are volleyballs, knee pads, backpacks, and sling packs. Add the cost of each gift item into your per-camper cost and price the camp accordingly.

Additional administrative costs might include website fees, cell phone use, database management, and accounting fees.

Pricing and Payments

Once you have identified your costs and desired profit, check the pricing of your competition to make sure you are right in line. If you decide to charge more than competing camps, make sure it is because you provide something the other camps do not: a special camp gift, extra training sessions, or individual skill videos.

Payment is an issue that should be clarified up front. We accept personal checks up to 14 days prior to the start of camp. After that point, we accept only cash, money orders, or cashier's checks. More recently, we started offering credit card payment options through our website, which has become the number one form of payment for parents. The parent is notified before they begin the credit card process that there is a credit card convenience fee added to the cost of camp. Requiring a deposit when the camper reserves their spot and then requesting the balance be paid 14 days prior to the start of camp is vital. Campers are less likely to cancel if they have made full payment.

Advertising and Marketing

If you provide a great camp experience for a fair price, word of mouth will be your best advertisement. Other things that you can do to market your camps are to advertise in the annual summer camp sections in local magazines; advertise on RichKern.com, AVCA.org, or other summer camp sites; print fliers and distribute them to every junior high and high school in your city or county; send e-mail blasts to clubs and players in your targeted area; and call high schools in your state and invite them to give your camp a try. Sending camp brochures to junior high schools and high schools in areas where there are strong recruits may pay off in the future.

One of the most important things you will do is create a website. You can hire a company to create, host, and manage a site for you, however, this option can be expensive. Your site should include camp descriptions and dates, sample schedules, check-in and check-out information, a list of what to bring, pricing, online registration, answers to frequently asked questions, staff biographies, information on your program and university, driving directions, and anything else you can think of that will help sell your camp.

Hiring Staff

Choose energetic and enthusiastic staff since they will be helping you create a camp culture that will attract campers back year after year. Personnel to consider when building your camp staff are head court coaches, assistant court coaches, administrative assistants, medical trainers, and residence hall supervisors.

Court Coaches

People who can serve as court coaches at your camp are other college coaches, club coaches, college players, and high school coaches. Club coaches do a tremendous job with skill camps because they are used to working with undeveloped athletes. Find coaches who are good teachers and hard workers, and who enjoy the camp setting. A lazy or negative head court coach can be a camp downfall. Put a lot of thought into your group coach assignments, and try to match your coaches and your groups according to their personalities and strengths. Although most coaches may want to work with the top group in camp, some of your most important groups are the beginners. You may want to assign some of your better coaches to those groups. Having groups spend a session or two rotating through stations gives campers the opportunity to work with multiple group coaches.

Administrative Assistant

The administrative assistant is an invaluable staff member. At many of the major college programs, a director of volleyball operations staff member is responsible for administering summer camps. If you do not have a director of operations, hire an administrative assistant to handle check-in and check-out, room assignments, residence hall staff supervision, payment collections, background checks, staff contracts, and any other administrative duties that need doing.

Medical Trainers

Your head athletic trainer can usually arrange for camp athletic trainers. It is important that you hire people who will be positive contributors to the camp experience. They must be qualified to deal with injuries ranging from sprains to sore forearms after passing sessions. The head trainer should be at registration to confirm medical clearance forms (submitted online during registration) and check for any allergies, medications, or other issues that may arise during camp. They need to make sure there is a signed parental consent form giving permission for medical treatment of minors in case of an accident. This should be collected at check-in if it is not part of the online registration process.

Residence Hall Supervisors and Floor Monitors

Residence staff members are critical to the overnight camper experience. It is vital that you hire people who are mature and generally care about the young people entrusted to your care. The care of campers is a responsibility that your staff must embrace and perform well. Develop a list of camp rules to distribute at registration that covers issues such as expected behavior and curfews.

TRAINING SESSIONS

Before you develop your camp training sessions, you need to explore the different types of camps you would like to offer, group sizes, and coach to camper ratio.

Types of Camps

Colleges around the country offer a variety of camps including individual skills camps, specialty skills camps, and team camps. Almost all colleges offer resident and commuter options for their multiday camps. The camp length can be anywhere from one 3-hour session that focuses on a particular skill, to a four- or five-day all-skills camp. Basketball programs seem to run more competition camps (existing AAU and high school teams attend and basically play tournaments), with some instruction and speakers thrown in here and there. Research the camps at institutions near you, and then find your niche so that you create a unique camp experience in your area.

All-Skills Camp

An all-skills volleyball camp usually consists of six to eight sessions in which all six skills (underhand passing, overhand passing, serving, attacking, floor defense, and blocking) are taught. If you choose to offer a tournament as part of your camp, I recommend that you schedule the camp over seven or eight sessions. The goal for this camp should be to introduce or refine the six basic skills necessary for playing the game of volleyball. Quality demonstrations and accurate repetitions are vital to the acquisition or refinement of each skill.

All Skills Camp: Sample Skills Camp Schedule —7 Sessions

Session 1 (3 hours)

Staff introductions and camp rules, gym culture, etc.

Ability grouping—Create a separate schedule for this—no skill instruction; evaluation only.

Two periods in which two skills are demonstrated and drilled (underhand passing and serving)

End with a combination drill and cool-down. Every session should end with a brief cool-down that includes stretching.

Sessions 2 & 3 (2.5 hours each)

Follow a similar time layout to session 1. Schedule review periods for each skill taught in the previous session. Demonstrate and drill the four remaining skills: overhand passing, attacking, individual defense, and blocking. End each session with some competition, usually coach controlled.

Session 4 (2.5 hours)

Have groups rotate through stations that touch on each of the skills taught previously. Keep the groups together and rotate them from court to court. The stations refresh the campers since they get to work with new coaches. I find that the stations provide an opportunity for coaches to be assigned to teach their best skill which improves the training experience for the campers. This also provides the opportunity for coaches to work with campers at a variety of skill levels. Each court is a station, and the staff assigned to that court teaches and drills only the skill assigned to that station. Examples include advanced underhand, overhand passing and advanced attacking and blocking (tips, rolls, shots, team blocking). Each group should rotate through five or six stations; work at each station should last 15 to 18 minutes. After the stations are completed, offer 30 to 45 minutes of competitive play.

Session 5 (2.5 hours)

Half of this session should be devoted to skill review within the groups; and the other half, to team concepts such as offense and defense. Team offense includes serve-receive patterns, coverage, and basic play sets. Team defense includes team blocking, types of defenses, and transitioning from defensive to offensive (attacking) positions. In younger groups, campers should learn multiple positions. Players 14 and older can begin specializing by position.

Session 6 (2.5 hours)

This session includes 40 to 50 minutes of skill review. The remainder of the session is devoted to creating teams that play controlled 6v6 games.

Session 7 (2.5 hours)

Create a round-robin camp tournament in multiple divisions. I recommend timed games so that you can start and end the session when desired. The session finishes with camp awards and check-out.

Specialty Camp

Specialty camps are popular with players who want to refine one particular skill. Because the high number of repetitions involved in specialty camps often results in overuse injuries, make sure to build plenty of recovery time into your schedule. Quality versus quantity is a good rule of thumb. An Internet search will turn up very successful specialty camps committed to a single skill. Evening serving camps are popular as well.

Team Camp

Team camps are for high school, club, and AAU teams who want to improve their team skills such as offense, defense, coverage, transition, and camaraderie. Such camps should not be just about tournament play; they should also provide competitive training sessions to help teams improve all facets of their game. Team camps succeed and grow based on their schedules, their competitive atmosphere, and the willingness of their camp administrators to make changes each year to meet the demands of repeat customers.

Team Camp: Sample Team Camp Schedule—8 Sessions

Prior to every training session, I have a staff meeting with all coaches and visiting coaches to make sure everyone understands the schedule. I also meet with all the campers prior to each demonstration so that we eliminate potential confusion about where their team rotates to and what they will be doing when they get there. Typically, a session consists of a five- to seven-minute information session, a demonstration of each drill and an explanation of how it is scored, and court assignments. You will need a staff of non-coaches to make sure each drill sequence starts and ends on time. Planning and organizing are vital to the success of any camp, but especially a team camp.

Session 1 (2.25 hours)

Out-of-System Training (the following schedule is for a pod of six teams on two courts)

10 minutes	Staff introductions and camp rules, gym culture, etc.
12 minutes	Demonstration of the three progressions for out-of-system training

Assign predetermined staff teams to demonstrate the drill, and then provide a detailed explanation of the drill during the staff meeting. Sometimes we choose participating teams from the camp to perform the demonstration to the rest of the camp.

1. Half court dig, set, approach, and catch
2. 5v5, no designated setter, attacker rotates out, fill from the center back
3. 6v6, first ball initiated to the setter, play out the points, first team to 3 points wins, then wave (bring on new players) the players

18 minutes	Teams break to courts and play three 6-minute time periods of drill 1. Coaches follow a round-robin schedule.
36 minutes	Teams continue with drill 2, play six 6-minute time periods
48 minutes	Teams continue with drill 3, play six 8-minute time periods

Note: Require teams to stretch and cool down at the completion of each session.

Session 2 (2.5 hours) Offense or defense theme

Session 3 (2.5 hours) Offense or defense theme

Session 4 (2.5 hours) 60 minutes of themed competition (director determines and provides a handout on the topic) and then 75 minutes of timed match play for the seeding of the tournament

Session 5 (2 hours) Controlled competitive games touching on all previous themes

Session 6 (3 hours) First round of the tournament (all sets are timed)

Session 7   **(3 hours)**   Second round of the tournament (all sets are timed)

Session 8   **(3 hours)**   Bracket play and camp awards

Note: I suggest that you schedule a practice for each team during either the lunch or dinner break over the first two days.

Group Assignments

Assigning groups is one of the most difficult tasks when preparing for an individual skills camp. It is also the area in which most camps receive the greatest number of complaints. Make every effort to group kids where they will be challenged, gain confidence, and if possible, be happy. You will encounter many young campers and their parents who are unrealistic about their skill levels. Your challenge is to meet their needs as valued customers while maintaining the integrity of your groups.

When grouping kids for skills camps, assign them a starting group based on two things: (1) the information they provided on the registration form (age, height, high school, and club experience) and (2) basic research into their club experience (the strength of the club or team). Also, keep in mind that about 75 percent of campers want to be grouped with their friends. Group assignments are made prior to their arrival and give a starting point for the ability grouping session at the beginning of the camp.

If you have a database program similar to FileMaker, you can sort campers by many of the aforementioned categories, which makes it quite easy to assign group numbers to each camper. Another suggestion is to assign your groups by the court coach's name so that the kids do not focus on the numbers of their groups. Many database programs also allow you to print name tags for the opening sessions that include the camper's name and the group coach. The campers then report to their assigned coaches and courts for the ability grouping session.

The ability grouping session is a 45- or 50-minute session in which staff members adjust the groups based on observing the campers performing basic skills such as passing, serving, setting, and attacking. The goal by the conclusion of the ability grouping time block is to have groups of 14 to 18 campers at similar levels. In many cases it is better to have a group of 18 with kids that fit than to move two kids down a level to have 16 in each group.

Do your best to begin and end every session on time and display the time period for every session on a clock that is visible to everyone. Schedule water breaks after each session of 30 minutes or more to break up the sessions and make sure the kids have time to recover. Prior to every session, conduct a staff meeting so that all coaches are on the same page. It is also helpful to begin and end every session with an entire camp meeting (only five to seven minutes) so that everyone knows where to be and when. Each court leader should take attendance at the beginning of each session. Make sure you have a plan for your administrator to check on any missing campers—check their dorm rooms or call their parents.

THE RESIDENTIAL EXPERIENCE

Quality, tasty meals along with safe and comfortable housing are vital to the camper experience. Food quality, taste, and variety are important ingredients for successful camp mealtimes. Take an active role in the food service, and develop a relationship with the director and staff. Meet with the director and ask about the menu for each meal. Make sure there are options such as fresh fruit, a salad bar, and ice cream available every day. Cafeterias make quite a bit of money from camps, so make them aware, in a kind way, that a quality experience helps grow not only the camps, but their income.

During the camp, walk around and ask campers if they have everything they need, if the food is good, or if you can do anything for them. Also, talk to the directors of the food service to make sure the campers are clearing their tables and behaving properly. You may want to assign your staff members to supervise the camper behavior during meal times. This goes a long way in creating a relationship with the cafeteria workers, and they will be friendlier to the campers.

The quality of your residential facilities and supervision can either significantly enhance or detract from the overall camp experience. Convince your administration (admissions and residence life) of the importance of providing clean, air-conditioned rooms for athletic summer camps. The positive advertising that summer camps provide for universities can be off the charts. Negotiate with the campus accommodations office to make sure that your assigned housing is within walking distance to the dining and competition facilities.

Room assignments are another critical part of the residential experience. Every decision you make in the residence hall should be about the welfare of the campers, while allowing for a fun experience. Take special care to meet campers' roommate requests. For example, if you have a group of three but your rooms have only two beds, move a bed in. If you have six kids who have requested each other, assign them to two or three adjoining rooms. The important thing for them is to be with their chosen roommates. Some campers will not have a roommate request, so put some effort into matching them with other kids their age and at their experience level. Keep an eye on campers who are attending by themselves to make sure they are having a positive experience; ask them to let you know if they need anything.

Residence hall supervision should be a top priority for your camp. Assign your administrative assistant to oversee all of the residence hall operations, especially the supervisors. One option is to require all collegiate volleyball players that you hire to serve as floor and room monitors. Your players should be accountable to you, and you should impress upon them how important this part of their job is. The staff should conduct room checks each night. Encourage the hall monitors to interact with the kids and be proactive in dealing with homesickness or room problems. It is a good idea to perform bed checks each night to account for every camper. You can also require your head resident (or administrative assistant) to collect the room check forms for an added layer of accountability.

Another option to ensure the safety of your campers is to hire a campus safety officer for three to four hours each evening to assist with the supervision and security of the building. The off-duty pay is attractive to safety officers, and these officers endear your camp to the entire security staff at your school, which pays off in additional eyes and ears during the camp period.

You will need an emergency plan for your camp in general, but especially for the residence hall. Have your floor monitors conduct a meeting during which they go over the emergency exit locations, staff room locations, emergency phone numbers, residence hall rules and violation consequences, and bed check procedures. Then have the staff escort the campers on their floor down the stairwells to simulate a fire drill.

CAMP STORE

Camp stores are a relatively easy way to supplement your camp earnings, but more important, they provide after-hours snacks and drinks for campers and staff. Most camps have dinner between 5 and 6:30 p.m., so the campers and staff are pretty hungry by the end of the evening session. Pizza, bread sticks, fruit snacks, water, and sport drinks are attractive items for your store. Try to limit or eliminate soda sales because the sugar will keep campers wound up well past bedtime. Some stores also sell volleyball-themed T-shirts, sweatshirts, and sweatpants along with knee pads, socks, and sometimes shoes. These items can be ordered on consignment from companies throughout the United States.

THE CHECK-IN AND CHECK-OUT EXPERIENCE

We are paperless; everything is listed on our website. Three weeks prior to camp, we send a confirmation e-mail directing parents to the website for information on when and where to check in, what to bring, a campus map, camp schedule, contact information, and any unpaid balance.

The first impression campers and those in their travel parties have of your camp will be set during the check-in process. Spend some time designing the steps for check-in, including the flow from table to table. It is vital to greet them, direct them to the starting point, and then process them as efficiently as possible. Let them know how excited you are that they are there. During your staff meeting, impress upon your coaches the importance of good customer relations. The more organized, efficient, and friendly the staff is, the more reassured parents will be that their children are in good, caring hands.

In addition to the staff members who are handling check-in, station your resident staffers on their assigned floors to greet and direct campers to their rooms. Give them a script to follow for greeting each family and providing all the information they need when preparing their rooms. As mentioned previously, have the residence staff host a 10-minute floor meeting just prior to escorting their residents downstairs for the walk to the courts or the cafeteria. Anything you can do to reassure parents and campers that their well-being is your highest priority starts the camp off on a positive note. If campers who have registered do not show up to check in, call their parents immediately to confirm that they are not attending the camp. Hiring a campus security officer to assist with traffic flow for drop-off and pickup will also help make the process go smoothly.

The campers' final impression of your camp will be their check-out experience. Plan the process so that is as organized and efficient as the check in experience. Provide trash bags on each floor for the campers to use. Staff members should be visible, checking each room to make sure kids aren't leaving electronic devices or sneakers behind, helping lug belongings to the elevators, and leaving them with a memory of a smiling face as they head home to catch up on sleep.

Camp Guidelines

Provide your staff with a detailed camp manual that includes your philosophy, camp goals, schedules, rules for staff and campers, emergency phone numbers, a campus map, a court layout, and a roster of assigned groups. The following lists provide clear directives to everyone involved.

Staff Expectations

1. Be on time.
2. Work hard.
3. Give constant positive feedback! Recognize campers' efforts as much as or more than the result.
4. Keep track of your group (always have your roll sheet). Each session begins with roll call. If anyone is missing, notify the directors immediately.
5. Have a practice plan for each session. If you do not completely understand a session, *please* ask the directors to explain.
6. Keep volleyballs off the floor, and keep the playing area safe. Have campers clear the ball to the end line, not sideways. Keep ball carts out of the attack area during play.
7. Wear proper attire including proper shoes (no flip-flops).
8. Always stand while working. The campers will work hard if you do.
9. Let us know how we can make your experience better.
10. Shag all volleyballs in your court area, and count them at the end of each session. Even out the numbers of volleyballs in each basket.

Staff Rules

1. No alcohol consumption while on campus. (Do not return to the dorms intoxicated.)

2. Do not provide rides for campers in your vehicle.

3. Do not use physical means for punishing campers. Do not drive between facilities.

4. Staff may not enter camper dorm rooms of the opposite gender unless for emergency purposes.

Weather Rules

1. Light rain and *no* lightning: walk the campers to the facilities.

2. Heavy rain and/or lightning: stay inside under cover until you hear from the directors.

General Camp Rules

These rules should be provided on the camper info sheet during check in.

1. No alcohol, drugs, or cigarettes allowed on campuses.

2. You may not drive your car anywhere during the camp.

3. Please do not leave valuables in your room while you are out.

4. You are allowed to be in only three places during camp: gym, cafeteria, and dormitory.

Residence Hall and Cafeteria Rules

These rules should be provided on the camper info sheet during check in.

1. No visitors (except parents) are permitted in the dormitory.

2. The cafeteria food is all you can eat while in the facility. You may not remove food from the café.

3. If leaving the cafeteria to use the bathroom, notify the attendant at the front desk.

4. Bed checks are at 10:30 p.m.; lights out is at 11:00 p.m.

Bad Weather

1. In the event of lightning or heavy rain, please stay indoors or under cover.

2. Lightning alert: One long horn blast for alert; three short blasts for all clear.

3. Safety first, please.

Fire Alarm

1. If the alarm sounds, leave the building through the nearest exit.

2. Do not use the elevators.

Keys and Key Cards

1. Lost room keys are $125, and lost building cards (white) are $25.

2. Do not leave your room without your key. You will be locked out.

CONCLUSION

Running a successful camp requires a lot of hard work from not only you, but by your entire staff and the university personnel running the support services (food and housing). The success from the camps can translate to positive marketing for your program as well as your university. Put in the time, hire good people, be clear on expectations, and have fun! There is no better feeling than getting the last key turned in and sending the happy campers home, looking forward to a return visit next summer.

9

Recruiting the Right Way

Salima Rockwell

I have had the opportunity to both play and coach volleyball at Penn State University. I have also coached at several other universities at many levels from a mid-major to a national championship team at the University of Texas, as well as playing on the national team. I have seen and done recruiting from all sides, but my recruiting philosophy is really simple: be honest, be exactly who you are, tell the truth, and develop meaningful relationships with the recruit, the family, and other coaches.

DETERMINING YOUR PROGRAM NEEDS

The needs of volleyball programs change all the time. Dealing with an ever-changing volleyball program and the unpredictability of very young recruits makes recruiting a challenge. Figuring out what you need by position may be easy, but predicting which positions will lack skilled players and what types of players you will need to replace those who are graduating is a complicated puzzle. One outside hitter is not the same as another (e.g., is she a passing outside hitter or not?). Needs also change based on the development of non-graduating players over the years. Because you may have a different void on the team every year, putting a team together is a very fluid process. Having a player who can play multiple positions is ideal for filling some of the holes that may occur when you are recruiting so far out. You need to consider players' ball control and whether they can hit on the right or the left side. Looking at setters and liberos is a little more specific. You usually know what class you want those scholarships to fall into, whether they are freshman, sophomores, or upperclassmen.

I keep track of all our players and potential recruits on a large whiteboard that is in a cabinet in my office. I have used this method for years. I have all the current players on it; those who are graduating are on the bottom and the top recruits (four or five deep) are listed for every class and position. We revisit it regularly and make adjustments as things change so we will know what it might look like next year.

IDENTIFYING TALENT

In my coaching career at several universities with programs at various levels, identifying talent has been a challenge. I learned a lot about identifying talent and potential from a coach I worked with early in my career. The characteristics he looked for were athletic ability and the drive and passion to play volleyball. It didn't matter if a player was 5 feet, 9 inches and an outside hitter if she had the drive and passion. Everyone knows that players can succeed in many ways. If a player was a competitive athlete who could fly around the court, that's who this coach was drawn to. I have the same attraction to such players.

Unfortunately, timelines in recruiting have changed as volleyball has become more competitive and athletes are being recruited at younger ages. As coaches, we have to look at different things because we are trying to project talent and ability three or four years out. Now we look at size, athletic ability, the potential for more growth, leg length, arms, even the size of feet and hands. We try to determine whether an athlete is going to grow or has peaked. Our projections don't always pan out, but we hope they do.

Some players clearly have the drive, but the younger they are, the harder it is to tell. Some young players seem disinterested or disengaged, but that may be because they don't quite know what they are doing or fully understand the game yet. Maybe they don't yet know how to show their emotion. I have seen such players several years later who have the drive they were lacking earlier. We have missed out on several athletes because they became comfortable in their own skins a little later in the recruiting process. When we were recruiting athletes as juniors or seniors, we knew what we were getting. Now that they are only freshmen in high school, we're not quite as sure. Sometimes their confidence develops a little later as well.

We film each recruit we are interested in with our iPads at tournaments and high school and club practices. We also share how players are doing with any of the other coaches on our staff who are not able to be on the road recruiting. This is a great way to compare players we may be looking at for the same position. We watch recruits on our list as many times as possible to see how they are progressing or changing.

ROLES OF HIGH SCHOOL AND CLUB COACHES

The best way for high school or club coaches to help athletes they are unsure about is to e-mail or call collegiate coaches directly to ask for advice on these athletes' levels. High school and club coaches should be familiar with as many levels of volleyball as possible so they have an idea of whether they are working with a potential high Division I athlete or an athlete who would be more successful in a more midlevel program. Collegiate coaches appreciate the honesty when a high school coach asks; they are usually happy to help identify the best level for an athlete.

High school and club coaches should film short YouTube videos (six minutes maximum) of their athletes. Mailing a hard-copy DVD delays the process of viewing a video. E-mailing a short film clip is the fastest and easiest way to get a college coach's attention immediately.

When sharing video clips with recruiting coaches, make identifying the player as easy as possible. Identify the player on the clip by providing her number, highlighting her with a circle or arrow, and identifying the team she is on, the color of their uniforms, whether she is on the near or far side of the net, and where she is starting on the court. Show a few minutes of actual game footage as well as a few minutes of individual skills or brief highlights. The best view is from behind the court so the coach can see how she moves around the court, her ball control, whether she can read the opponents, and how she moves within the team system. Remember, you are trying to get the college coach's attention quickly, so show the player's strengths or her best moves early in the footage. This could be great jumping ability, an awesome kill, a stuff block, a defensive save, or any other type of move that will grab attention.

The objective of film clips is to help recruiting coaches determine whether athletes will fit into their programs and whether they need to see them play in person, either during the high school or club season. These clips can be made simply with an iPad by coaches, friends or family members. They don't need to be expensive Hollywood productions with slow motion or fancy graphics. Just show the athlete playing volleyball, and let that action speak for itself.

High school coaches should understand that they are an integral part of the recruiting process. They may feel left out because of all the club volleyball teams, but we have found more and more that high school coaches have good relationships with the athletes we are recruiting. We always reach out to high school coaches even if we don't see them when we are recruiting at club tournaments. Another critical part of the high school coach's involvement in recruiting is making sure the athlete is on track academically, taking the correct core courses and entrance exams to be admitted to a university. Working closely with guidance counselors, coaches can ensure that student-athletes get the best advice on initial eligibility requirements for NCAA schools.

Both high school and club coaches need to know the recruiting rules of each school that is recruiting their athletes. These regulations can be found on each sport governing body's website, which are listed at the end of this chapter. Because they are always changing, coaches should review them each year as their athletes are being recruited. Schools differ in many areas including contact and evaluation periods, eligibility, financial aid, and their use of phone calls, texts, e-mails, and letters. Many high school coaches, club coaches, prospects, and their parents do not realize that some college coaches may not be allowed to return phone calls to athletes or their parents, and as a result, assume that a coach is not interested. All coaches need to know the rules and provide video clips to get the attention of college coaches, although club coaches are usually more aware of the magnitude of recruiting because they see coaches recruiting at their tournaments every weekend.

Club and high school coaches need to help their athletes do their homework on each school and coach they are interested in or is showing an interest in them.

They should help athletes and their families navigate through what can be a very intense process. Athletes in the 9th grade may be recruited by several high-level programs and may get scholarship offers early. They could be pressured by some programs to make an early commitment; however, if they are great student-athletes, they need to know that those opportunities will not go away. College coaches often pressure athletes and their families because they are afraid the athletes will choose other schools and they want the process to be over. High school and club coaches need to help their athletes understand that they do not need to accept the first scholarship offer they receive. It is sad for everyone when young people are pressured to make decisions when they haven't taken the time or had the support from coaches and club directors to look at academics, athletics, the college coach's style, playing time, their aspirations, and so many other variables that should be important to them, such as visiting the college campus.

Club coaches should not act as agents and restrict communication between universities and their athletes. It is important for athletes and their families to hear from every program that may be interested in them because the decision is theirs. Coaches would do better to educate them about questions to ask and the type of research they need to do on each university and coaching staff.

If the prospect is overwhelmed and distracted with e-mails, letters, phone calls, and texts, and needs to focus on the rest of the season, it may be time for the high school or club coach to ask the collegiate coaches to back off until the end of the club season. They may just need to focus on playing volleyball and enjoying the rest of the season. University recruiters who honor that request are obviously thinking about the athlete first and their programs second. If they don't back off from recruiting, the family will know that they may not respect their wishes in the future.

PROMOTING YOUR UNIVERSITY AND VOLLEYBALL PROGRAM

What is important to athletes at this young age? They want to feel special and know that they are the one. You have to show them enough interest that they know it is all about them, which it is. They are looking for interesting and new things on social media sites and your school's website. They like personal stories. Is your marketing department doing cool things on Twitter? Can they follow your program on Instagram, Twitter, and Facebook? Somebody needs to be in tune with all of this and keep it interesting—someone on your staff or from the marketing or sports information office. The person or people in this role must understand how important it is in recruiting and be all over it. The recruits know how to follow all the programs they are interested in so they will get all the automated updates. You can see the recruits all on their phones between matches, so you know it is important to stay connected with them by providing as much information as they want. You could even provide an online prospect questionnaire for any athletes who may be interested in your university along with a summary of critical recruiting rules.

RECRUITING STRATEGIES

Phone calls and text messages are all allowed at certain times and may change. In 2015, a college coach can call an unlimited number of times during a contact period. The junior year is usually the heaviest recruiting time. It can get a little crazy with unlimited texting and people wanting to be texted back immediately. Top schools are the outliers because they recruit so young.

I have done only one home visit in the last eight years. In-person contact is allowed after July 1, but the rules may change each year. Sometimes I wish we could slow down recruiting by backing up home visits and official visits for a year so they would occur during their junior year instead of their senior year. Maybe the parents would be relieved not to have to pay to go to all of the universities on their own; they could simply wait for official visits during their junior year, which might slow things down a little bit.

Some athletes grow up wanting to go to a certain school. Perhaps it is nearby, or the whole family has gone there. If these athletes want to decide early, I think that is great. I worry about young players who haven't seen a lot of schools and are recruited by schools across the country where they have no real ties. These athletes seem to transfer more. De-commitments don't happen often, but they are most likely when athletes get to a school and find out it is not at all what they thought it would be.

Unofficial visits are very important now, but can be a challenge. Club volleyball is very time-consuming and expensive. Many parents can't afford to go to all the club tournaments, send their children to camps, and visit numerous college campuses. A lot of players regionalize; that is, they attend colleges they already know and feel comfortable with. However, they cannot make the most informed decision when they can't afford to visit all the schools that may be interested in them. Unfortunately, the official visit, which the university pays for, has become a formality during the senior year, after athletes have already made commitments. Families need to think about visiting college campuses as they vacation while their children are young. When they are driving around the country or flying to tournaments and cities, they can take time to stop by nearby campuses and get a feel for the schools. Athletes need to start early and see as many as colleges as they can.

Developing Trust

Once you have identified the athletes you are interested in, you should begin the relationship by making sure athletes, their parents, and their coaches trust you. They must believe that you are genuine in the recruiting process. I tell recruits to call me anytime, even if it is not about being recruited to the university I am working at. I tell them, essentially, that if they need help with anything about volleyball, playing on a summer USA Volleyball team, deciding which camp to attend, or anything at all, to call me.

As coaches, we need to open ourselves up as mentors to these young players. Parents will start to lean on us if they can tell that we care about their children as people. Every conversation isn't about a hard sell, but about getting to know recruits and their families. Witnessing the lack of honesty in some coaches is very frustrating. We need to know where these athletes are coming from. We need to put ourselves in their shoes and understand what they are looking for and what they need, and understand the stress involved in trying to make the best decision of where to go to school and play volleyball.

I learned to recruit from the head coaches I worked for. I was kind of a natural recruiter because I love to talk to and help people, and that's really what recruiting is. The communication part was easy for me. Great recruiters have magnetic personalities. People want to engage with them; they are trustworthy and honest, and they love to talk about volleyball. They love the game and sharing their passion for it. Most great recruiters don't have huge egos; generally speaking, they just love volleyball and are outstanding people you want to hang out with. Since recruiting is all about selling the university and the volleyball program, it is key to have someone who the players can relate to on your staff. If coaches don't have that type of personality themselves, they may be the ones who stay back in the office and take care of the tremendous paperwork with recruiting.

Offering Scholarships and Maintaining Commitments

Generally, we offer scholarships when we are 100 percent sure that an athlete can help us, which could be as early as 9th or 10th grade. Letting an athlete know that a scholarship is on the table is totally different from pressuring her to make a decision.

The head coaches I have worked with don't pressure anyone to make a decision or give them a deadline, and neither do I. The offer is theirs until the bitter end. Sometimes, during a junior or senior year when things are feeling a little tight with our second or third choices, we have to let an athlete know that we are under some pressure to make a decision. However, we want athletes who want to be here. We want to make sure they are coming because they want to, not because we forced them to make a decision.

After athletes commit to our school, we keep in touch with them. We do this for the sake of the relationship, but also because other schools may not honor that verbal commitment and continue to try to recruit them. We want to protect our prospective athletes from this pressure. We may communicate less frequently at this point and talk more about day-to-day things. We are getting to know them personally, letting them know that they can contact us anytime, and staying engaged with them. This helps athletes feels as though they have made the right decision and will be comfortable at our school. It shows we care. It is also very important to stay in touch with parents as well.

TRACKING RECRUITS

It is critical that you identify a system for tracking all prospective recruits and where you are in the process with them. We use University Athlete (www.universityathlete .com) as a database to house most of our information. With this program you can look up any athletes and learn more about them. It allows you to also add notes under recruits' names and look up their schedules at tournaments, which is very helpful. A club that registers with University Athlete submits its schedules, which are uploaded so you can find times and the number of the courts athletes will be playing on. Every club gives its information to University Athlete, and university coaches pay an annual fee to access the service. This has made the data management side of recruiting much easier than it used to be.

International Recruits

I prefer to recruit domestically; I believe there is enough talent in the United States for a lot of teams to be good. However, international athletes can be good additions to your program if you are looking to move up quickly in the national rankings. The opportunity to have a great athlete with playing experience who is not afraid to compete because she has been there is hard to pass up. Most international athletes want to play volleyball and get an education. It is sometimes tough to determine whether an athlete is eligible to play on your program because of that athlete's professional experience. One recruiting service that can help identify international recruits is American Volleyball Scouting Report Global (www .avsrglobal.com/coaches).

Is an Athlete Being Recruited by a School?

The definition of a recruited athlete is defined in the 2014 NCAA rule book as follows: A prospect is considered a recruited athlete if the college takes one of the following actions:

- Provides the prospect with an official visit.
- Has off-campus contact with the prospect or the prospect's parents or legal guardians.
- Offers the prospect a national letter of intent or an athletic scholarship agreement.
- Initiates a telephone conversation with the prospect or the prospect's parents or legal guardians more than once.

Ironically, a college coach can have frequent communication (letters, e-mails, texts, phone calls if the athlete initiates the call) with a prospect without that person being considered a recruited athlete if the college coach does not take any of the preceding four actions.

Recruited Walk-Ons

We have a number of recruited walk-ons. Russ Rose, women's volleyball head coach at Penn State, loves to have a nice-size roster. Some athletes love the program and are super invested in what the school has and they are good enough to play and contribute, but at the time they applied, there was no scholarship for them. They are treated the same as athletes with scholarships in terms of academic services, equipment, and meals on the road. You would never know who is on scholarship by the way our athletes are treated. We have even had starters who were recruited as walk-ons.

NEGATIVE RECRUITING

Negative recruiting is my biggest pet peeve in the world, and it happens a lot. I tell our recruits that if they ever hear anything negative about our program or rumors about what one of us has done, they should ask us about it and we'll be happy to explain. We emphasize that we will always tell them the truth or give more information on what they are hearing. We like to tell them this up front before it happens so it puts the possibility on their radar. We do not negatively recruit—never have and never will. It doesn't help the recruit and it doesn't put the program in a good light. If an athlete you have recruited buys in to negative recruiting against you, that's OK; maybe that wasn't someone you wanted in your program to begin with.

Doing your best to sell your program is what you need to focus on. If someone tells me she is looking at another school, I tell her how awesome that program is, but here is what we have to offer. I let her know that there are other great programs, but explain what separates our program and why she should come to our school. If the negative recruiting by someone in another program is totally untrue and can damage our reputation, we call the person to discuss it.

CONCLUSION

Recruiting is an essential part of every college volleyball program. Take time to enjoy the process of meeting young players, their families, and other coaches. To be successful, you have to identify the right type of recruit for your program. If you are losing too many recruits to other schools, you may need to reconsider how you are identifying the athletes you are recruiting. Remember, you want to establish connections among your recruits, your school, your coaching staff, and the athletes on your team. See you on the road!

RESOURCES

NCAA I: www.ncaapublications.com/productdownloads/CBSA.pdf
www.ncaa.org/student-athletes/resources/recruiting-calendars?division=d1

NCAA II: www.ncaapublications.com/productdownloads/CBSA.pdf
www.ncaa.org/student-athletes/resources/recruiting-calendars?division=d2

NCAA III: www.ncaapublications.com/productdownloads/CBSA.pdf
www.ncaa.org/student-athletes/resources/recruiting-calendars?division=d3

NAIA: www.playnaia.org/d/NAIA_GuidefortheCollegeBoundStudent.pdf

NJCAA: http://www.njcaa.org/njcaaforms/140605_2_Prospective%20student%20brochure%2014-15.pdf

NCCAA: www.thenccaa.org

CHAPTER

10

Developing a Five-Year Plan

Bill Ferguson

When in the market for a new job, or your first job, it is important to align yourself with an organization or athletic department that has the foresight and patience to understand the benefits of a five-year plan. In many cases, five years will be the term for your first contract. My plan had a three-pronged approach called the three Ps: people, principles and process. In addition to allowing you the time you will need to implement your principles, the two major strengths in your plan are people and process. The people involved are your student athletes and staff. The process is, quite simply, time.

If you are building a program from the ground-up, the five-year plan means that you will have a longer period of time to build your brand with your chosen people from the start. If you make an error or two, which is quite reasonable, you will have time to make corrections in your recruiting approach for both student athletes and your staff.

Let's assume, for the purposes of this chapter, that you are taking over a program that has struggled and you have been chosen to right the ship. This timeline will allow you to weed out those people from the previous regime who will not buy into your new set of plans. You will also be able to identify those possible gems of people you may have inherited from the previous regime who are on board with your plans. These people will meld with the new people you bring in to form the core of your program. If you are establishing a program at a new school or taking over for a great coach who is moving on, the content is still applicable, but with a tweak here and there.

PEOPLE, PRINCIPLES, AND PROCESS

People, principles, and process are the three keys to your five-year plan for establishing excellence. People and principles work hand in hand to establish the process by which you establish excellence. Depending on how your brain works, you may want to switch the order of *people* and *principles*. Your five-year plan will mostly be set up by year 1; you will then tweak, improve, and maintain it through year 2 and beyond.

TIME LINE

The men's volleyball program I had taken over at the University of Southern California had finished the season in 11th place (12 teams) in conference play for four straight years, before moving up to 9th place the year before I took over (I came on board as an assistant coach that year). Following is a time line showing how our teams finished in the Mountain Pacific Sports Federation (MPSF) tournaments in my first six years as head coach:

Year 1: 2007 MPSF Tournament (8th place)

Year 2: 2008 MPSF Tournament (8th place)

Year 3: 2009 MPSF Tournament champions—NCAA Final Four

Year 4: 2010 MPSF Tournament (6th place)

Year 5: 2011 MPSF regular season champions—NCAA Final Four

Year 6: 2012 MPSF regular season champions—NCAA Final Four

Year 2 is highlighted because it is the year that all the athletes who had been coached by the previous head coach graduated. The team became completely my team in year 3. I discuss the importance of that later in the chapter.

In the first two years of coaching, sleep is a luxury and holidays are for banks and the post office. You will likely have an unhealthy love triangle with sleep, energy drinks, and coffee. Holidays are your time to catch up on administrative work. Are you ready to go now?

Year 1

This chapter focuses on year 1 because it is the year in which you will have to collect the most information to assess the situation, find out what questions you need answered, and triage those questions and answers. If you have a set of principles, your question/triage process will be streamlined already. If your principles are clear and you have executed your plans properly, you may find your five-year plan reduced to a two- or three-year plan. Following are some of the questions I asked when I was interviewing for my job and, quite frankly, some of the questions I wished I'd asked when I got the job:

1. What is my message and vision for the team, and what kind of culture do I want to create?
2. What is the current culture of the team?
3. Who am I? What type of coach am I?
4. What types of assistants and staff members should I hire based on question 1? (Based on questions 1 and 3, hire to your weakness!)
5. What type of system do I want to run?

6. What are the skills of the team I am inheriting? What types of people do I have?

7. What can we be good at immediately?

8. What types of players do I need to recruit?

The following sections address these questions.

What Is Your Message and Vision for the Team, and What Kind of Culture Do You Want to Create?

Your staff and players have to know exactly what you expect of them. The program I took over had had a ton of success, but not in the cognitive lifetime of those I was going to recruit. The trick for me was to present a vision that would galvanize players, staff, administrators, and, very important, alumni by conveying the ultimate respect for those who had made the program so great in the past and inspire them for the future. I came up with two teams: the current New York Yankees and the 1980s San Francisco 49ers. Both teams very much mirrored the greatness my school desired in the way they achieved and maintained their greatness and went about their business. The Yankees were winning at the time, so the current players and recruits could relate to them, and the staff, administration, and alumni could relate to the 49ers.

Establishing and maintaining a team culture is crucial. Your message and your team culture go hand in hand. You must envision a culture, make a road map to get there, and maintain that map. That road map must be simple; its strength is its simplicity. We articulated our road map as follows:

Be above reproach

Academically

Athletically

Socially

Once we devised our simple road map, we reinforced it using one of our university's established messages:

The ideal USC Trojan is

Faithful

Scholarly

Skillful

Courageous

Ambitious

One important factor in creating the team culture is getting buy-in from juniors and seniors on the team. This is critical. They are unlikely to be on the team that ultimately attains excellence, so you must make them feel like part of the solution, rather than blaming them for causing the problem. Our message to the juniors and seniors was twofold:

1. You will be the group that got the ship sailing straight.
2. You may not be on the team that makes it to the Final Four, but when we do, it will be just as much because of you as it will be because of the guys on the floor.

What Type of Coach Are You?

As a head coach, you must have a clear idea of what your strengths and weaknesses are. Better yet, you need to know what you are willing to delegate if you can. We are all control freaks, I know. Are you a fierce motivator, or the quiet scientist? Are you a CEO/big picture/recruiter/administrator type, or a total hands-on nuts-and-bolts nerd in the gym?

In my case, I had to do a little of everything. As a junior club coach for both boys and girls, I was comfortable training any technique, position, or system. I had also trained coaches and handled administrative duties. As a collegiate men's assistant coach on two occasions, I had acquired a broad base of experience. Under my first head coach, I had trained the setters, yet ran our block and defense during matches while also helping spearhead recruiting and assisting with the administrative duties. My second time around, I had been almost a chief of staff–type of assistant, overseeing almost every aspect of the program. Now, as head coach, I had to decide which way to go with my first two hires.

What Types of Assistants Should You Hire?

My big decision with my coaching team was to hire an assistant coach who had been through the rebuilding process. I wanted my assistant to have a very different personality than I did, so that our athletes would have a choice of coaches to connect with.

The other major factor in choosing my coaching team was my home life outside of volleyball. I was on my way to getting married and starting a family, so I looked for assistants who were a little younger with more flexible schedules. Because your coaching team will play a huge part in determining the success of your team once you are off and running, you should do what you can to ensure that you complement each other.

Lastly, give some thought about whether the people you are considering hiring are people you can live with every day and rely on in a foxhole. You have to get along—not always, but mostly. You are going to share office space, buses or vans, airplane rides, and possibly hotel rooms. You need to like and trust these people.

What Type of System Will Your Team Run?

Pat Riley's Los Angeles Lakers ran the fast break and were "Showtime." The Phil Jackson Lakers ran the triangle offense. Oklahoma University's football teams coached by Barry Switzer ran the option. Bob Stoops' Oklahoma teams find success with the spread offense. The Dodgers were all about speed, finesse, and player development through their farm system. The New York Yankees were all about power baseball and were built through free agency.

What Is Your Team Identity?

You have to make a decision about your team identity and go with it—choose a staple, a principle. In a huge twist of irony, I chose flexibility. I wanted the best volleyball players available to fit our university. Some would be power players. Some would be finesse players. We were always going to plug a system that fit our personnel and allowed us to run a game-plan offense and a game-plan defense no matter what. This decision helped our program accelerate our time line by about a year and a half.

What Are the Skills of the Team You Are Inheriting?

Eventually, you will have your fingerprint on the entire program and be running the system you think works best. At our program's zenith, we were a very big, powerful team—skilled, but big and powerful. On either end of that period of time, we had a little bit of finesse in there too. In years 1 and 2, our best attacker was a 6-foot, 2-inch ultra-fast jumper with a quick arm. We needed to set him everywhere (three positions) on the court, and we did. In year 2, we added a 6-foot, 8-inch high-ball hitter, but we didn't have a reliable third attacker, so 6-2 and 6-8 had to hit three spots on the court…all at sets of different tempos. It wasn't until midway through year 3 that we had reliable attackers at all three pin positions. If we had established a high-ball offense, we would have been killed in years 1 and 2. If we had run a fast offense, we would have been killed in year 1 and mediocre in year 2. The moral of the story is to maximize the personnel on hand, which helps to answer the question, "What can we be good at immediately?"

What Types of Players Do You Need to Recruit?

Recruiting is and always will be the most important part of coaching sports. Dwyane Wade, Chris Bosh, and LeBron James all recruited each other.

Our recruiting had to be driven by academics, admissions, and the cost of attendance along with athletic excellence. Having a smaller pool of athletes to draw from drove our decision to be flexible when it came to our team identity. If we were ever unsure about which person to recruit, we always fell back on our road map: Be above reproach academically, athletically, and socially. That would break ties and settle discussions. If there was still a tie after that, we would bring both athletes in!

Once we had our people and principles in place, we were able to move forward with our process.

Year 2

The honeymoon is now over. You now have some athletes on your roster that you recruited with your vision in mind. Year 2 is often the most rewarding for coaches, because the team is beginning to take the shape they intended.

Remain steadfast with the implementation of your culture at this time. Last year's juniors are deciding whether you are for real, and whether to buy in one more time. If you are not resolute, they will turn into lame ducks, and you will have to decide whether you want them around. Recruiting will continue to be at the top of your list. If you can secure back-to-back, solid recruiting classes, your program will be set for several years.

The second year is critical for your coaching team as well. You will begin to see how the team gels. Sometimes coaches begin to excel at certain tasks while drifting away from others. Maintain solid communications with your coaching team as preferences shift.

Year 3

Year 3 may be an up-and-down year. Remain steadfast. This is the third year of the same message for some who may be finding it a bit old. Your program may take a bit of a step backward as the higher-level players from the previous coach depart, and your younger, less-experienced players take over. These bumps in the road will test the team as players naturally begin to think that success should be here by now.

If you have hit it out of the park recruiting, you should see the fruits of your labor pay off in year 3. In 2009, my year 3, we had lost three 4-year starters—one a team captain and two our best attackers. We lost some matches that were absolutely maddening, but ended up in our first Final Four. Things began to click for our team. Our coaching team had changed by one. Our starters consisted of one freshman, three sophomores, one junior, and one senior.

Years 4 and 5

As you move into years 4 and 5 of your plan, beware! Little things can turn big at this point. Make sure to continue to recruit winners. At this point, the success of your team will attract players who believe they can belong without having to prove themselves—these are known as *attachers*. Attachers arrive on the upswing of the program, when things are already good. There is really no way for them to personally feel the blood, sweat, and tears of those who were with you from day one. It will be your responsibility to protect the team when you recruit during year 3 and beyond. Once those athletes are on campus, you must also make sure they fully understand what is at stake and what has been built. The attachers will have the largest impact on your team in years 6 through 8.

Success with a young group can also lead to some issues. Our early success led our juniors to be attachers, not to our team, but to winning. They had lost sight of the process that enabled them to win.

Also, keep in mind that you will not always be able to attract the best of the best for every spot on your roster. You will have to pay much attention to the quality of the players who are your backups. These backups, or support players, sometimes end up being better at tearing a team down than the superstars are at building it up. The bottom line is to recruit character, not characters!

ADDITIONAL CONSIDERATIONS

When you become the coach at another school, you will need to take some time to learn the past culture of the program, seek out a mentor who can help you through some tough adjustments, and respect the coach who was there before you, whether that person was successful or not.

Culture of Your School or Organization

When I accepted the head coach position, I recognized that some of the practices at other universities where I had coached wouldn't fly at this one. To learn about the school or organization culture, seek out a stalwart coach from another sport at your organization or a former coach. What are the traditions, nuances, sacred cows? Depending on where you place yourself in the organization (yes, I said *place yourself*—you have a ton of control in this process), the school or organization may have established traditions or cultures that can help you deliver your message. Use them to your advantage instead of looking at them as dark clouds or pressure.

Finding a Mentor

Look outside of volleyball for some of your answers. There aren't as many volleyball programs and coaches that have been around long enough to be resources as there are football, basketball, baseball, and soccer coaches. There are many different coaches at many different institutions and professional organizations who will have relevant information that can help you. I would suggest asking them for advice as often as it is relevant. Remember, they were most likely in your shoes at one point in their careers. Make sure you present them with direct questions. Though sometimes the best information may come from free-flowing conversation with these coaches, getting to that point must be earned by being organized with the questions you ask. You must respect their time. In my case, I would research those coaches' careers, their teammates, and the coaches they played under to find out how their experiences were relevant to my situational need or curiosity. All of these people were more than gracious with their time. Remember, when your team is doing well, it reflects well on the other teams in your athletic department. I am fully aware that such a cadre doesn't exist at every institution, but there are bound to be countless people who have insight and have had success at your institution and in the surrounding community.

Following a Legend

If a great coach is leaving your program and the torch is being passed to you, it is very important that you stay true to yourself, be yourself, and not try to imitate your predecessor. That being said, you still have to honor existing traditions and cultures as long as they are productive. If you must institute any kind of fundamental change, tread lightly and do it slowly and respectfully.

OVERALL FIVE-YEAR PROGRAM PLAN

Following is table 10.1 with many items to consider in your five-year program plan. It can be very rewarding to plan ahead and check items off as you accomplish them. Certainly, you will need to adapt this chart to your program by adding or deleting items as needed at the end or beginning of each year.

TABLE 10.1 Mapping Out a Five-Year Program

Program Areas	Year 1	Year 2	Year 3	Year 4	Year 5
Coaching staff	Paid assistant(s) Volunteers GAs Interns Fifth-year athletes Future staff Athletes				
Support staff	Director of operations Administrative assistant Secretary Statistician Videographer Athletic trainer Strength coach Academic adviser Nutritionist Sport psychologist				

Program Areas	Year 1	Year 2	Year 3	Year 4	Year 5
Facility—practice and competition	Availability Maintenance needs Seating Flooring				
Facility—ancillary areas	Weight room Locker room Training room Academic area Equipment area Laundry Equipment storage				
Office space	Furniture Conference room Whiteboard Technology				
Equipment	Apparel contract Sport equipment Office equipment Computers, laptops, iPads				
Team roster—recruiting	Current athletes by position and year Needs by year				
Recruiting travel	List of tournaments School visits Practices Budget Recruiting services				
Budget	Current budget by line item What you need to be successful				
Schedule	Conference RPI Out-of-conference Off-season				
Team travel	Mode of travel Travel party size International trip				
Camp	Objectives Facility Staff Recruits Schedule				

(continued)

Table 10.1 *(continued)*

Program Areas	Year 1	Year 2	Year 3	Year 4	Year 5
Home events	Event staff Promotions Marketing Setup Half-time activities Match management Officials				
Contracts	Annual or multiyear Salary Benefits Courtesy car Country club membership Bonus Camp Apparel Other benefits				
Technology	Software Statistical programs Video review				
Consultants	Sport psychologists Specialists				
Annual training plan	Current plan What do you want to be doing next year? What do you want to be doing five years from now?				
Booster support group	Fan support Education Travel party				
Fund-raising	Needs Responsibility Plans Endowed scholarships Naming opportunities				
Community service involvement	Athletes volunteering Coaches volunteering Annual charity to support				

Program Areas	Year 1	Year 2	Year 3	Year 4	Year 5
Communication	Newsletters Websites Blogs Twitter Facebook Instagram Other social media Speaking engagements				
Team-building activities	Preseason Weekly activities Ropes course Ethnic dinner Others				

CONCLUSION

Surrounding yourself with the best *people* and remaining steadfast with your *principles* will allow you to create a five-year *process* that will help you earn success at any level. Such a process will give you flexibility for growth and growing pains. There will undoubtedly be bumps in the road, but a five-year timeline will allow you to remain steadfast with your approach and application of your plan without having to resort to shortcuts. If you are fortunate to have five years to implement your plan, stay the course. There will be many opportunities to "jump the gun" and get greedy. Stay with your plan. Rome wasn't built in a day.

PART THREE

POSITIONAL TRAINING STRATEGIES

11

Training Middle Hitters

Ben Bodipo-Memba

We've all heard stories about choosing middles, or been in the situation ourselves: *Who should play middle? How about that player over there? She's tall.* Hopefully, we have moved past that type of thinking. As tempting as that solution may be, the tallest players do not always make the best middles. Although being tall definitely helps, many more characteristics and attributes make up good middles. Even more important, however, is how they are trained.

NAME FOR THE POSITION

Before we get into what to look for in an athlete to play middle, you must identify what you are trying to get out of that position. It's interesting that there are four predominant names for the middle position. Sometimes what a coach or a player calls it (e.g., middle blocker, middle hitter, quick hitter, middle attacker) provides insight into what that person believes is the primary responsibility of the position. Your name for the position sends a message (maybe even subliminally) to the players as to their primary role on the court. My college coach used to say, "You are a middle blocker, so it is your job to shut down their hitters. Any kills you get are gravy." Of course, I was more concerned with getting kills!

EXPECTATIONS FOR MIDDLES

Middles' primary focus should be blocking, because the team will not always be in system (i.e. passing or digging close to the setter) and able to set the middle up offensively. That being said, offensive effectiveness is critical. So what exactly are the expectations for middles?

Offensively, middles need to be able to score in many ways through a variety of sets: quick sets, slides, shoots, pushes, and step-outs. They should also be able to use a variety of swings: power, cross-body, wrist-away, pinky-down (no look), and tips (short and deep).

Defensively, you obviously want your middles to stop or slow down the opposition with blocks. This requires a lot of skill and knowledge. First and foremost, these players must be able to read the play (see the game) as it develops, move laterally quickly, and get their hands across the net at the right time. All of that requires coordination, discipline, and patience.

CHARACTERISTICS OF EFFECTIVE MIDDLES

Now that we have identified what you want out of your middle, it's important to look at the characteristics that constitute an effective middle. Some skills you can train and improve, but some . . . well, you know how the saying goes: You can't teach height! Not all good middles are 6 feet, 4 inches tall, and not all 6-foot, 4-inch players are good middles, but height obviously helps. Two features that may go unnoticed are arm length and hand size. Being a good blocker requires getting one's hands across the net far and fast. A player can make up for a lack of height with long arms, and take up more space with big hands. Being quick is more important, in my opinion, than height. I would recruit a quick, 6-foot, 1-inch middle over a slower, 6-foot, 4-inch middle any day. Speed wins games. The middle should be able to close the block. Coaches prefer a fast arm swing that can frustrate opposing defenses with expertly placed shots over a straight downswing from a taller, slower middle.

Middles should have fast-twitch muscles and be easy jumpers. They need to be able to change direction and cover ground quickly. Most important, they need to work *hard*. If you have an athlete who is looking for the glory position, middle is not for him. Middles are expected to be up in the air and ready to hit a ball on every offensive rally and to block on every opponent attack. They are not always going to get set on a perfect pass, but they will often be set when the pass is a little off the net. Great setters are taught to "force" the middle. A strong transition (getting back off the net and back in to hit) is what separates great middles from good ones, and this all requires a lot of hard work.

From an offensive perspective, middles are primarily responsible for hitting the quick set. All sets are given a tempo that correlates to how high or how quickly a hitter attacks a ball (figure 11.1). Most of the middle attacks are at a zero tempo (the hitter is in the air with his arm extended as the ball is in the setter's hands, as in figure 11.2) or a first tempo (the hitter is leaving the ground as the ball is being set). Slides are considered a second tempo.

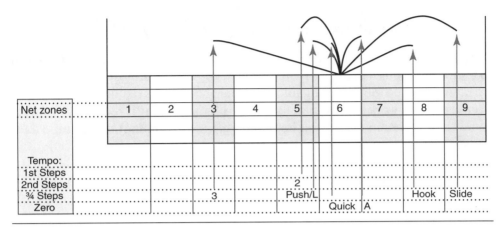

Net zones	1	2	3	4	5	6	7	8	9
Tempo:									
1st Steps									
2nd Steps					2				
¾ Steps			3		Push/L			Hook	Slide
Zero						Quick A			

FIGURE 11.1 Middle hitter sets and tempo.

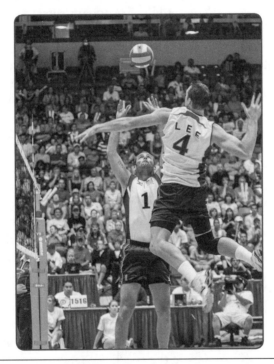

FIGURE 11.2 The hitter is in the air with his arms extended for a zero-tempo set.

TRAINING MIDDLES FOR OFFENSE

Let's look at how to train specific attacks, starting with the quick. I encourage you to train your middles to hit a zero-tempo ball, knowing that most middles, in reality, hit first-tempo sets. Training middles to be good hitters requires a progression from arm swing work to transition footwork. The great thing is that you can always come back to certain drills (e.g., nonjumping, spacing, timing) to fine-tune their skills. The components of a good quick attack that we address in this section are arm swing, spacing, tempo, and timing, which includes watching the ball from the passer or digger to the setter.

Arm Swing

Because of its importance, the arm swing should be practiced every day. A middle's arm swing is very different from an outside hitter's swing—outside hitters have time to wait for the set to get to them; middles are not afforded that luxury. Middles are all about speed, so it is imperative that they make their swings compact. They can practice speed in a drill as simple as hitting back and forth with a partner.

Encourage middles to focus on each swing and pay attention to what they are doing. The swing starts with the toss: they should always toss the ball up with two hands. This forces the nonhitting hand to go up as well, which is a simple, but often overlooked practice. The toss should be out in front of the hitting arm, so that the player can take a step and swing at the ball. Middles should also try to toss low to simulate a first-tempo attack. Most important is that they keep the elbow of their hitting arm high. We coach players to keep the elbow back instead of up. Too many players put the elbow up; the result is that the hand is lower than the elbow, defeating the purpose of getting the elbow high. When players pull the elbow back, the hand stays high. As a result, they pull the nonhitting hand down (instead of just letting it fall), which helps rotate the torso and takes pressure off the shoulder. (The abdomen is a bigger muscle—use it!) Middles need to let the hip of the hitting-arm side (i.e., right hand, right hip) lead naturally; then finish with the elbow so that the arm follows through naturally. The partner catches the ball, then hits back, repeat for time or amount of reps.

Another good way to train the arm swing is to stand on a sturdy, padded box. The drill starts with a toss from the coach to the hitter on the box and then progresses to a set from a setter off a toss from the coach. Coaches stand as close to the setter as needed to ensure an accurate toss with minimal movement by the setter. This is a great time to emphasize keeping the nonhitting hand up and open, as a target for the setters. The middle hitter's goal should be to exchange the nonhitting hand with the hitting hand.

Box work is a great way to get more repetitions while saving the legs. Hitters should start with both arms already up and ready to swing. This focuses on the exchange move (nonhitting arm, then hitting arm). Then progress to driving their arms up and swinging to work on timing and the exchange. Using a cell phone, iPad, or video camera and a playback system, you can film players swinging a few times, let them watch themselves, and then have them swing a few more times to make any necessary corrections.

Spacing

Correct spacing (from the net and from the setter) is an essential part of being a good middle hitter. Being too tight (too close) to either will hamper the ability to terminate the ball. Players should progress from hitting on the box to working on the last two steps of an approach. This forces them to work on proper spacing.

A simple "hit off the toss" drill can help players focus on arm swing and spacing at the same time. In this drill, the middle stands on the left leg with the arms in front, ready to be thrown back. The coach tosses the ball to the setter, and as the ball crosses over the middle's shoulder, the middle pushes off the left foot to create the last two gathering steps of the approach (a quick right-left step). The player should be at a 45-degree angle to the net and an arm's length from the setter and the net.

The more attention you give to detail on your middles' technique during the early training sessions, the better off they will be when the speed of the game takes over. Make sure to give focused feedback (e.g., keep the elbow back, left arm up). Spacing from the setter takes priority over (and solves the problem of) net spacing. A general rule is to have middles be an arm's length from the setter and the net (on a perfect pass). Staying off the net (or keeping the setter in front of them) is essential, and visually tracking the ball from the pass aids in accomplishing that. Tracking the ball also determines the middle hitter's timing of when to start the approach to hit.

Tempo

Most coaches are always telling their middle hitters to get up early. Players hear this (all hitters, actually) all the time, but if you were to ask them what *early* means, or when they should be in the air, you would probably get a wide range of answers. Train your hitters to think in terms of what step they are on when the setter is touching the ball. For example, outside hitters who are hitting a fast, or go, tempo set should be on the second step (of a four-step approach) when the setter is touching the ball. If they were hitting a higher (hut) set, you would want them to be on the first step as the setter is touching the ball.

The same concept applies for middles. To determine timing for the quick set, however, you must first decide what tempo you want to run your quick attack while considering the skill level of your players. The three basic tempos for a quick attacker are zero, first, and one-and-a-half; the choice should be based on your preference as well as the ability of your middles. Experiment with all three and see which ones work best for your athletes. Also, have them continue to train at least one of the other tempos, because they may become better at it after more repetitions.

We see all three tempos run with success at high-level NCAA Division I programs. Zero tempo means that the middle is in the air right before the setter touches the ball, forcing the setter to shoot the ball up to the hitter's hand. In a first-tempo attack, the middle is on the last step, or close step, as the setter is setting the ball and, essentially, rising up in the air as the set is leaving the setter's hands. This is the most common quick-attack tempo. Even though teams strive to run a zero-tempo quick attack, in reality most middles (even at the international level) attack at first tempo. There are many reasons for this, but mostly it has to do with ball control and, of course, the comfort or trust between the middle and the setter. The advantage of zero-tempo quick sets is that the hitter is in the air before the opposing blocker jumps and therefore has the advantage of hitting against no blocker or one blocker jumping late. That being said, it is not a bad thing to be working on zero tempo even if it becomes first tempo. It's a lot easier to slow down than to speed up.

A one-and-a-half-tempo quick set is not seen much at the high levels, but it is very effective if done properly. St. Mary's University, an NCAA Division I volleyball program in Moraga, California, uses this tempo and consistently gives opposing teams' defenses fits of frustration. Assuming that the middle is using a three-step approach (left, right, left, step close), then the middle is on the second step as the setter is setting the ball. This is a higher set and works well with middles with good jumping ability and vision.

Timing

Regardless of which set tempo you use, the key to timing is tracking the pass and approaching at the correct time. Get the middles to open up to where the pass is coming from and track (watch) the pass from the passer toward the setter, instead of glancing over their shoulders. This helps them find the pass, which alleviates timing issues. Advise them to wait for the volleyball to cross the plane over their shoulder before they start their approach. They should be chasing the ball to the setter. This is a very important concept. One of the biggest mistakes middles make with timing is starting the approach too early. Remind them that they are faster than the ball and don't have very far to travel. Not watching the ball being passed or dug and leaving early are the most common problems that are easily corrected. Tell them to be patient; then slow to fast on the approach and small to big on the steps. You want your middles to be dynamic, explosive, and fast twitched.

SITUATIONAL ARM SWINGS

Because middle hitters need to rely on their quickness and vision to hit the ball by the block, they should develop a variety of swings. We have already discussed arm swing warm-ups on the ground (i.e., hitting back and forth). Middles should now practice a variety of situational swings and then advance to box hitting and then to live hitting. They need to focus, once again, on using the whole body (nonhitting arm up, hitting elbow pulled back, hip leading, hip of the hitting arm moving forward to create torque before finishing with the swing) while now varying the contact points. Have them practice swinging straight ahead to where they are facing, while also developing no-look swings. A player hitting a quick or a shoot set (3) will be opened up to the setter at about a 45-degree angle (see figure 11.3).

The Wrist-Away Swing

Middles should practice a wrist-away swing (the wrist-away swing is one form of a no-look swing) by approaching and swinging as normal. They should be striking the middle to top of the ball (see figure 11.4). If hitting right-handed, they pull with the left arm and lead with the right hip, but on the swing, they finish with the thumb down, following through outside the body (parallel to the side). Another way to think of it is to finish with the right hand in the right pocket. It is critical to stress good control and solid contact over power. The power will come as they get more comfortable swinging. This is a good swing to teach advanced or older players; it may cause a little more stress on the shoulder, so don't overdo it with younger players.

The Cross-Body Swing

Another no-look swing is the thumb-up, pinky-down, or cross-body, swing. Players use the same approach as in other swings, but stay opened up to the setter the entire time. This swing can be used only when the set is pushed a little past the middle's hitting arm or in front of the nonhitting shoulder. Contact should be made on the top or a little on the right side of the ball (at the 1 o'clock position). On the swing, the

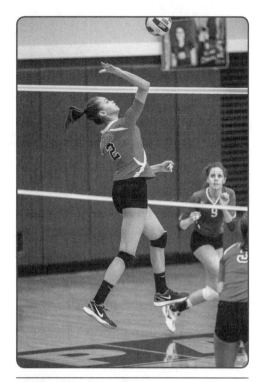

FIGURE 11.3   Player hitting a shoot set.

FIGURE 11.4   Player using a no-look swing.

Photo courtesy of Don Feria/goldenbearsports.com

hitter should finish with the thumb up (or pinky down), and the finish should be across the chest and not much lower than the shoulder (see figure 11.5). This is another swing that requires good control and contact over power. The power will come as players get more comfortable swinging. This is another swing probably best taught to more advanced players; it may overstress the shoulders of younger players who rely on the shoulder muscles, rather than the abdominals, to propel the ball.

Off-Speed Hits

Well-placed tips and off-speed hits are also important to have in middles' tool boxes. An open place on the court is usually right over the block, in the deep corner, or out toward the sideline. Players must understand that a kill is a kill is a kill. The crucial issue is not how

FIGURE 11.5 Player performing the cross-body swing.

Photo courtesy of Don Feria/goldenbearsports.com

hard they swing at the ball, but whether the ball hits the floor in the opponent's court! With all tips it is essential that they approach thinking *swing first*! Teach them to tip the good sets as well as the ones they have to because of poor timing or an inaccurate set. They should use the same mechanics, focusing on keeping the elbow up. Again, hitters need a variety of swings or "shots" at their disposal.

SLIDE ATTACK

Another popular swing used primarily in girls' and women's volleyball is the slide. This is an exciting attack to hit and very tough to defend against if done correctly. Many of the swing mechanics are the same, but the approach and finish are very different from those used in swings that have a traditional two-foot takeoff. Like the quick set, the slide can be run at a variety of tempos. With this attack, the player either chases the set or has the set catch up to her (the latter is faster). The approach is what makes the slide attack unique. It is parallel to the net, and the player jumps off one foot (the left) as in a basketball layup. This is tough for the block to defend against because blockers' natural tendency is to drift out toward where the hitter is going. The hitter, meanwhile, has various points of contact from which to attack. The two types of approaches commonly used in the slide attack are explained in the next section.

Slide Footwork

The slide is used primarily to beat a team either by speed or misdirection (or both) depending on the tempo. Although both approaches are interchangeable (with misdirection and speed), one is better suited for misdirection. In the first approach, the middle makes a plant step toward the setter with the left foot. This makes the blockers think that the middle is attacking in front of the setter. The middle then pushes off with the left foot going parallel to the net. Then, with a quick (and big) right then left step, the player launches into the air (off one foot, as in a layup) to attack the ball. The approach is basically in the shape of an L and is usually used on a set in which the hitter catches up to the set. It is possible to use a faster tempo in which the hitter is past the setter before the set is made, but that requires a very fast middle and a very accurate setter.

The other approach forgoes subtleties and is used primarily for pure speed. The footwork is similar except there is no jab step toward the setter. The middle goes directly toward the pin as fast as she can. I like to tell my middles to aim for the pole, which helps to keep them from getting too tight to the net. As a result, their pattern is more of an arc, and the left-foot plant is usually on or one step behind the setter.

With both approaches, the player's natural momentum carries her laterally. The key is to transfer as much lateral energy as possible to vertical energy. A couple of things that help lessen floating are driving the right knee up while planting the final left step, and turning the right knee around in the direction opposite to the direction of travel. This not only helps slow down the float, but also allows players to use torso power to hit crosscourt and line.

Slide Swing

Because middles have more time to swing on a slide, they must focus on keeping the left arm up and the hitting elbow up and back. The tendency is to drop the right elbow for a longer swing, but doing so gives the blockers more time to set up and adjust. Middles want to swing quickly, and a high elbow helps them also swing deep (a very tough swing to stop). As in the quick set, middles should use tips to keep the defense guessing. The tip down the line in the deep corner and the tip back inside to the middle of the court are generally the most effective. The progression used for a quick set should be used for slide attacks. The third basic attack for middles is the shoot set in front of the setter. The approach is the same as in a quick set, as is the timing, generally using a zero- or first-tempo set. Other sets middles can hit are step-outs, slides directly behind the setter, slides halfway between the setter and the antennae, and slide footwork in front of the setter. These are all fun to experiment with, but I recommend that players perfect two or three attacks before getting fancy.

BLOCKING KEYS

Blocking is an essential part of a middle's game. As we alluded to earlier, they are called middle blockers for a reason. Blocking is also one of the skills that takes the longest to develop. Some of this can be attributed to limited practice time at the high school and club levels, but a lot is attributed to poor technique and "the ends justify the means" type of thinking, which is negatively reinforced. How many times have we seen blockers slap or swing their arms to get the big "kaboom" block, and when they send that ball back faster than it was hit, the crowd goes wild? Middles like this and will to continue to block like this. The block looks great, when they get it. As such, they are rewarded for poor technique.

Blocking is one of the most, if not *the* most, frustrating skills in volleyball. Middles want to block every ball—which is a good thing, don't get me wrong. The problem is that, if not trained properly, players sacrifice technique for result. Slapping at the ball, reaching, guessing, and truncated footwork result in general frustration when they don't block every ball. Even before you start teaching technique, sit your blockers down and explain two concepts: (1) they are not going to block every ball and (2) you would rather they be late and right than guessing and occasionally early.

Telling your blockers to try to block everything and then saying that they can't block everything may seem like contradictory messages. However, this will help them put things in perspective. I once coached a middle blocker who was one of the hardest workers I'd ever coached. She was not the most skilled, definitely not the most talented, but she worked *hard*. She believed that she was supposed to block every ball and was very disappointed when she didn't. She trusted her technique, as I like to say, so it was a good type of determination. One match, she made her rounds in the front row; then the libero came in to serve for her. She came to the bench (she was coming in hot!), sat beside me (we had many of these meetings), and started freaking out: "What am I doing wrong? I missed that last block! Is it my footwork? Eyes? Hands? I don't know what I'm doing wrong!" I turned to her slowly and said, "Um . . . it's 2 to 1." The match had just started, and the girl had taken a good swing, but she wanted to block everything.

Break it down for your blockers in practice. The NCAA Division I team blocking leaders blocked 3.06 balls a set. The individual leader blocked 1.81 balls a set. That does not constitute a lot of the 25 points needed. Help your players accept that they're going to miss some.

Reading the Situation

The most important blocking skill for a middle (and actually for all volleyball players defensively) is the ability to read the situation. This is yet another reason blocking can be frustrating and tedious. Many hours must be devoted to blocking, especially the reading part, for a person or a team to become great blockers (figure 11.6). The basic mantra of successful blockers is, "Know before you go." Players must study and read instead of guessing.

To be good readers, players must read the correct cues at the correct time. Let's break that down a bit further. When reading, blockers should follow a pattern: passer, setter, ball, hitter (PSBH). There is a difference between looking and seeing when it comes to blocking. Looking is short, a glance—picking up information such as trajectory, direction, and speed quickly and moving on to the next skill. Seeing is longer; it involves studying cues such as a hitter's approach angle and a setter's tendencies.

We use a drill called PSBH to train reading. This is a great drill for the whole team because everyone needs to get better at reading. The number of players in the drill is up to you; it works

FIGURE 11.6 Players put blocking training to the test.

with 12 people or 2. The focus is on the eyes, making sure players are watching the right cues, but you can add other components as you see fit (e.g., eyes and first step, arms across the net). I recommend having the setter start setting pin to pin and then adding a middle. Designate another coach to focus on one blocker, in this case the middle, from the end line so you can see the blocker's eyes. As a ball is chipped into a passer, the blocker calls out "on," "off," or "over" based on the platform angle and the passer's body position (looking). This gives you feedback about what the blocker is seeing. It's very important to stress that it is OK to be wrong on the call. In fact, there is no wrong or bad call (as long as the blocker recognizes an overpass in time to adjust). An "on" call just means that the blocker needs to stay in the middle longer because of the middle attack potential. The purpose of this drill is for you to see what your players are watching and train them to get better at reading cues.

By looking at the passer, the middle immediately sees the setter. This step is crucial. The tendency for blockers is to watch the flight of the ball, whereas picking up the setter is much more important. As soon as they have determined that it's not an overpass (which should happen a few seconds in), they need to find the setter and, more specifically, the setter's arms. Good setters can fake out opponents with their body language (e.g., leaning back or forward); however, faking with the arms and wrists is very difficult. Train your middles to see those parts of the setter. Basically, if you were to draw a box for where to focus on the setter, it would encompass the hands down to the shoulders or elbows, whichever is lower. Constantly remind your middles to find the setter as they are going through the drill.

Blocking Balance

Just as important as watching the correct cues is staying balanced. Once your middles have seen the setter, they will be very tempted to lean one way or the other based on what they have read. Get them used to anticipating *then* reacting. If they start leaning or, even worse, moving, for example, to their right, you immediately give the advantage to the setter. Good setters can see or feel this movement and will capitalize on it by setting the other direction. This is when you need to hammer home the message: Better late and right than guessing. Get them to understand that on a perfect pass the setter has the advantage; it's OK to be late, especially on fast-tempo sets to the pins.

Blocking Vision

Your middles have now looked at the passer, seen the setter, and maintained their balance. Now they need to look at the set. This requires a very quick glance. All they need to determine is the trajectory of the set. Making sure it's not set over, mainly, but also determining the speed of the set will also influence the type of blocking footwork to use. Once again, stay on your middles and keep them from spending too much time on the ball in flight. One way to remedy this is to change PSBH to PSH—take the ball right out of the equation. Yes, there will be an occasional set over, but you will find that the majority of the information the blocker gets comes from studying the setter and hitter. In fact, I have sometimes changed the name of this drill to passer, setter, ball, hitter, hitter, hitter!

The sequence is: passer (look), setter (see), ball (look), hitter (see). After a quick glance at the ball, the middle needs to pick up the hitter. Let's assume that the ball is set to the left-side hitter. The middle needs to make a dynamic block move toward the hitter. Studies have shown that the majority of hitters hit in the direction they are facing and approaching. Middles need to study that approach, go where the hitter is going, and get the ball. If you can get your middles to understand the concept of surrounding the hitter's shoulder, they will progress as blockers quickly. After the middles do one rep, they shuffle back to the middle and repeat for a certain number of balls. You can also make this a continuous drill in which both sides are going for kills; or semi-continuous in which the hitting side is going for kills, and when the defensive side transitions, the players just free ball it over the net. Continue for a certain number of balls. Again, the key to coaching this is to focus on the blocker, be a stickler for detail, and praise as well as critique (e.g., "Good eyes; now stay balanced"; "Find your setter earlier, but great footwork").

Blocking Footwork

As mentioned in the characteristics section, fast middle blockers who may be a little shorter can be more desirable than slow-footed tall players. Put those two preferable qualities together, though, and such a player would obviously have a great career and make you look like a great coach! However, being a fast middle is about much more than getting from A to B. It's going from A to C and then to B back to A, changing directions quickly, being relentless, and patrolling the net from antenna to antenna. This requires discipline in eye sequencing and, just as important, in footwork.

Many types of footwork can be used in blocking: swing blocking, shuffling, crossover, turning and running, and numerous combinations of all those. Which ones are best? It depends on the situation, and all middles should practice and be comfortable using all of them. In the end, it's about getting to the hitter as fast as possible and being dynamic enough to penetrate across the net. We train swing blocking because we believe that it allows our players to be the most dynamic, but also because we start in a bunch block (closer to the middle of the court). However, we also want our middles to shuffle to defend against certain sets. The basic rule we use is: If the set is higher or slower, use a big, dynamic swing block. The faster the set, the less time blockers have, so they have to shorten their arms or use a crossover or shuffling footwork technique.

We train blocking going both left and right, but the percentages are 60/40 to 70/30 for right and left, respectively. The majority of sets are made to the right, so we play percentages and make sure we close to the outside. Our players train with static footwork and coach-initiated drills, which we combine with game-type drills that incorporate more random blocking.

Regarding footwork, it's important to get a big push in the first move. I prefer to use the word *push* instead of *step* in training. I find that when I say, "Take a step" or "You need a bigger step," all I get is a big lift of the leg (maybe 3 inches, to prepare for the big step) or a backward (negative) step. So when players are blocking right, I tell them to push with the left foot; this helps them cover more ground. This concept can be used with both shuffle and swing blocking footwork.

Both shuffling and swing blocking require getting to the hitters quickly. When shuffling, players must make numerous quick shuffles while staying square to the net in a crouched, or loaded, position so that they can jump fast when they get to the hitter. In swing blocking, the middle uses a crossover footwork technique (in the same crouched, or loaded, position). The basic swing move is a three-step pattern similar to a hitting approach. Going to the right, the player pushes off with the left foot (creating a step with the right foot). The blocker should be perpendicular to the net at this point. They then make a big push with the right foot (arms should draw back now, as in a hitting approach). Planting the left foot at a 45-degree angle (this is the braking step and important to keep from drifting), the player pivots on it, squaring up to the net and finishing the block with their hands over the net.

Blocking Strategies

In addition to the many types of blocking footwork, various strategies are used in blocking. It's up to you to develop one that fits your style. Obviously, you would like your players to block every ball straight down, but in reality . . . well, you know. Do you want your blockers funneling the ball to an area? If they are late to close, do you want them to reach into the gap or press straight over (allowing defenders to fill the gaps)? There is no correct answer; it comes down to the system. The only absolute is getting their hands across the net. We want our blockers to seal the net low and tight. Reaching up high at the ball gives the hitter more angles to attack and makes it harder for the back row to defend. A block straight down is always good, but forcing a hitter to hit a shot they don't like to hit, making them hit out, funneling a swing to your best defender, slowing down a swing with a block touch—these do not show up in the box score, but they are all what I like to call positive blocks, and they are just as good.

Blocking can be very frustrating (perfect pass = advantage hitters) and requires discipline and repetitive training in technique. The great thing about training is that the players can (and should) work on footwork daily, even without a coach. Taking 10 minutes out of practice daily goes a long way in becoming an effective middle blocker.

CONCLUSION

Playing middle requires a unique mind-set. These players should have more of a workhorse mentality (steady, consistent, relentless) and value team glory over personal glory. These traits combined with great physical tools are essential for becoming a great middle.

12

Training Outside Hitters

Erin Mellinger

In our volleyball program, we train the whole athlete. In the case of outside hitters, we train them to be six-rotation players in any offensive system so they will contribute in every rotation. Ideally, we want to be able to use them in both the frontcourt and the backcourt during serve receive, defense, attacking, and serving.

CHARACTERISTICS OF EFFECTIVE OUTSIDE HITTERS

The ideal outside hitter jumps well, is dynamic and athletic, and has good arm speed and ball control. We like our outside hitters to have a jump approach in the 9-foot, 7-inch range or higher. We are constantly recruiting athletes who work well or can be trained to work well against a big block. Height can vary based on the jump approach. Obviously, the bigger or taller the athlete the better, but jump reach and speed are more important than size.

Good foot speed in both offense and defense is also crucial for an outside hitter. A player who can transition quickly to dig a ball and then move out and back in to hit the ball makes an ideal outside hitter. Coaches are always looking for speed and athleticism—that is, for players who can move quickly forward, backward, and laterally. Correct footwork, knowledge of the game, and agility training can increase foot speed.

Importance of Ball Control

Ball control is the number one priority in our system. For this reason, we consider passing the most important skill in volleyball and spend much time and energy on serve-receive and ball-control drills. Athletes must understand that ball control leads to good setting and hitting. Serve receive and passing are not only physical skills; they also involve a mind-set. Outside hitters need to have a mind-set that they are passers before they are hitters. Outside hitters who want to be six-rotation players need to serve receive well in every rotation. This is especially true for the player in the O2 position. This player must be able to serve receive, must play dynamically, and must not be afraid to take control of the tri-line in conjunction with the libero.

Defense

Outside hitters are constantly playing defense in both the frontcourt and back-court. The constant transitions from serve receive to hitting, hitting to defense, and defense back to hitting require mental toughness. In our offensive system, our outside hitters play defense in middle back, although we do switch it up when specific players warrant a change. However, the majority of the time, the outside hitters play middle back and are used in the offense as attackers from the backcourt.

Outside hitters attack from the back row using the BIC set. The BIC set is a two-height, or second-tempo set about a foot inside the attack line towards the net. The hitter is on the second step of the approach as the setter is setting the ball. In the middle-back defensive position, outside hitters are responsible for deep corners and lateral movement, but have free rein to move to where they read the hitter. Understanding the movements of the game and focusing on hitters instead of the ball helps outside hitters defensively. Outside hitters who are six-rotation players can be good defenders and also assist in the offense from the back row.

OFFENSIVE SYSTEMS

We like to keep our outside hitters on the court for a complete match to contribute not only physically, but also mentally as a result of the consistency they develop. The more they pass with one another, the more comfortable they are and the more consistent their passes become. A few offensive systems that can be used are the 5-1 and 6-2 systems.

5-1 Offensive System

The O1 and the O2 have different roles in the 5-1 system. The O2 should be a low-error player—someone who is really good at tooling hands (using the block), swinging line, and mixing up attack shots. In the 5-1 system, the O2 has to be a six-rotation player with good ball-control skills who can serve receive as well as attack well out of the back row. The O1 is a more physical player who can be an offensive threat. The O1 hits a heavier ball, could have a higher jump, and is considered a go-to player who can terminate in one-one situations. It is critical that the O1 be able to score points when given an opportunity.

If the setter (S) is in right back, the O1 starts in right front (figure 12.1). The O1 is in front of the setter because she will

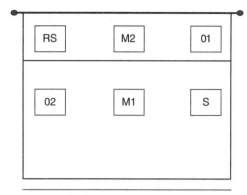

FIGURE 12.1 The 5-1 offensive system.

be in the front row with only two hitters (M1) and the setter for two rotations. The M1 starts in middle back. The O2 starts in left back, opposite the O1, and is in the front row with the right-side hitter (RS) for two rotations. The RS starts in left front opposite the setter. The M2 starts in middle front opposite the M1, which means that the O2 is only in the front row with the M2 and the setter for one rotation.

6-2 Offensive System

The O1 and O2 may have different roles in a 6-2 offensive system, but it really depends on the makeup of the team. The player who has more ball control for serve receive and plays better defense would be the one staying in for six rotations; outside hitters or right-side hitters. There are many options with a 6-2 offense. You can substitute middles for setters instead of right sides or run a standard 6-2 and substitute right-side hitters for setters (figure 12.2).

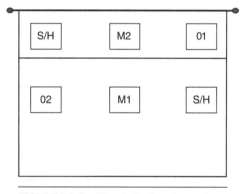

FIGURE 12.2 The 6-2 offensive system.

Either way, we like outside hitters to play six rotations. Given the makeup of our offense, running a 6-2 gives our outside hitters more opportunities to score; hence, we keep three hitters in the front row at all times.

CREATING SCORING OPPORTUNITIES FOR OUTSIDE HITTERS

Our team uses more of a middle and right-side hitter–driven offense, so the majority of the sets go to the middle and right-side players. This obviously puts the outside hitters in more one-on-one situations against the block so they can score often. It is interesting that when you look at many rosters, players are listed only as outside hitters. We have specific players that play right side. Sometimes there are players that can play all three positions (O1, O2, and right side), but we like the right side to be successful hitting off one foot.

Sets for Outside Hitters

The sets we use in our system for outside hitters are: hut, hut-go, 32, gap, and BIC. The hut set is about a three-tempo set that should land in the last panel of the net inside the antenna (see figure 12.3). The hut-go is about a two-and-a-half-tempo set (the antenna height and a half), which means the ball goes through the last panel of the net (five panels away from setter) and would land outside the court if the hitter did not contact the ball (see figure 12.4). This ball is very different from a shoot or a faster ball to the outside. The setter should hold the set in the last panel (fifth panel of the net) and create a lift on the ball so it does not die out before it reaches the last panel.

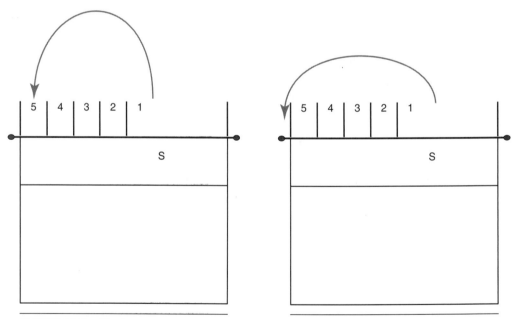

FIGURE 12.3 The hut set.

FIGURE 12.4 The hut-go set.

The 32 is an inside set that is mostly used when the outside must play defense on a tip or roll shot ball from the opponent (figure 12.5). It gets its name from being in the third panel of the net (three panels away from setter) at about a second tempo (the height of an antenna). The gap set uses a one-foot takeoff approach between the third and fourth panels of the net. It is a ball that is set in the third panel (three panels away from setter) at a two-and-a-half-tempo set and is positioned just inside the opposing middle blocker's left hand. The outside hitter should be able to swing hard crosscourt or cut back toward area 1 (figure 12.6).

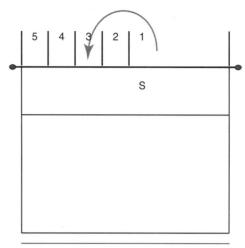

FIGURE 12.5 The 32 inside set.

The last set for the outsides is the BIC set, which is used when the outside hitter is playing back row and in middle back. The BIC is a two height or second-tempo set about a foot inside the attack line (figure 12.7).

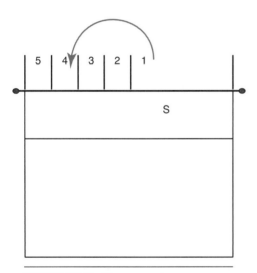

FIGURE 12.6 The gap set.

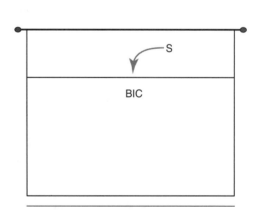

FIGURE 12.7 The BIC set.

Sets for Right-Side Hitters

The sets we use in our offensive system for right-side hitters are A, black, red, C, swing, zone, and D. The A set is similar to a back 1 (one panel behind setter, see figure 12.8). The black set is two panels behind the setter as a second-tempo ball (see figure 12.9). The C set is the highest right-side set, which is pushed to the antenna at a two-and-a-half-tempo set (see figure 12.10). The red set is also a second-tempo set, but instead sets two panels in front of the setter (see figure 12.11). The swing set is a one-foot takeoff ball that is pushed to the C zone (to the antenna) at about a two-and-a-half-tempo set (see figure 12.12). The zone is set in the middle of the net at a two-and-a-half-tempo set (the height of an antenna plus half) (see figure 12.13). The zone set is used as an outlet ball to keep the right-side hitter involved in the offense when the setter is pushed out of the setter position. The D set is the back-row attack for the right-side hitter who plays right-back defense (see figure 12.14). The D set is about a foot inside the attack line at a two-and-a-half-tempo set (the height of an antenna plus half).

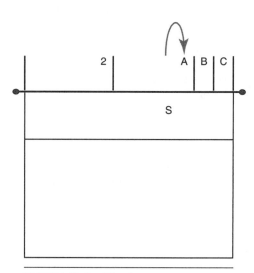

FIGURE 12.8 The A set.

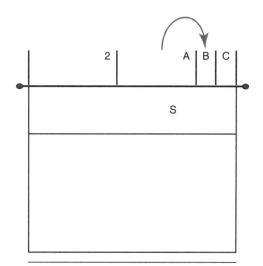

FIGURE 12.9 The black set.

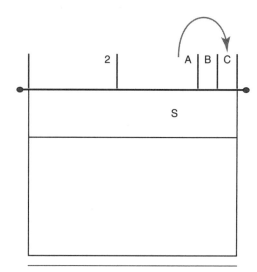

FIGURE 12.10 The C set.

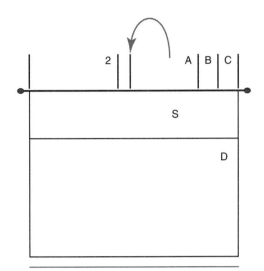

FIGURE 12.11 The red set.

Note: The net is divided into five panels out to the outside hitter position and three panels behind the setter.

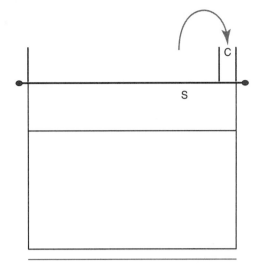

FIGURE 12.12 The swing set.

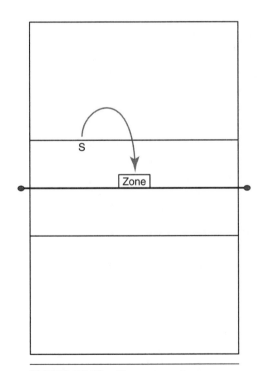

FIGURE 12.13 The zone set.

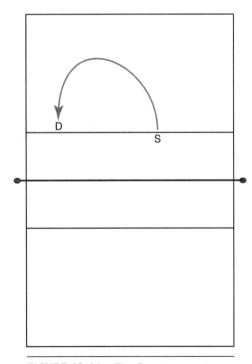

FIGURE 12.14 The D set.

TRANSITION

Transition is a very crucial part of an outside hitter's game. A deep and wide transition allows an outside hitter to evaluate a set, see the block, and make the necessary adjustments before swinging at the ball. Ideally, an outside hitter should transition 10 feet outside the court and 12 feet deep off the net. The transition from serve receive to attacking a ball has two possible options:

1. Serve receiving the ball: The outside hitter must perform three large shuffles to try to get outside the court to the 10-feet-deep or 12-feet-deep range.

2. Not serve receiving the ball: The outside hitter must perform five large shuffles and must get outside the court to the 10-feet-deep or 12-feet-deep range.

Transitioning from a serve-receive position to attacking a ball is different from transitioning from defense to attacking a ball. In serve receive we train to have specific footwork, whereas in defensive transition we train to turn and go. Turn and go means opening up to the court, tracking the ball, and running to transition to the 10-feet-deep or 12-feet-deep range.

We spend a significant amount of time each week training outside hitters in transitioning. More important, we use a specific drill that can be modified or used as a progression to help in that training. This drill can be used out of serve receive, during defense, while using the block, and while working various shots.

TRAINING OUTSIDE HITTERS

Learning to hit a variety of shots is an important part of an outside hitter's offensive training. Examples are the roll shot (shallow or deep), open-handed tip, hard crosscourt shot, tooling blockers hands high and tooling the outside hand (right hand of the outside blocker if hitting from left side) of the opponents, hard line shot, and high, deep ball to area 5. The most important shot we train is the tooling of the opponent's hands. When training to "tool the block," outside hitters obviously must first locate the block. After locating the block, they must decide what to do with the arm swing to manipulate the blocker's hands. For example, when attacking the block or swinging line, the outside hitter looks to use the outside hand of the opponent. Repetition is the key to training tooling the block. Athletes sometimes want to avoid the block, but training them to manipulate the block is more effective. When training to hit a hard line shot, we teach athletes to use shoulders, hips, and abdominal muscles. The whipping of the hips speeds up the arm swing and allows a full range of motion and the use of the abs, shoulder, and hips, which is more effective than using just the shoulder.

To train the high over-the-block shot to area 5 deep, outside hitters practice aiming just above the block and finishing the middle finger through the top of the ball to create more topspin on the ball so that it drops. When attacking sharp crosscourt, our outside hitters finish thumb down toward the net. The roll shot requires a wrist motion starting from the bottom of the ball and finishing through the top simulating a popping sound. Most important when mixing up shots is the ability to approach with the same speed, have the same arm swing, and change only the wrist or hand at the end. The following drill can be used to train outside hitters in all shots.

Outside Hitter Drill: Various Shots

Purpose

This drill can be used to train outside hitters to work various shots on the court.

Setup

Place one or two players on the sturdy box with their hands in a blocking position.

Execution

Using the same footwork explained in figure 12.15, the OH either passes and transitions or transitions and hits a hut or hut-go set. Coaches give instructions on the focus of the drill (e.g., tool hands [swing high off the hands or use the outside hand of the blocker], hard line, roll shot deep, roll shot short, tip area 1 deep or area 2 short, swing high over the block to area 5, or swing hard cross).

Coaching Points

We also add floor markers and have hitters aim for those areas. There is always a focus in this drill.

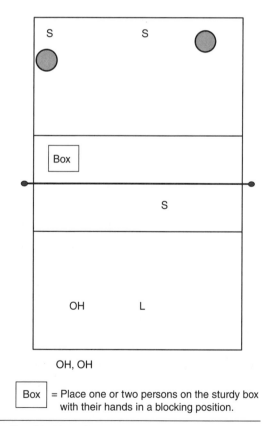

Box = Place one or two persons on the sturdy box with their hands in a blocking position.

FIGURE 12.15 Outside hitter drill: various shots.

TRAINING RIGHT-SIDE HITTERS

In our offense, right sides may be more dynamic in their ability to hit several tempo sets. Their transitions are significantly different from those of the outside hitters: they are 2 feet behind the attack line and lined up inside the court near the T of the attack line and the sideline. Right-side hitters must choose a set based on the position of the pass.

Several sets move with the setter, which is how sets are implemented into the offense. In an ideal situation, a black set is set in the B panel of the net, which is two panels behind the setter. However, if the setter moves forward toward the 3 panel on the net, then the right-side hitter must position herself two panels from where the setter will set the ball. When the setter is pushed back two panels from the target position, the right-side hitter must position herself to attack two panels in front of the setter for the red set.

The right side is always lined up with the setter and square to the net. In our offense, right-side hitters approach straight forward, not at a diagonal. The movement in the right-side offense allows the right side to attack regardless of the pass.

BLOCKING EXPECTATIONS

Ideally, we like our players to defend opposing hitters with just blocking; however, channeling balls to our defense is just as important. An outside hitter's base blocking position is two arm's lengths from the middle blocker. The outside hitter is responsible for blocking in every offensive scenario except when the opponent's outside hitter is attacking. Most important is defending the hitter directly in front (i.e., the opponent's right-side hitter or setter) or any hitter that crosses into the blocking zone (e.g., middle hitter hitting a slide). In addition to blocking in their own zones, outside hitters are also responsible for blocking with middle blockers on a quick (i.e., 1) attack as well as a crossing X play. A crossing X play is when the opponent's right-side hitter leaves her immediate zone and enters into the middle of the court; the outside hitter must follow the opponent's right-side hitter to set up a double block with the middle blocker.

Figure 12.16 shows the base defensive position for the outside hitter and right-setter. Lines are showing primary responsibility for the blocking area on the net.

The right-side hitter's primary concern is to defend the opponent's outside hitter. This player's base blocking position is one arm's length from the antenna or pin. However, the right-side hitter is also responsible for assisting middle blockers with blocking. The right-side blocker must consistently set a block in the correct position along the net so the middle blocker can close the block.

Hand positioning for both outside and right-side hitters is very important. In blocking, one hand is considered the fronting hand; the other hand is the directing hand. The fronting hand must be in front of the ball. The directing hand directs or redirects the ball into the opponent's court. For pin players (outside and right-side hitters), the hand closer to the antenna is the directing hand. If the directing hand is not strong at holding its position, then pin players usually are "tooled" (when hitters hit the ball into the block and score for a point) by the opponent's hitters.

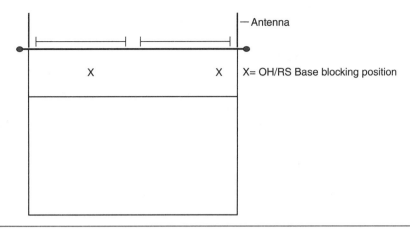

FIGURE 12.16 OH and RS blocking responsibilities.

Pin players (outside and right-side hitters) are very important in the blocking scheme. Pin players have full responsibility for setting the block in the correct position along the net, staying there, and allowing the middle blocker to close shoulder to shoulder. It is just as important for the block to funnel balls to the defense as it is to have a stuff block (a ball that is blocked for a point).

SERVING

Serving is a crucial tactical part of the game of volleyball. Tough serving helps manipulate the opponent's offense. We use a variety of tactics to manipulate certain positions or opposing players. Serving is another important duty for outside and right-side hitters. Repetition is the best way to develop good serving skills. We work on serving every day for at least 20 minutes of practice time. Jump serving has changed the pace and the speed of the game. A great server can be a tactical point in the game by manipulating the other team's serve receive with her serve, which makes it easier to play defense.

We practice serving into the last two feet of the court using mats. To briefly demonstrate the importance of serving seams, put three chairs out on the court with mats between them. The objective is to hit the mats and not the chairs. Hitting the chair simulates serving directly at the serve receiver; players should instead try to serve in the seams.

VIDEO

We use video for various reasons in our program. Video gives athletes the opportunity to truly evaluate themselves. We use video to evaluate athletes' serve receive and defensive postures, offensive and defensive transitions, and hand positions for blocking. Visualization can sometimes be a helpful tool for improving and adjusting technique. The spring season gives us more opportunities for individual training and video evaluations.

SCOUTING

Scouting opponents is also an important tool for helping our outside and right-side hitters. We focus on several things when scouting: how to assist hitters in manipulating the defense, opponents' weaknesses, how to control go-to players, and serving tactics. Focusing on these four things prepares our athletes enough without overwhelming them with too much information. We watch films as a team. Our athletes complete their own scouting reports, and then we discuss the opponent's weaknesses. The coaching staff obviously spends more time scouting opposing teams than the athletes do. We try to keep it simple by providing enough information to help them without overwhelming them.

STATISTICS

Statistics plays a large role in the game of volleyball. It is important to record statistics in both practices and matches. Statistics help both coaches and athletes evaluate performance. As a coach, I expect certain numbers from certain positions. I like primary passers (outside hitters, right-side hitters, and the libero) to be passing at 75 percent or higher. That means that 75 percent of serve-received balls are a three-option pass (i.e., give the setter the option to choose to set middle hitters, the right-side hitter, or the outside hitter).

Not only do we have serve-receive statistical numbers for passers to reach, but we also have hitting percentages for the O1 and O2. The O2 ideally is expected to hit in the .250 range to be consistently contributing to the offense. More important, the O2 has to be a low-error player—a player who keeps the ball in play and hits shots. The O2 should also be able to use the opponent's block to score. The O2 is expected to terminate for a point, but ideally mixes up shots and commits very few hitting errors. We look for the O1 to hit in the .350 to .400 range. The O1 is continually contributing to the offense as a go-to player. The O1 is expected to score, especially because that position is in the front row with the setter for two rotations if we are playing a 5-1 offense.

CONCLUSION

We recruit to have four or five outside hitters on our roster each year. Depth creates competitiveness and challenges each athlete to constantly improve. Our program has won several national championships, and depth is the reason. Creating a competitive atmosphere in which players develop, improve, and push one another is so significant to their training. The main reason we won a national championship in 2013 is that we had good athletes who challenged themselves and their teammates.

Our outside hitters help us win in a variety of ways. Most important is their ability to play all six rotations, which creates consistency. We train outside hitters to score in one-on-one situations and to be low-error players. They are not just front-row hitters in our offense; they also serve as hitters in the backcourt which in turn obviously creates more offense. Outside hitters play significant roles on the volleyball court.

13

Training Setters

Wayne Kreklow

The setter is arguably the most important player on any volleyball team. Not only does the setter touch the ball more than anyone else on the floor, but she also decides who attacks the ball, what kind of ball they are attacking, where along the net they are going to attack, and how often they are going to attack. The setter controls the tempo of the match and has a more influential role in the outcome than any other player on the floor. All great teams in any team sport have one thing in common: a great facilitator. Championship football teams all have great quarterbacks—Brett Favre, Tom Brady, Peyton Manning. Championship basketball teams all have great point guards—Magic Johnson, Tony Parker, Maurice Cheeks. Championship volleyball teams, likewise, all have great setters—Lloy Ball, Lindsey Berg, Robyn Ah Mow-Santos, and Courtney Thompson just to name a few from recent U.S. Olympic teams. All of the great athletes and players have one thing in common: They make those around them better players. They are facilitators. By virtue of the physical, technical, tactical, and leadership skills they possess, they make it possible for a collection of talented individuals to become a great team.

In this chapter we take an in-depth look at how we can identify and train setters to be the facilitators and leaders that are so critical to the success of our teams. We must be knowledgeable about the offensive systems we can run and what is required of setters in those systems. We must also be aware of the physical attributes needed to be a great setter and also be well schooled in how to train them. In addition, we must also examine leadership qualities and determine the activities and drills we can use to help our setters develop into the leaders our teams need. We address the question, "Are leaders truly born that way, or can we develop them?" Finally, we discuss how to prepare setters for competition—performing in the heat of the moment when all eyes are on them and the outcome rests squarely on their shoulders.

OFFENSIVE SYSTEMS

The two basic systems of play that most teams use are the 5-1 offense and the 6-2 offense. A brief explanation of each is helpful because the process of choosing and developing a setter depends on what is asked of that player. We need to know what physical and mental characteristics are essential and what setting skills are required to implement your offensive system.

5-1 Offensive System

The 5-1 offensive system simply means that one setter plays both front row and back row. Because the setter is on the court all the time, this player must be not only proficient in setting, but also reasonably good at all the other skills. The 5-1 setter has to block and defend (and sometimes attack) just like your other front row players.

6-2 Offensive System

The 6-2 offensive system uses two setters, each normally rotating into the back row and out of the front row. They can rotate in for any front-row player, but most teams normally rotate them in and out with front-row players who usually play right front, or position 2. Some teams rotate their setters in and out with their middle blockers. Because setters in a 6-2 system do not usually play across the front row, it allows for a well-skilled but smaller setter to be a significant contributor because she does not have to worry about blocking against a much larger opponent. There are a number of teams, however, that choose to keep one of their setters in across the front row because she might also be a very effective attacker.

Choosing a System

Knowing the basics of these common systems, how do you decide which is right for your team? This million-dollar question does not always have an easy answer. However, looking closely at the skills setters need in order to do well in either of these systems should help you understand what to look for in setter candidates and how to train them.

The advantage of running a 5-1 offense is that you have one setter (one quarterback) to facilitate play. This promotes consistency in terms of tempo and rhythm on offense. Also, from a coaching standpoint, working and communicating with only one setter during play can be easier than working and communicating with two setters. The most often-cited concern with running a 5-1 is that a setter may not be big enough to put up a good block. Using a 6-2 offense allows you to substitute a smaller setter for a bigger block, but your hitters will have to get used to hitting off two setters. Also, using two setters could potentially disrupt your tempo and rhythm on offense. In addition, two setters require more practice time (which is often limited) for setter training and hitting repetitions.

When making the decision to run either a 5-1 or a 6-2 offense, ask yourself, "What does *our* team need to do to win?" At the end of the day, it doesn't matter what the U.S. national team does or what the Chinese are doing or what the Brazilians are doing. What matters is what will put your players and your team in the best position to win.

At Mizzou, we look very closely at what other successful teams do offensively. What are they doing that makes them good? What are they doing to beat other teams, and why are those things working? What we have discovered has been very helpful in putting together our own philosophy of offense and working with setters.

Over the past several years, there has been a push to make the game of volleyball more exciting and appealing to fans. Making the switch to rally scoring, lowering game scores from 30 points to 25 points, and loosening ball-handling rules have all had the effect of shifting the focus from defense to offense. If you look at team statistics in the NCAA Division I conferences, you will usually find that the league leaders almost always either lead or are very near the top in some key statistical categories: team hitting percentage, kills per game, assists per game, or service aces per game. They are also usually at or near the top in fewest reception errors per game. What also jumps out when looking at team statistics is that the best blocking teams are not always at the top of the league standings, unless they are also very proficient in one or two other offensive statistical categories. Knowing these trends helps us choose our offensive system and understand what type of setter we need.

Whether you choose a 5-1 or 6-2 system, your team must be an efficient offensive team. Your players must be able to terminate play at a high level and side out at a high level. To do so, your team must be able to handle the ball well and your setters need to be able to put your attackers in a position to be successful. Knowing the importance of offense over defense, we focus more on becoming the most efficient offensive team we can be and less on becoming the best blocking team. At Mizzou, we made the choice to go with a 5-1 system because our setters have been outstanding at running our offense and getting our hitters great swings. In the 2013 season, Mizzou led the nation in team hitting percentage, kills per set, and assists per set and committed the fewest attack errors per set. Our setters have not always been the best blockers or the best defenders, but they have been among the best facilitators, and that has allowed our Mizzou teams to consistently win at a high level and succeed.

Some great teams employ a 6-2 offense because they want to generate more offense. Traditionally, teams have used a 6-2 offense because they had two small setters who were a liability at the net blocking. Bigger players were brought in to block. With the current emphasis on offense, more teams are running a 6-2 offense to use more attackers. The strategy is to have more attackers, more speed, and more points of attack along the net. Teams that employ a 6-2 offense always have three hitters in the front row and can always attack the opponent's left-side hitters, traditionally the weakest blockers.

Take an honest look at the personnel on your team and consider which system would give your team the best shot at winning, not what is currently most popular or even what you would prefer to use. Consider not only what your setter is capable of doing, but also how many attackers you have and what they are capable of doing. One of the keys to winning is fitting your system to your players' strengths, not trying to make your players fit a particular system.

CHARACTERISTICS OF SETTERS

No two setters are exactly alike, but when we are evaluating setters, we find it useful to examine certain characteristics we feel are most important. We separate those key characteristics into four main areas: physical skills, technical skills, tactical skills, and leadership skills.

Physical Skills

Physical skills are those unique physical traits that setters are simply born with. Over the years, there have been many debates about what physical attributes help to make great setters. We all want tall, quick, agile setters with great hands who are strong leaders and straight-A students! Unfortunately, because such players are few and far between, most of us have setters who have only a few of those attributes and it is our job to maximize their strengths and minimize their weaknesses.

When deciding on a setter, consider again what your team needs to do to succeed. Because we already know the importance of being a great offensive team, we focus on the physical attributes that facilitate an efficient offense. We need a setter who can get to errant passes and keep us in system as much as possible. This means that we need someone who is quick and agile. Obviously, we are going to look for someone who can, first, consistently deliver a hittable ball and, second, run an efficient offense.

If you are a high school coach with limited time to train setters, keep it simple. Identify a player who can get a ball to the same place consistently and let your hitters go to work. I have often seen high school and club teams beat themselves with errors because they were trying to do too many tactical things that their players were not skilled enough to execute. Remember the adage, "Don't attempt to do tactically what you can't execute technically."

Our teams have competed against many great setters of all sizes, shapes, and levels of athletic ability, and all have been very good. The key is that they were all *really* good at something, and that was, more often than not, setting the ball. We have competed against tall, great blocking setters who were not particularly quick or agile, but had great hands and could put a ball anywhere. We have also competed against shorter, slower setters who were likewise great because of their ability to consistently get their hitters great swings. In addition, they usually had great coaches who recognized their limitations and knew how to play around them. Slower setters had ball handlers who put the first balls higher to give them time to get there, or the team played a rotation defense so that the slower setter did not have to cover as much court.

Technical Skills

All good setters must be technically proficient. This requires the investment of a lot of time on the part of both the setter and the coach. The time required to develop a really good setter, more than anything else, is what makes a great setter so hard to find. Most high schools and clubs simply don't have the time to train a great setter. Even college coaches, who are restricted by NCAA by-laws governing allowable practice hours, have difficulty training setters.

Knowing that we have limited time to train setters, we again need to ask ourselves as coaches, "What are the most important things my setter needs to be good at for our team to succeed?" Most of us would answer—setting the ball! Thus, we should use every allowable minute we have in the gym to train setters to set the ball. We must organize and prioritize our setters' training so we don't waste precious time in the gym.

In training, regardless of position, I believe in progressions. We start with the fundamentals and work toward more advanced techniques. That doesn't mean that we never expose players to more advanced techniques before they master the basics, but making sure players feel confident and good about themselves is important. We never want them to walk out of the gym feeling bad about themselves.

In training our setters, we focus on front sets, back sets, and jumps sets every day. It is very important that every setter master these three basic skills. Once the setter feels comfortable with them, we incorporate movement. We all know that setters spend more time chasing down errant passes than setting from perfect passes, so they must spend time training those movements. We do this for 30 minutes before practice, every day! At the NCAA Division I level, we obviously train more than simple front sets and back sets, but the principle of concentrated repetitions is the same regardless of level.

During the individual setting sessions, we rarely spend time on blocking, serving, or defense. We save that for regular team practice. During these 30-minute blocks, we often have to remind our setters of the concept of *mindful repetition*—paying attention to what they are doing and striving for perfection even when the task seems mundane.

Tactical Skills

We obviously look for setters who understand the game of volleyball. This understanding takes the longest to master, and you could argue that it is never fully mastered because the game is continually evolving. A high-level setter needs to be thoughtful and have a desire to really dig into the game on a deeper level than other players. Much like NFL quarterbacks, setters need to understand not only their own team and what each player is doing, but also the opponent players and tendencies. Once again, extra time is required to really study videos, digest the stats, and process the information.

Leadership Skills

Leadership in a setter is extremely important to the success of the team. Again, just like the quarterback, the setter needs to be respected and trusted by the entire team. Leadership and trust, however, are concepts that players can misunderstand, particularly younger players. In my opinion, leading means showing the way rather than pointing the way. Leading means being out in front, not bringing up the rear and telling everyone where to go and what to do. To garner the trust of the team, a player must first prove himself trustworthy in both what he says and what he does.

When evaluating setters, watch them setting, but also watch their interactions with teammates and coaches. Setters need to be steady and consistent, both mentally and physically. I have never been a fan of loud, emotional, and intense setters (the only exception has been when they were incredibly positive). Players look for the setter to be under control and steady at all times—not too crazy when the team is on a roll and not too down when things aren't going well. I have often compared the emotional requirements of a setter to those of a ship captain. When things are going well, no one needs the captain. When the ship is sinking, though, everyone looks to the captain to save them. They need to see a calm, composed person in charge and giving direction, not someone who is panicking!

TRAINING SETTERS

When training setters, addressing the four skill areas just discussed (physical, technical, tactical, and leadership) is crucial. Training in some of these skill areas can be done separately; some can be done in combination. As with all training, one of the most important things you can do as a coach is to be sure that your setter is clear on exactly what is being asked of him or her and exactly how you would like it done. I highly recommend using video as often as possible. Nothing is more powerful than your setter being able to "see" what you're talking about rather than trying to "imagine" what you are talking about. There are countless studies that show learning is greatly enhanced through seeing and doing, rather than simply listening.

When addressing the physical training of our setters, we focus intensely on the physical demands and movements required in the position. We do this through direct observations of our own setters and others as well as by watching a lot of video. If you do this, you will find that setters repeat many movement patterns. Knowing these patterns makes it much easier to design drills that will help your setters become better at getting to the ball and thereby delivering better sets. We separate our physical training into generic strength, quickness and agility work, and setter-specific movement training.

In our generic physical training, we focus on developing quickness, agility, speed, and vertical jump. These are all obviously explosive movements so they must be trained accordingly. Explosive movement in sport requires strength. Strength alone, however, does not really help setters be quicker, faster, or more agile. At Mizzou, we focus not on how much setters lift, but on how fast they can move what they are lifting. We monitor the weight they lift to make sure they can move fast and explosively. We also have them lift as often as possible from upright or unstable positions rather than from a bench, while seated, or from a machine. Again, the primary purpose of our strength training component is to make sure the body is strong enough to exert the force necessary for moving explosively and also to prevent injury.

Along with strength training, we obviously must focus heavily on the speed, agility, and quickness (SAQ) of our setters. All of our generic SAQ activities are in the confines of a 30- by 30-foot area, the same dimensions of the volleyball court we compete in. Again, thousands of drills are available in print and video, but I urge you to look at the movements your setters make on a regular basis and be creative in designing your own agility drills. What we find is that our setters tend to repeat patterns of movement over and over. Through direct observation and more often, video analysis, we identify those patterns and look to create drills that replicate those patterns.

Setters must be able to accelerate quickly. They are generally stopped in right back and must cover no more than 10 to 15 feet in reacting to a transition opportunity. In addition, while they are accelerating to the setting position on the net in anticipation of setting a pass or dig, they must quickly change direction to pursue an errant play on the ball. Setters must train for movement in all directions! In addition, they must be trained to use a variety of footwork patterns. In this case, I'm not talking about specific footwork patterns when setting so much as I am about generic agility. Being proficient in a variety of movement patterns in multiple directions, such as shuffling, sprinting and moving into a shuffle, shuffling into a sprint, and performing a crossover step into a shuffle and then into a sprint, is critical. Visualize a great tennis player moving during a rally. Tennis players have some of the best footwork and agility in the world of sport.

Technical Training

We have our setters come in every day for 30 minutes of training before practice. This allows us to give them the concentrated repetitions they need to become proficient in their role. There are many philosophies out there pertaining to training setters. Some coaches use thousands of very controlled and scripted repetitions with a coach tossing; others advocate a more random approach. I believe that each method has merit, and we tend to take a more balanced approach in our setter training.

Our setters spend the first part of every 30-minute training block setting a weighted volleyball against a wall to develop strength. They usually do no more than five minutes of this, but we believe it builds skill-specific strength.

When our setters move to the net, they normally progress from simple to more difficult drills. I have always been a big believer in creating a feeling of competence in players by starting with simple drills that provide a lot of touches and a high success rate and gradually making them more difficult and more challenging. We use hundreds of drills during these sessions, but the most important thing to remember when working one on one with setters is to recreate movements and situations that they will encounter in live play. For example, we usually start with a coach tossing to the setter because we can control how fast we move and where specifically we want the setter to set from. Determine the skill your setter needs to get better at and have her repeat it. It might be using a simple setting technique, finding the ball after she blocks, setting a tight ball, or moving a ball off the net to set. We've encountered all of them over the years!

Our staple drills include having our setters set multiple balls from multiple spots in a series. A sequence example is (1) on the net, (2) forward along the net to zone 4, (3) turn and run back to the setter position on the net, (4) off the net to finish—four balls in a row all set to zone 4 (left front). You can create any combination of movement patterns for your setter to move through while tossing balls for him to set. All great setters need to be comfortable being uncomfortable and to be able to deliver a hittable ball.

We spend a lot of time making sure setters are comfortable receiving balls from all spots on the court, not just from the middle of the court where most coaches toss from. We make sure to toss from left front and left back as well as right back. In addition, we have our setters set balls that are tossed very high in the air so that they have to wait for them. Likewise, we also toss flat, fast balls to set. Setters should also be required to set balls that are spinning (topspin, backspin, sidespin). In short, be creative and look to recreate what your setter is doing during live play.

Tactical Training

Learning the tactical part of the game is arguably the toughest part of training for a setter. There is no shortcut; a certain amount of exposure to situations is required to consistently recognize them and respond correctly. Seeing what the other team is doing and making the right decision in a split second is not easy. The fact that there are very few great rookie quarterbacks in the NFL or junior-aged setters leading their national teams in the Olympics speaks to the difficulty of learning the tactical part of the game. This is why great young setters from clubs that train and play at high levels are so valued: there is no substitute for the number of games they have played and the amount of experience they have had. Those of us who are not fortunate enough to have one of these young, elite setters can close the experience gap with training.

A combination of seeing and hearing is required to develop the tactical part of the game for setters. Coaching feedback is great, but without actually seeing what the coach is talking about, the setter's learning is limited. Video feedback is very effective in training setters in the tactical aspects of the game.

When we look at videos with our setters, we ask that they pay attention to specific things. First is to look at themselves as they are setting. We ask them to notice whether they are giving their set away early through poor ball position or body posture. We also point out situations that often occur during games: do they have a favorite hitter or set that they always use in certain situations? Do they tend to attack second balls on only certain passes or in certain rotations? When they run a play set, do they always run the same option? We also ask them to watch the opponents to see how they react to what they are doing. Did the play set have the desired effect? If not, why? Did they get the right hitter against the right blocker? Being able to see what happened and how their decisions affected the game is priceless.

In addition to watching videos, we also give our setters strategies for creating opportunities for our hitters to score. Following are some examples:

Going against the flow. This simply means that the setter tries to set away from the direction in which she is moving to get the ball. If she is moving toward left front, she sets to right front; if she is moving toward right front, she sets to left front. The idea is that the opposing middle blocker will tend to follow the setter; if the setter sets against the flow, the opposing middle will not be able to close the block to the outside hitter.

Overloading. This involves bringing multiple hitters into a zone on the net to have more hitters than blockers.

Creating movement. Moving hitters either into or out of another zone is another great way for setters to create scoring opportunities for the team.

Creating movement and setting away from that movement. Creating movement by having attackers move into and out of different zones along the net requires blockers and defenders to make decisions and communicate assignments. This preoccupation with movement often gives an uninvolved attacker an opening at the net to score. An example of this is an X play, in which a middle hitter runs a slide and the opposite hitter attacks in front of the setter. However, instead of setting one of the two obvious choices, the setter sets the ball to the outside hitter.

All of these strategies are based on the idea that the more defending players have to think and the more decisions they have to make, the more slowly they will react, thereby creating more gaps to score from. This concept is very similar to a football team using misdirection and movement to freeze defenders, opening gaps and creating opportunities to score.

Leadership Training

Your setters have to be leaders on your team. By virtue of the position and the fact that the setter is so heavily involved in directing the team, she must gain the trust and confidence of her teammates. We have discovered many types of leaders over the years, and they all have strengths and weaknesses. However, some traits and behaviors that we have noticed lend themselves to effective leadership more than others do.

To lead, setters must earn the respect of their teammates. Notice the word *earn*. Respect cannot be given—it must be earned. To earn respect, a setter must be one of the hardest-working players on the team. He must consistently show that he will *bring it* every day for the team.

Your setter needs to be a positive influence in your gym. This does not mean that the setter does not hold teammates accountable for lack of effort, focus, and so on, but any feedback to them must be delivered in a nonjudgmental manner. We as coaches need to work with our setters so that they understand how to give feedback in a positive, nonthreatening way rather than in a negative, destructive way. At Mizzou, we tell all of our players that their job is to encourage each other and compliment great play and great effort. No player likes to have a teammate telling him what to do and how to do it—that is the coach's job. The only exception to that rule at Mizzou concerns effort. I believe that a teammate calling another out because of a lack of effort is fair game, because effort (or lack of it) is a choice! We want our players to choose wisely.

You can develop leadership skills in your setters by allowing them to practice leading and giving feedback on how they are leading. Put them in situations in which they have control of the team or activity, and then give them feedback on how they interacted with the team. For example, having your setter lead warm-ups or stretches gives her an opportunity to direct the team in a nonstressful activity. Directing the team to huddle up periodically during drills and scrimmages, calling a time-out during a scrimmage, and choosing the team's practice on a certain day are all ways setters can practice leadership. Don't make the mistake of assuming that your setter knows how to lead! There are countless ways to help your setter solidify her place as a leader on a daily basis. As a result, when the team gets into a stressful match environment, the players will trust the setter and follow her with confidence.

DEVELOPING TACTICAL SKILLS

As coaches, we need to work very closely with our setters to help them develop a good understanding of tactics. They need time, on-court practice, and meaningful feedback to see the game as we see it. You and your setter must be on the same page about what you are trying to accomplish and how you want your team to play. Every coach has a philosophy that dictates how the team plays; setters must understand that philosophy. At Mizzou, we play an up-tempo offense and we want attack options in multiple positions. When thinking in terms of tactics, our setters must account for the impacts of their decisions not only on our opponents, but also on our team. Once again, setters need to remember the adage, don't attempt to do tactically what you cannot execute technically.

The two main activities that we use to help our setters gain a better grasp of game tactics and strategies are video analysis and game-like drill work. Video analysis gives the coach and setter time to really pick things apart, whereas game-like drill work involves replicating game situations in practice so that setters are better prepared come match time.

Spending time with your setters watching videos of practices and matches is essential for helping them develop a grasp of effective tactics. Getting a clear sense of what the opponents are doing and how they are responding to the setter's choices is very difficult during live play. Video is a great way to help your setter understand the effects their decisions have on play and whether those decisions are getting the team the desired results. When we watch videos with our setters, it is a very two-sided exercise. We ask lots of questions to get them to think through all of the scenarios they are faced with during competition. For example, we ask them to pay attention to what the opponent blockers are doing in each rotation. Are they committing with certain hitters? Are they shading one side? Are they rotating defensive players a certain way? How did the blockers and defenders respond to the play set you called? Did they move the way you wanted? If not, why? We ask lots and lots of questions!

Setters need to think about what they are doing offensively as well—what each attacker does best and how that fits into the framework of the offense. A major part of the setter's job is knowing the type of set each hitter needs to be a good attacker. Attackers have different sets they can hit well. When calling play sets, the setter must understand which attack options are available and what types of sets the attackers are proficient at attacking. Our team is often in a situation in which we would like to run a particular play set, but we don't because it does not optimize the strength of our available attacker. In that case, we defer to the attacker's best swing; we would rather have our attacker take her best swing, even if it is against the opponent's best blocker.

SITUATIONAL TRAINING

On-court practice in gamelike situations is best for helping setters develop a clear understanding of tactics and strategy. As in most of our other drills, we progress from simple to more complex to give both our setter and our hitters a chance to feel good about what they are doing and how they are connecting.

Our first priority is making sure our setter and hitters are comfortable executing the play sets we like to run. We also want to be sure that setters and hitters understand why we run certain play sets and what we hope to gain. This helps them understand why certain hitters get set more than others do. We have found that it motivates the hitters who don't get set to really sell their fakes because they understand their role in the larger play set. Working with the setter and hitters off a simple toss allows coaches to focus on the spacing and timing needed for running the play well. Once our players understand what we want, we practice the same play set off a free ball pass and work our way to a pass off a live serve or dig—once again, moving from simple and easy to more difficult and complex. Even using this type of progression, we often have to return to simple and easy drills if the players are struggling. Again, we want them to feel good about what they are doing rather than frustrated and angry.

Setters also need to feel comfortable working with multiple attackers when play is moving pretty fast. To do this, we use what we call our three-ball, three-hitter drill. We use this drill quite a bit, even in pregame warm-ups to get our setters and hitters moving and thinking. It is very basic, but initially very difficult for our setters. In this drill the setter has to set three consecutive balls, passed from our defensive specialists, to any of three hitters (LH, MH, RH) who are attacking and transitioning. A coach tosses the balls over the net to the defensive specialist to pass. The three hitters stay until after the third ball is attacked and then rotate out as a group. What makes this drill particularly difficult for the setter is that the coach is sending the next ball over as the previous ball is being attacked; hitters are calling out what set they want, and things are moving pretty fast. Our intent is to make things chaotic for our setter so she can practice making good decisions under pressure.

We also find it very helpful to use drills that create blocking situations that we commonly see, to help our setters make good decisions. For example, we add blockers to our three-ball, three-hitter drill to slow it down a bit. We ask our blockers to make a series of obvious overloads and commits to, again, give our setter practice at making the right decision. When we do this, we quietly but constantly ask our setter questions such as "Why did you set that hitter? Are you attacking a certain blocker, and if so, why?" No matter what our setters set, we want to be sure they always have a plan!

Another exercise that has worked well for us in developing setters who think tactically is weighting scoring in drills to either reward or penalize the outcome of the setter's decisions. We use bonus points in drills to reward things such as getting an attacker a one-on-one situation or scoring with a particular play set we have been practicing. Likewise, we also assess a penalty point if, for example, the setter sets a middle hitter into a double block. The bonus, or penalty point, scoring works well because it allows us, the coaches, to focus on a particular part of the game during live play and it can be easily used for just about any drill.

CONCLUSION

Your setters are arguably the most important members of your team. Just as all great football and basketball teams have great quarterbacks and point guards, all great volleyball teams have great setters. As coaches, we must be heavily invested in our setters and be willing to spend the time and energy needed to help them develop into the great players every great team needs. By focusing on their physical, technical, tactical, and emotional development, we can prepare our setters for the physical and emotional challenges they will face during competition. Patience is a key! Training the setter is a complicated and slow process, but also an extremely rewarding one that forges a bond between setters and coach that lasts forever.

14

Training Liberos

Erik Sullivan

What do great liberos look like? Most coaches would agree that they are strong, athletic, and explosive; they can move around the court easily and quickly; they have a great touch when they contact the ball and can control it to the spot of their choosing; and they can communicate at a level that demands the attention of everyone on the court. Most players excel in one or, if they are lucky, maybe a few of these areas, but finding players who are great in all of them is very difficult. The question then becomes how to help athletes grow to excel in all of these areas.

PASSING

We use passing as the example of how to train for all the skills a good libero needs. The other skills are discussed more specifically later in the chapter, including how to train them. It may be best to first explain how I think about passing and my philosophy of training athletes to accomplish this skill, as well as the mechanics behind it.

At the end of the day, controlling the ball is a physics problem. How do we take a ball in space that has some direction and velocity and redirect it to a particular area of the court without catching and throwing it? If you think about it, every skill in volleyball can be addressed in this manner. Once we have figured that out, the next issue is how to repeat the mechanics of this skill over and over at a high level. The best way is to make the mechanics and movement of the skill as simple as possible. We have a tendency to overthink and overcomplicate things.

Players who can create a large, flat platform with the forearms and hold it in space at the right angle can redirect the ball to where they want it to go. Problem solved! Great ball controllers can do this while keeping the platform still, or quiet, relative to the angle they are trying to create to redirect the ball—regardless of how much movement there is in the rest of their bodies. We spend a lot of time in practice trying to calm players' platform movements down. Most of the time, the ball has enough energy to take it where it needs to go. A libero can take away or give some energy in subtle ways, but most of the time, the platform should be fairly still. It should not be swinging in either the vertical or horizontal plane.

Above the Waist in Passing

Let's start by looking at what is happening above the waist as we analyze the mechanics of passing and playing defense. At the time of contact, the posture should be forward and slumped. The back should be rounded both vertically and horizontally. Imagine sitting comfortably at the dinner table, just before your parents yell at you to sit up straight. This is the correct posture: shoulders forward and relaxed, elbows straight and locked, and hands held together with fingers overlapped and thumbs together in the middle. This is the most common and probably the easiest way to hold the hands when putting the platform together. However, it is not the only way.

The shoulders should be shrugged forward and pushed out away from the body. This brings the elbows closer together to create a nice, flat surface. The player can also rotate the thumbs out, thus rotating the radial bones out and exposing the less boney parts of the forearms to create a flatter, softer platform. Once the platform is formed, there should be fairly little movement at the point of contact.

There should not be any swinging in the vertical plane while pivoting from the shoulders. The angle of the platform to the torso should remain fairly constant, and any movement to give energy or take it away from the ball should come in a bunting motion, not a swinging motion. The same goes for the horizontal plane: the platform should not swing across the incoming path of the ball. Players who create the proper angle with their shoulders and platform do not have to swing the platform to get the ball to go where they want it to go.

This swinging motion is probably the most common mistake we see during passing. It also leads to the most catastrophic errors, typically ending the play or not allowing the team to run its offense. When players swing the platform, they increase the amount of motion and add a timing element to passing mechanics that makes the skill much more difficult to perform consistently. The best analogy is that of a baseball swing: batters who swing hard make contact, but they have a hard time controlling where the ball goes and hit a lot of foul balls. When they want to make sure to control the ball, they bunt. I want our passers to bunt!

How players get to this passing position is just as important as the position itself. The movement used to establish this position should be minimal, or as quiet as possible. There is no reason to be flailing all over the place. More movement creates more chance for error and less chance for repeatability. Remember, players have to be able to do this over and over and over. Their movements should be quick, concise, and mechanically efficient. They should begin in a position that closely resembles the final position. (This is described in more detail in the following section, Below the Waist in Passing.) The shoulders should be relaxed and forward, and the arms should also be relaxed and almost straight. It is a mistake to have the elbows bent and tucked up next to the body. The motion to get the platform out should begin by straightening the elbows and reaching the arms out to the proper position and angle to deflect the ball to where it needs to go (see figure 14.1). This is followed by putting the hands together to finish the motion of creating the platform. This should happen with one move, without much motion or swinging of the platform. Again, more motion equals more chance for error.

The head should be still, with the chin up and eyes forward. The player shouldn't look at the ball contacting the platform, but rather, see it in peripheral vision without moving the eyes. It is OK to play the ball in many positions relative to the body. The ball does not have to be between the knees or played at the midline, as long as it is in a plane that is away from the body so the player can create angles with the platform by dropping a shoulder and rotating around their trunk (see figure 14.2).

The ability to create this angle without lifting the platform is instrumental. If the player's platform rises and becomes more parallel with the floor, there is a greater chance for the ball to skip off to the right or left. With the right angle, the ball will deflect to where the player wants it to go. Again, very little movement is necessary when the angle is right.

Below the Waist in Passing

Now let's look at what is going on with the lower body during passing. Being in a good position of balance helps players create the proper mechanics above the waist. The most ideal position is to have the feet a little wider than shoulder width and the toes pointed slightly in (pigeon toed); the knees and hips should be bent, and the back should be

FIGURE 14.1 Good forearm platform.

FIGURE 14.2 Creating a good angle by dropping a shoulder.

at about a 45-degree angle relative to the floor. One way for players to easily get into this position is to place their hands on their knees and rest their weight on their hands (see figure 14.3). As the ball is being served, they take the pressure off the hands and let the arms relax in front of the body.

FIGURE 14.3 Resting position, ready to receive a pass.

This position is very close to the desired final position when contacting the ball. From here, players can accomplish the mechanics of this skill with very little movement.

Unfortunately, not all balls are served right to passers. The question then becomes how to move to get into position to pass the ball. When players are moving around the court, they should be able to maintain a balanced position. They should shuffle their feet, moving them in unison to keep a wide base, so that when they do contact the ball, they can quickly be in a good position without a lot of extra movement. Their weight should be slightly forward and on the balls of their feet; keeping the feet slightly pigeon toed helps keep the posture forward and the body balanced. After determining where the serve is going, passers should try to establish a good, balanced base with the feet, legs, and lower body before the ball gets there. Once there, they should use the mechanics described earlier in a concise move with their platform. If they create a proper angle and hold it true at the point of contact, the ball will deflect to its desired position.

What if the passer is unable to establish a position of balance relative to the ball? The player can still pass successfully by maintaining the mechanics above the waist. It becomes much more difficult, but good passers can hold the platform still and create good angles in unbalanced positions or when having to move through the ball. The ability to move quickly around the court obviously reduces the occurrence of these situations and helps passers be more constant. However, even the best players in the world have to play some balls from unbalanced positions.

A big point of emphasis in training passing is quieting down players' movements. Passers should be quick, concise, and mechanically efficient. Adding movement to the mechanics of the skill (e.g., swinging the platform, bending the elbows, moving the head) increases the chance for error and makes the skill much more difficult to repeat at a high level.

DEFENSE

The mechanics used when playing defense are very similar to those used when passing. The platform mechanics and movement to the ball are the same. Again, athletes should be trained to be calm and still. Often, the increased speed of the ball when someone is attacking tends to cause defenders to be more aggressive in their movements. The concept of being quiet with movements and creating a good angle with the platform is the same for defenders as for passers. Defenders should be trying to deflect the ball back to the target with the platform. Typically, we ask our players to be a little more conservative with their ideal targets when playing defense, and we want their digs to be a little farther off the net and a little higher than what we would classify as the ideal pass. The posture when playing defense should be slightly lower than when passing, but again, the idea of having a solid, balanced base with the weight slightly forward is the same.

Above the Waist During Defense

During defense, players' shoulders and arms should be relaxed and hanging in front of the torso. They should have the slumped posture used when passing. If they are in the proper ready position, the platform should be almost formed. The defender should be stopped and balanced when the attacker is contacting the ball to have the best opportunity to react and be in the best position to play the ball. The motion to dig the ball should begin with the elbows and then the hands making one move to the ball. Players need to be ready to dig a ball driven hard in their direction as well as to move and pursue balls that are not hit directly at them.

Below the Waist During Defense

When moving, players should be able to control the platform from an unbalanced position (see figure 14.4). They should also be able to get to the floor easily. There has been a lot of discussion about the technique for getting to the floor in the men's game versus the women's game. Historically, men tended to dive and sprawl, and women tended to roll. Today, the way of getting to the floor is less defined between the sexes because many women dive, sprawl, and pancake. We don't prefer a specific way; we just want every player to have a couple of safe, quick, and efficient ways to get to the floor and get back up quickly. Our players work

FIGURE 14.4   Moving to the floor to dig a ball up.

on four or five ways to get to the floor, so that they are comfortable with these options as situations arise.

SERVING AND SETTING

In some situations, it makes a lot of sense for the libero to set the second ball when the setter digs the first. Typically, the libero is the best ball handler and may create the best opportunity to generate offense in out-of-system situations for the team. A libero with this duty as part of the job description must be efficient at setting both with the hands and with the platform. Good court position awareness is also crucial, so that the libero knows when to set with the hands (behind the attack line) and when to set with the platform, bump set or setting with the platform (in front of the attack line). When bump setting, liberos should square up to the target when possible and use the mechanics they would use when passing (i.e., keep the platform fairly still, do not use much platform movement or swinging, and use the legs and body to move up through the ball to shape the set). We expect them to set the ball high off the net, so the attackers have the best chance to generate a good swing out of it.

Liberos are also allowed to serve under certain rules and should be part of the evaluation process to see how they fit into the team's serving rotation.

TRAINING LIBEROS

Before we address how to train liberos, you should consider the merits of coach-driven repetitions versus learning to play by playing. Coach-driven repetitions allow you to increase the quantity and quality of the contacts of all players on your team; however, because you are initiating most of the contacts, your players have fewer opportunities to read and see the game. On the flip side, drills initiated by the athletes have some inherent inefficiencies that diminish the quantity and quality of contacts, but they will learn to see the game better through their experiences.

Some coaches firmly believe in one training method over the other and train their teams accordingly regardless of age or skill level. I do not. I believe that there is a time and a place for both training methods. I tend to believe that with younger athletes the coach should be more involved, and as players get older and more skilled, the training method should shift to more of a playing style.

For example, players who are just beginning to pass need a lot of contacts and feedback in a controlled environment, off a coach's toss, to learn proper mechanics and the fundamentals to build the proper motor skill patterns. As they get more comfortable and efficient in their mechanics, they should transition to passing from a tossed ball to a server. There is a definite advantage to players learning to pass the way they will pass during a match. Last I checked, not too many matches are played with a coach initiating the first ball. These skills are developed by seeing the server and recognizing things about body position, ball contact, and slight variations of the skill, which allows passers to read, or feel, where the ball is going before it is even in motion. These skills become more important as the level and speed of the game increase.

Unfortunately, I do not have any magic ball-control or special drill that creates the perfect libero. This is why I thought it was important to explain my philosophy. The following sections describe the activities I do with beginners as well as players at the highest level.

Beginner Training

With players just beginning to play volleyball, we try to separate the mechanics above the waist from those below the waist. We work first on simple platform formation, hand grip, straight elbows, contact point, and so on. At this point we introduce a ball from a coach's toss about 5 to 6 feet away. Players should have good posture with the lower body, and the ball should come right at them so they do not need to use any lower-body movement. We then have them move without introducing a ball, to get an idea of necessary posture as well as foot movement patterns. Then we bring back the ball and move them around with the toss.

As the movement increases, it is important to stress good fundamental mechanics. As movement and variability increase, mechanics tend to break down, so players must create patterns that are desired and mechanically efficient. As they get more comfortable, you can add more unpredictability and maybe have them pass back and forth.

The concept of teaching simple, isolated mechanics and then adding movement and variability can be used at every level, but the starting point is more advanced for higher-level players. The same concepts apply for teaching defense, serving, setting, and so on. As players progress, you can increase the distance of the initiated ball, progress to a served ball, and add other players to increase unpredictability and variability. Eventually, the progression would lead to more live playing situations, live serves, passing with multiple players, and passing serve-receive situations.

Advanced Training

As players develop and begin to show some mastery of skills, more repetitions should come from actual servers. Passers need to learn to pass off a live serve so that they can learn to see the game. The server gives a lot of subtle cues as to where the ball is going before and during contact that are important for the passer to identify. The only way a player can begin to identify these cues is with live repetitions.

On our team we create situations that put the passers at a disadvantage, such as positioning servers on a stable box a few feet into the court. Even though it is not gamelike, the passers are still getting repetitions from live servers. Putting the servers on a stable box makes the passers have to receive tougher serves because they are contacting the ball from a higher point and the trajectory of the ball tends to be flatter and therefore more difficult to pass.

DIGGING TRAINING

When training digging, we also progress from coach-driven repetitions to more live repetitions as players develop. We like to separate what is going on above and below the waist for players who are just beginning. At the lowest level, we hit balls right at diggers, so that they are not required to move much and they can focus on platform formation, position, body posture, and good platform angle formation to deflect the ball. Players also practice some movements without the ball: shuffling out of base position to other desired defensive positions, sprawling, rolling, and pancaking (see figure 14.5). As they get more comfortable with mechanics, we combine the two training methods by adding movements to coach-driven repetitions and changing where the ball is hit relative to players' body positions.

FIGURE 14.5 A player uses a pancake move to play the ball up.

Proper Stance for Diggers

Like passers, diggers need to have quiet, concise movements. Very often, players, especially young ones, have a lot of movement going on that is unnecessary. At the point of contact, the feet should be stopped and on the floor, the shoulders should be relaxed with a forward posture, and the elbows should be relatively straight and hanging in front of the body. Again, as in passing, players' platform movements to the ball should begin with locking the elbows, moving the arms to the desired position (good angle) in one motion, and then locking the hands together to complete the platform. A common mistake is locking the hands together first and swinging the platform to the desired position. This can lead to a lot of variability in ball contact, especially as the speed of the game increases because it creates timing and extra motion issues. Diggers need to be still for as long as possible to be able to see the game. We see many players who are moving a lot but not really going anywhere when they are defending. Players should be still, see the play develop, read the attackers, and then react.

Advanced Digging Skills

As diggers progress, so should live repetitions. The ability to see hitters and read the mechanics and body positions of attackers are very important skills for defenders and are very often undeveloped. At the higher levels, diggers should still get some coach-driven repetitions, but only for a short period of practice. There is some value in refining skills in a controlled environment (e.g., off a coach-driven ball), but the majority of training should be in more live situations with a full defense on the court because diggers need to be able to function within the team defensive systems and concepts.

Although this chapter is not about training setting and serving, both can be parts of liberos' duties. When this is the case, both should be trained extensively.

Liberos in Training Sessions

Liberos should be part of every drill and active throughout team training sessions. There are always ways to incorporate them into drills even if the focus is not part of their required duties. For example, when we are doing an out-of-system hitting drill, we may have our libero set the ball to create the out-of-system situation, or we may have her contact the first ball and control it to a position on the court that allows us to function within the drill parameters. If it is impossible to involve liberos in practice, make sure they are active, maybe peppering among themselves or getting repetitions from a coach in another part of the gym.

MENTAL TRAINING

Liberos also need to develop their mental game. This can be a very big asset not only for them, but also for the team. If your libero is the best ball controller on your team and you can teach her to be aggressive and take more balls in a bigger area on the court, this can dramatically increase your first-ball contact results. Also, if you can teach your libero to share your mind-set in terms of what you would like to see from your passers and defenders, she can be a court coach for you and your team. A libero who can help direct traffic in the back row and in serve receive can be invaluable.

CONCLUSION

Great liberos are huge assets to their teams, although they are often overlooked because they typically do not score a lot of points. However, more often than not, great teams have great liberos who prevent a lot of points from being scored against them. These players can be the ball-control glue that holds their teams together. Many act as back-row coaches on the court directing traffic during the game. Spending time and effort on training your libero can definitely make your team better.

PART FOUR

MATCH PREPARATION AND STRATEGY

15

Deliberate Practice Concepts

Gylton B. Da Matta, PhD

Considered by many to be the ultimate team sport, volleyball is very challenging to teach, learn, and play. The skills and fundamentals of the game—such as jump serving, passing a 60 mph ball, setting with high accuracy, spiking using advanced shots, triple blocking, and digging using a dive or roll—require complex instruction. As such, practice must be deliberate. Anyone can learn volleyball skills, but exceptional performance requires a systematic teaching regimen through clinics, camps, classes, or courses. Players and coaches must plan for the deliberate practice of prioritized tasks and skills to achieve their goals (Ericsson, 1996).

Practice is the key wherever volleyball is taught. Applied, deliberate practice takes place at schools, clubs, and national development centers to develop fine motor skills, volleyball-specific speed, and the motor ability to perform in game situations. This chapter introduces deliberate practice theory as applied to volleyball.

VOLLEYBALL DEVELOPMENT AND THE ROLE OF PRACTICE

Over the past 20 years, some countries have consistently performed well in world-class volleyball competitions. The key to their success has been a commitment to quality and quantity in terms of practice (FIVB, 2014). For instance, from 1992 until the present, the Brazilian Volleyball Federation has been ranked one of the top in the world. Deliberate practice has been a primary reason.

In the early 1980s, the former USSR team as well as the U.S. men's team showed the world that expertise could be maintained using scientific training principles and a strong social support system. High levels of commitment, effort, resources, and practice (both quantity and quality) explain the gold legacy of volleyball teams in the past and present. The literature shows that deliberate practice can positively affect the development of volleyball across all ages and levels.

Volleyball athletes reach their peak performance at approximately age 26. Thus, the volleyball community needs to understand that winning a national championship at age 12, although fun, is not as meaningful as developing a player who can play for a lifetime. Also, because the neuromuscular system determines the outcome of motor performances, more practice is only helpful if it is quality practice.

I recommend intensive training for young players who express a willingness to put in the effort, time, and resources to work toward playing on national volleyball teams. All volleyball players should practice no less than three times per week, and additional physical conditioning and technical practices should bring their total commitment to five times per week. This is important to acquire the physiological adaptations for fine motor skills (Ericsson, 2000). Also important to consider are critical windows of learning, maturational factors, and balancing other variables such as social life and schooling (Knudson & Morrison, 1997).

WHAT IS DELIBERATE PRACTICE THEORY (DPT)?

Scientific evidence suggests a direct relationship between practice and expertise. To achieve expertise, a performer must engage in many years or thousands of hours of practice specifically designed to enhance performance. Such practice requires a substantial commitment of resources and effort as well as inner motivation. Performers must also balance their active practices with proper rest to prevent injuries and maximize their neurophysiological adaptations.

Expert coaches consistently develop elite athletes (e.g., John Wooden and Dean Smith in basketball). According to Bloom (1985) and Ericsson, Krampe, and Tesch-Römer (1993), expert coaches use a deliberate practice theory framework. Many say that coaches coach the way they were coached; however, expert coaches produce expert players consistently by adopting effective teaching strategies from a motor development and motor learning stand-point.

In the volleyball community, a common term related to expertise is *effective coaching*. Coaches view it as coaching that results in outcomes related to win–loss records (or percentages), individual player development, or success at the national or international level. In deliberate practice, however, long-term athlete development is a major focus. Positive psychological responses such as a perception of good court skills; high self-esteem; personal best scores at elite competitions; intrinsic motivation to practice for long periods of time; and high levels of enjoyment, enthusiasm, and satisfaction are considered deliberate practice achievements.

An important educational notion is that play requires skills. To develop motor skills, athletes need to learn them properly and in the context in which they will perform them. So, teaching volleyball skills requires planning, changing the environment, providing simulations, and creating situations that elicit the acquisition of those skills. Elite players should experience a process best described as play-practice-play:

1. Play: Athletes develop intrinsic motivation through playing the game.
2. Practice: Athletes embrace the commitment to practice smart and to refine sport-specific skills.
3. Play: Athletes enjoy greater abilities at play throughout their careers.

The Link to Teaching Games for Understanding

One way to develop game literacy in students is to use the Teaching Games for Understanding (TGfU) model. Steeped in constructivist approaches to teaching, the TGfU curricular model was originally introduced to address concerns expressed by Bunker and Thorpe in 1982 surrounding student illiteracy in games (Werner, Thorpe and Bunker, 1996). In this approach, students learn games by playing them rather than learning isolated skills and sport-specific tactics. Using tactical problems and solutions that transcend a variety of games as the backbone, this model helps students learn not only what they need to succeed in games, but also, and perhaps more important, when and why to make certain decisions in dynamic game contexts. The TGfU model creates better and more knowledgeable game players, but also motivates participants as they take part in a variety of games.

According to DPT in volleyball, play-practice-play should also be the structure of one practice session aligned with the goals and objectives planned by the coach. We know that playing volleyball without the proper skills is not ideal. More exposure to the game enables children to understand it and develop a passion to play the sport for a long-term (Lund & Tannehill, 2010).

Players who acquire the confidence to perform through practice are the ones who succeed at high-performance camps and national tryouts. They are the ones recruited to play in college, at the international level, and professionally (Côté, Baker, & Abernethy, 2003).

Skill acquisition requires motor prerequisites and fundamental motor skills. Players without a proper motor foundation have difficulty learning skills and therefore playing the game. Skill learning that is not stored in long-term memory is often forgotten after short periods of time without practice. Many expert coaches believe that teaching skills randomly (e.g., technical circuit training) increases retention (Newell, 1986; Morrow, Jackson, Disch, & Mood, 2010). Technical circuit training presents the most critical tasks, from simple to complex, in practice sessions that involve 9 or 10 tasks at 12 to 15 stations. Following is an example:

1. Footwork for spiking, transitioning to block, and going back to play defense.
2. Footwork for passing, transitioning into a player's hitting line, and approaching to spike.
3. Side landing on a mat after simulating digging a volleyball using a side lunge.
4. Stationary arm swings in an 8-inch box using a tennis racket to elicit maximal reach and the midline follow-through.
5. Footwork for blocking, with and without jumping, as a progression for dynamic blocking; landing on a mat to practice safety and accuracy.
6. Passing simulation with elastic bands while keeping the body leaned forward and maintaining proper forearm position.

7. Dynamically catching and pushing a medicine ball (3 lb) to simulate setting.

8. Catching and pushing a basketball while focusing on finishing the follow-through position of hands and body extension.

9. Serving a volleyball from an elevated plane or safe box to develop tossing accuracy and contact accuracy for a floater serve.

10. Hitting a ball hanging from elastic (adjusted to the player's reach) while landing on a mat.

11. Acquiring advanced shots; hitting mini-volleyballs in and out of the midline to spike around blockers.

12. Passing forward against a wall with and without a bounce.

An example of applying deliberate practice to a volleyball situation involves teaching players how to perform dynamic blocking without drifting. The players execute the dynamic blocking movement and land on a mat. Another example addresses problem solving for hitters spiking against a blocker. Coaches teach their players the advanced skills of hitting across or outside the lines of their bodies so they can hit around blockers. Some coaches believe that players are born with certain cognitive and psychomotor abilities; however, according to deliberate practice theory, those who do not learn the skills of hitting will not be able to hit around blockers (Da Matta, 2004).

Coaches have not succeeded at teaching a given task or skill until their athletes can perform it consistently. When a player is learning, for instance, how to set properly, the coach must use the deliberate practice strategy of having the player repeat the skill in different ways (variability of practice). Balancing the frequency and intensity of practice to optimize learning can be difficult. Elite coaches often use breaks in their practice sessions to control the dosage and intensity of effort (Ericsson, 2000; Morrow, Jackson, Disch, & Mood, 2010).

Rest, both during and between practice sessions, is an important factor in long-term athlete development.

EXPERT COACHES DEVELOP EXPERT ATHLETES

One of the tenets of DPT applied to volleyball is that athletes learn through observation. For volleyball players, learning and improving relies on the ability to see important details on a player's own technique as well as in the playing styles of other role models. They learn from watching each other, but primarily from modeling, for instance, seeing experts playing, even by closely observing their own coaches. A smart and expert coach creates an environment in which performance with proper form is visible to all learners. If seeing is believing, then doing is practicing! The specific motor skills of volleyball are acquired through practice that engages multiple senses. People learn motor skills by doing, repeating, and engaging in meaningful, effortful, and specific movement tasks.

Ideally, coaches should modify the environment for their athletes. In volleyball, each skill (serving, passing, setting, attacking, blocking, and digging) is unique; however, many other abilities are required to play the game well. For instance, a player must understand the game, have body and ball control, and avoid making unnecessary mistakes (i.e., unforced errors). Sport fundamentals, physical abilities (e.g., vertical jump, agility, coordination, timing, dexterity), and mental (or cognitive) skills are critical at all levels of performance. The practice environment should elicit motor responses that directly transfer to the motor skills in volleyball. For this reason, coaches must create practice situations that best resemble the game (Morrow et al., 2010).

Spiking a ball in a closed skill situation might help young and late-maturing players acquire proper spiking form. The environment can promote finesse and expertise by having posters of top performers exhibiting excellent technique. Proper modeling and video feedback are highly recommended when teaching both elite and beginner players.

BRAZILIAN MODEL OF TRAINING

In Brazil, very experienced athletes teach youth so that young protégé athletes can emerge. The athlete pool in women's volleyball is very limited in this country, where soccer and social roles represent two huge constraints on women's sport participation. Nonetheless, Brazil has one of the top volleyball programs in the world. It has embraced deliberate practice that focuses on (1) early initiation and late specialization, (2) assigning elite coaches to develop athletes at the grassroots level, (3) compensatory movement training, (4) volleyball-specific injury prevention, and (5) an elite system of training based on sport science principles and sport pedagogy (Da Matta, 2004).

An example of how Brazilian coaches start players early and specialize them late is the age at which players serve. Players at the U12 level underhand serve only; those at the U13 and U14 level use overhead serves only, and jump serves are allowed only for players 16 and older. Brazilian gold medalists revealed that they had experienced the compensatory development of motor skills and special physical abilities programs designed for volleyball. In this sense, "compensatory" means that when a late-maturing player commits to his or her process of training, practice represents a "catch-up" process. Therefore, coaches must assess what motor patterns or motor skills are missing in order to teach them in a timely manner. As a result of constant testing and self-improvement, most elite players in Brazil understand the importance of reviewing their basic skills both in practice and competition. Moreover, the same gold medalists reported being trained under developmentally appropriate systems of play (e.g., nine players on a club team with equal playing time, using varying net heights for younger players, no jump serves under 14). In fact, the acquisition of proficient skills such as timing, full body extension in the air, and understanding the flow of the game represent some of these building blocks in athletes' physical and cognitive repertoire. One example of cognitive skills is an athlete's ability to understand the game, know about tactics, and develop critical thinking skills under pressure. Thus, the balance between practicing and playing (tactical development) is the key concept in deliberate practice in volleyball (Werner, Thorpe & Bunker, 1996).

Elite Brazilian players reported that when learning volleyball, they proceeded through a sequence of phases that represented stages of tactical development (Da Matta, 2004). With its simple-to-complex approach, deliberate practice exposes players to the game on day one, during which they learn some critical volleyball fundamentals. Following are the five levels of learning proposed by the FIVB through mini-volleyball.

Five Levels of Mini-Volleyball

1. Catch and throwing game (1v1; 2v2).
2. Setting and passing with a bounce (1v1; 2v2).
3. Serving, setting, passing, and spiking with and without a bounce (3v3).
4. Same as level 3 with no bounce, but adding rotation. When the ball is over the net, players rotate.
5. Underhand serve, all skills, no bounce (4v4 up to 6v6).

The skills of a volleyball player can be compared to those of a violinist or piano player. If a young piano player misses a note, would it be appropriate to slap the child's hand? Would it be effective to punish him by making him run the steps of a stadium? The answer is clearly no. Coaches should reflect on the consequences of punishment in elite volleyball training. More than 8 out of 10 expert athletes reported that they had never been punished for making a mistake during a game. Their coaches likewise reported that they found corporal punishment unnecessary and obsolete.

Brazilian volleyball teams have been successful in the past two decades for a variety of reasons. Both athletes and coaches have reported success with using sport-specific movements during training along with analysis and technical and tactical assessments. Volleyball programs also use a coach development program that is aligned with physical education. Adult programs have become privatized and professionalized with corporate support, and children's volleyball programs have been created at the grassroots level.

DELIBERATE PRACTICE IN ACTION

In essence, volleyball players who want to achieve greatness must practice a lot. Practice improves performance. A player learning how to set needs to perform setting tasks that rely on the whole spectrum of setting skills, all possible situations, and all possible modified equipment such as a volleyballs, lighter volleyballs, basketballs, medicine balls, and trainer volleyballs.

Quality of Practice

Variable practice, skills assessments, individualization, and customized approaches are some of the basic DPT principles for volleyball. For instance, to develop a follow-through at the midline, players use dumbbells and tennis rackets to create the desired outcome (elbow high, contact at maximal reach, and follow-through at the midline). Practice quality is directly related to teaching practices that result in the permanent learning of correct (effective and efficient) movement patterns.

Good planning is one characteristic of a quality practice. Other characteristics are appropriate coach-to-athlete ratios, enough equipment, quality space, enough time allocated to optimal practice, and an atmosphere that promotes learning. Volleyball is an ideal sport for elementary, middle, and high school age children. Good coaches are good teachers, but to achieve excellence, coaches must be experts in designing practice sessions. I have asked 12 top coaches to design 10 practice sessions that they would recommend for clubs and for schools.

The following are some examples of lessons plans in a very condensed format.

Teaching Volleyball with Expertise in Mind (10 practice sessions)

Practice Session 1

Show a master's volleyball video

History and development of the modern volleyball game

Ball-handling and manipulative drills for setting with a basketball: mimic setting (catch/throw)

Ready position game floor ball (strike in low position)

Coordination, body posture, and footwork for spike approach without a ball (moving dynamically)

Macro game (attention "change" focus) warm-up with spike approach sequence with tennis balls

Arm swing progression: volley balls against a wall

Setting form and technique progression with a basketball

Multiple-contact setting (add pressure from a partner)

Sitting: pass with a partner (lying and sitting)

Constantly moving or changing positions

Talking aloud what they do

(continued)

Practice Session 2

Sitting sets from a partner: Placement-draw-hold-push

Setting on knee from a partner toss

Setting back and forth with a bounce

Mini-volleyball: 2v2 Changing positions and focusing on talking aloud

Video on mini-volleyball

Warm-up: review spike

Review setting and establishing parameters. Setting from P3/P2 facing to P4S1: Multiple contacts from various points close to the center court, squared to P4:

– S1: Multicontacts
– S2: Catch and throw a basketball
– S3: Set back and forth with a bounce and set to

Practice Session 3

Introduction to passing

Video on passing: Show the whole skill

Ready position: Describe and explain preparation phase, execution, and follow-through

Run-through; catch volleyball before it goes off court

Catch tennis balls on the floor

Teach grip pattern, arm positions, shoulders, and base of support

Practicing platform without a ball; then self-passing with a bounce and then self-passing with no bounce

Passing against a wall I: Multiple contacts close to the wall

Passing against a wall II: Passing off the wall, but let it bounce once

Passing against a wall III: Passing 10 feet away from the wall, no bounce

Mini-volleyball 2v2: setting only three bounces

Warm-up: blocking, attacking transition routes

Passing and setting I, II, III

Pass-set: Pass it over triangle drill. A back row player passes the ball to the setter, who sets to an attacker, who passes the ball over the net; the coach initiates this ball control drill will a toss, a downball, or a serve

Play 2v2 doubles

Practice Session 4

Underhand serve progression: Base of support, hitting arm fully extended back, contact the ball with hands open, follow through with hitting arm pointed at the target

Play, play, and play class: A whole practice dedicated to playing volleyball (Play 1v1 with modified rules; play 2v2 like beach volleyball, play 4v4 and then play 6v6)

Mini-volleyball: 3v3 bounces, use motivational fun scoring system (1 point for opponent's mistakes, 2 points for aces, 3 points for three hits followed by a kill, 4 points for blocking, and 5 points for exceptional plays such as long rallies)

Practice Session 5

Warm-up: Shadow drill routes and movement training (no balls)

Blocking and attack routes

4v4: Setting and following the ball (passing)

Ball control drill: Pepper with a pass, set, spike; Pepper using tips, roll shots, then ball control with down balls and finally with a jump at the moment of the spike

Hitting lines off a partner's tosses

Ball control drill over the net, playing in half-court

Mini-volleyball: 4v4, one bounce

Three touches

Underhand serve, then serving from the ground, then jump-serving

Center front sets and blocks

Practice Session 6

Warm-up: Arms

Butterfly drill

Ball control I, II, III

Pepper 2 v 2, three hits mandatory

Mini-volleyball

Right-side sets

Only left front hits

Practice underhand serve on targets

Cool-down, homework, official rules

Practice Session 7

Warm-up: History of volleyball

Arm warm-up against a wall (focus on reach and snapping the wrist)

Overhead floater serve, then overhead jump-floater serves

Hitting lines: 2s and 4s followed by playing queen of the court 3v3

Mini-volleyball: 5v5 right-side sets, left-front hits

Practice overhead serve

Cool-down: relaxation

Health-related fitness: Aerobic resistance and cardiorespiratory foundation for fitness and for life

(continued)

Teaching Volleyball with Expertise in Mind (10 practice sessions)   *(continued)*

Practice Session 8

Warm-up: Video on 6v6 (teaching the 4-2, 6-2 and 5-1 systems)

Hitting review: Focus on reaching the ball at the peak of the jump and landing properly

Setting sequence I, II

Passing sequence I, II

Pepper 3v3 I, II

Volleyball game: 6v6, center-front sets

Homework: Compare beach and indoor volleyball

Conditioning for volleyball: Muscular strength, muscular endurance, flexibility, and body composition

Practice Session 9

Warm-up: 6 × 6 shadow drill

Front-row block and off blocker cover

Pepper I, II, III

Triples: King of the court

4v4 motivational scoring system

6v6 modified game, situational training, lower net/higher net, and special scoring (3 points for stuff blocking or 5 points for winning long rallies)

Homework: Volleyball website research (Visit www.usavolleyball.org)

Self-assessment

Practice Session 10

Warm-up: Playing triples; back row exchange or queen/king of the court

Volleyball tournament or volleyball festival

Assessment, rules, strategies and technique, theoretical test

Video or rubric: Assessment process or product

Health-related fitness: Volleyball for a lifetime; why is volleyball a lifelong sport?

Strategies to Prevent Injuries

Proper equipment is crucial for preventing injuries; mats can be used for tumbling and practicing landing and rolling, and a blocking net can prevent balls from coming under players. Using easy tasks, progressing to more difficult tasks, and using analysis from simple to complex leads to permanent learning and build players' confidence as they move toward learning tough skills such as emergency landing on defense. When doing extensive jump sessions in practice, it is recommended to use mats or simply implement the randomized training approach.

Redefining Fun in Volleyball

Using clean, colorful, and purposeful equipment that is safe and facilitates learning is highly recommended in applied deliberate practice in volleyball. Attention, finesse, and good decision making are required in deliberate practice tasks. Good coaches use their training, but they also use common sense during their practices. Variability of practice, creativity, and science can go hand in hand. Practice tasks must be challenging and realistic enough to be translated into game situations. A whole technical circuit can be implemented at low cost by using typical middle school physical education equipment.

The organization of practice depends on the available space, equipment, time, and personnel. At national-level practices, many volunteer coaches might be available to create one-on-one deliberate practice tasks in the gym. However, both in colleges and clubs, normally one coach or a coach and an assistant must deliver all training sessions. Redefining fun also means that it can be fun to learn challenging skills. Volleyball is a sport that requires a high level of proficiency in order for players to have fun. Practicing complex skills may not always be fun, but the fun can only last so long without those skills. Coaches can explain to players that learning new skills is a new way to define fun.

PRACTICE VARIABILITY AND TASK SPECIFICITY

Volleyball is a fun and complex sport to learn, but this does not mean that it is difficult. According to modern sport principles, athletes should experience game-play situations in which they can succeed during the first day of practice. When I asked the top four coaches in Brazil which skill they would teach first, they were unanimous: spiking! For expert coaches, motivation and readiness to learn are keys to success. When a player demonstrates high motivation to learn a skill, the coach can associate other skills to that one and create deliberate practice tasks in which the player can succeed in the whole spectrum of content.

For instance, from a tactical approach, a coach can show a player who loves spiking (the motivational task) that without a good set and a good pass, a good spike is unlikely. The practice can present the chain of skills that happen before and after the motivational task, which can then be translated into a game situation. From a technical development approach, all prerequisites (e.g., understanding the whole skill, moving toward the ball, properly using the arms to jump, mastering timing, contacting the ball with the hands open, and landing safely) are critical in spiking situations. The association of spiking with other skills becomes the next building block based on the fact that spiking is highly fun and motivational. When planning practice, coaches must list all content they intend to teach and then organize the content in a way that the athletes can easily assimilate and apply. Expert coaches understand the importance of teaching volleyball skills adopting a "random training" versus a "block training" approach. However, the combinations of skills can be organized in a logical order that directly represents game situations and can be presented according to their complexity. In DPT, task presentations can be very specific to the performance context, therefore it is better to associate the skills in the order they happen in the game than in a scattered way. For instance, in a randomized approach, it makes sense to prescribe a player to serve-receive, attack a ball, and move into a home-base position (complex 1) or to serve, then get onto the court to perform a defense and after that, attack a ball from the back row (complex 2). Other skill associations could be: spike, block, defense; serve, serve receive, set, and spike; or block, transition off the net, dig, and spike. These associations of skills characterize the situational training in DPT applied to volleyball.

In a research study in which I interviewed 18 experts players about how they learned to play volleyball, 60 percent answered that they played with physical educators at the age of 11 to 14 using the following sequence: catching and throwing concept games; floor ball (low body posture and striking game); change (inclusion, movement, and attention game in dynamic volleyball settings); introduction of the spike; serve and manipulative skills using highly organized progressions; and introduction of setting, passing, and ball control in modified games that allowed long rallies (Da Matta, 2004; FIVB, 2014).

To understand the process of learning a complex skill, let's consider the spike. Every volleyball player wants to spike, but being an all-around player is the new volleyball standard. A player learning to spike must understand the relationships among all skills, movement patterns, and situations. A single analysis of a complex skill can be deceiving. When teaching volleyball, coaches must understand that open skills require control and reduced parameters. Closed skills, however, require task extensions toward teaching progressions. In the case of spiking, coaches often design tasks with too much information for the nervous systems, making them far too difficult for learners. When beginners see a single picture of a spike movement, they often store that picture in their minds. To learn the appropriate movement patterns, however, they should see the whole skill. So, it is highly recommended that coaches use video clips instead of still shots when teaching complex skills. Pictorial analysis and posters showing the whole sequence of movements are also adequate. The FIVB (International Volleyball Federation) in collaboration with USA Volleyball has issued a series of posters depicting all fundamental skills. These graphic instructional materials are powerful tools for beginner and intermediate level players. As players move into higher levels of expertise the use of e-tutorials (electronic video clips) and the use of videos become more appropriate. The advancement of video technology accessibility allows coaches to use e-tutorials to provide a better model for learners because they show the whole movement as it really happens in the game.

BIOMECHANICS AND MOTOR LEARNING THEORY

Teaching analysis, skills acquisition, and knowledge of performance must be followed by an assessment to document improvement (Robertson, Caldwell, Hamill, Kamen, & Whittlesey, 2014). That means that after a sequence of three-four weeks of practice, athletes should be assessed on their level of improvement. Therefore, coaches and athletes can use any video devices such as smartphones, tablets, or mini-cameras to film practices and games in the beginning of the season and then film it again at the end of the season. Technology becomes an essential tool to facilitate learning. In DPT, coaches use video technology to provide visual feedback and to prime learners to acquire new concepts and skills in the near future. In order to better understand the use of video clips in assessing athletes' performances, expert coaches adopt rubrics or checklists for fundamental skills (Gabbett, Georgieff, & Domrow, 2007). The following checklists can be used to assess players' performances on a few skills. They can be helpful in tracking players' progress throughout the season and in planning practices (Robertson, et al, 2014).

Assessment Rubric: Floater Serve

Skill performance

Name: _____ Score: _____ / 36 points

E-mail: _____ Phone: _____

Evaluator: _____

Task: _____

Preparation phase: goal setting, imagery

- Base of support (wide, feet staggered) _____
- Body leaning back (weight back, ready to shift forward) _____
- Holding ball at chest level; elbow of holding arm extended; hitting arm open; hands pronated (facing out) _____

Execution phase: hip action, javelin, palm out

- Simultaneous lift and hip extension; inhalation _____
- Lift ball toward forehead _____
- Shoulder rotation (fully) _____
- Compact contact at the midline, in front of the body _____
- Freeze and continue arm action at the midline _____

Follow-through phase: midline, extension

- Finish weight transfer _____
- Exhale; extend body to target _____
- Get low and relax for next action _____
- Move into court (go to base) _____

0 = absent; 1 = inconsistent; 2 = consistent; 3 = proficient

Assessment Rubric: Passing (Underhand or Overhead)

Skill performance

Name: _____ Score: _____ / 36 points

E-mail: _____ Phone: _____

Evaluator: _____

Task: _____

Preparation phase: tracking and anticipating

- Ready position (good judgment of server; wait to get low)   _____
- Tracking and staying calm; confident!   _____
- Lock out early and watch ball   _____

Execution phase: finesse, square to target

- Wide base of support   _____
- Hunch back, shoulders shrugged   _____
- Elbows completely extended   _____
- Heart-shaped grip   _____
- Contact at forearm; looking at target   _____

Follow-through phase: freeze and transition

- Push to target   _____
- Move forward   _____
- Hold platform 2 seconds   _____
- Transition into new action (prep to spike, cover)   _____

0 = absent; 1 = inconsistent; 2 = consistent; 3 = proficient

Assessment Rubric: Setting

Skill performance

Name: _____ Score: _____ / 36 points

E-mail: _____ Phone: _____

Evaluator: _____

Task: _____

Preparation phase: read, track, relax

- Tracking ball—reading pass _____
- Shape ball with wrists in dorsiflexion _____
- Ready position (coiled) _____

Execution phase: see and analyze (whole picture)

- Get under ball and hold ball _____
- Bend elbows and knees _____
- Square to target _____
- Spring into action (extend knees and elbows) _____
- Finish with hands wide open (pancake) _____

Follow-through phase: freeze and transition

- Freeze 1 second _____
- Step in target direction _____
- Relax _____
- Transition _____

0 = absent; 1 = inconsistent; 2 = consistent; 3 = proficient

Assessment Rubric: Spiking

Skill performance

Name: _____ Score: _____ / 36 points

E-mail: _____ Phone: _____

Evaluator: _____

Task: _____

Preparation phase: see, anticipate, relax

- Pass, get ready _____
- Shuffle, shuffle, read the set _____
- Relax, balance forward _____

Execution phase: relax and relax

- Approach: foot pattern (right, left, right-left) for the right handed player or (left, right, left-right) for the left handed _____
- Wide backward arm swing _____
- Breaking step (heels, toes) _____
- Upward arm swing, hands out, telescope, karate, snap wrist _____
- Maximal reach, shoulder upward _____

Follow-through phase: relax and finish

- Snapped wrist _____
- Arm at midline _____
- Land softly _____
- Transition into new action _____

0 = absent; 1 = inconsistent; 2 = consistent; 3 = proficient

Assessment Rubric: Blocking—Dynamic Action

Skill performance

Name: _____ Score: _____ / 36 points

E-mail: _____ Phone: _____

Evaluator: _____

Task: _____

Preparation phase

- Watch pass, setter, hitter _____
- Front projection of hitter's approach _____
- Load and delay (explode if late) _____

Execution phase

- Extend and mark quick set _____
- Giant step outside _____
- Close step, jump, and arm swing _____
- Front net; penetrate block _____
- Push to middle of court _____

Follow-through phase

- Keep arms high _____
- Outside hand turned in _____
- Land softly and balanced _____
- Transition into new action (base) _____

0 = absent; 1 = inconsistent; 2 = consistent; 3 = proficient

Assessment Rubric: Defense

Skill performance

Name: _____ Score: _____ / 36 points

E-mail: _____ Phone: _____

Evaluator: _____

Task: _____

Preparation phase

- Base, read, release _____
- Low posture _____
- Body balanced forward _____

Execution phase

- Move forward _____
- Heart-shaped grip _____
- Crown (cross thumbs back) _____
- Dig ball up to middle of court _____
- Good use of shoulder roll or side landing _____

Follow-through phase

- Continuity of movement _____
- Base to release _____
- Talking _____
- Relax; be cool on hard-driven spikes _____

0 = absent; 1 = inconsistent; 2 = consistent; 3 = proficient

CONCLUSION

Volleyball players have achieved a level of performance never seen before. The technical training, physical conditioning, and technology adopted by top teams in the world have established a new paradigm as well as new standards that top coaches have adopted, adapted, and incorporated into their practices. Teams that invest in research, technical development, and long-term athlete development will advance their performances and stand out from their opponents and counterparts.

REFERENCES

Bloom, B.S. (1985). *Developing talent in young people*. New York: Ballantine Books.

Côté, J., Baker, J., & Abernethy, B. (2003). From play to practice: A developmental framework for the acquisition of expertise in team sports. In J.L. Starkes and K.A. Ericsson (Eds.), *Expert performance in sports: Advances in research on sport expertise* (pp.175-209). Champaign, IL: Human Kinetics.

Da Matta, G. (2004). The role of deliberate practice and social support systems on the expertise development of women volleyball players in Brazil. Unpublished doctoral dissertation, University of South Carolina, Columbia, SC.

Ericsson, K.A. (1996). Expertise and deliberate practice research issues. *The road to excellence: The acquisition of expert performance in the arts and sciences, sports, and games*. Hillsdale, NJ: Lawrence Erlbaum.

Ericsson, K.A. (2000). How experts attain and maintain superior performance: Implications for the enhancement of skilled performance in older individuals. *Journal of Aging and Physical Activity, 8*, 366-372.

Ericsson, K.A., Krampe, R.T., & Tesch-Römer, C. (1993). The role of deliberate practice in the acquisition of expert performance. *Psychological Review, 100* (3), 363-406.

FIVB. (2014). *FIVB operational manual IV—Extended theoretical information* (pp. 122-139). Lausanne, Switzerland: Author.

Gabbett, T., Georgieff, B., & Domrow, N. (2007). The use of physiological, anthropometric, and skill data to predict selection in a talent-identified junior volleyball squad. *Journal of Sports Sciences, 25*, 1337-1344.

Lund, J., & Tannehill, D. (2010). *Standards-based physical education curriculum development* (2nd ed.). Boston: Jones & Bartlett.

Knudson, D.V., & Morrison, S.S. (1997). *Qualitative analysis of human movement*. Champaign, IL: Human Kinetics.

Newell, K.M. (1986). Constraints on the development of coordination. In M.G. Wade & H.T.A. Whiting (Eds.), *Motor development in children: Aspects of coordination and control* (pp. 341-361). Amsterdam: Martin Nijhoff.

Morrow, J., Jr., Jackson, A., Disch, J., & Mood, D. (2010). *Measurement and evaluation in human performance* (4th ed.). Champaign, IL: Human Kinetics.

Robertson, D.G., Caldwell, G.E., Hamill, J., Kamen, G., & Whittlesey, S.N. (2014). *Research methods in biomechanics* (2nd ed.). Champaign, IL: Human Kinetics.

Werner, P., Thorpe, R. and Bunker, D. (1996). Teaching games for understanding: Evolution of a model. *Journal of Physical Education, Recreation and Dance, 1* (67), 28-33.

RELATED LINKS

www.fivb.org

www.fivb.ch/EN/Programmes/minivolleyball.asp

www.volleyballadvisors.com/volleyball-blocking-drills.html

RELATED ARTICLES

Mandigo, J.L. (2003). Using problem-based learning to enhance tactical awareness in target games. In J. Butler, L. Griffin, B. Lombardo, & R. Natasi (Eds.), *Teaching games for understanding in physical education and sport: An international perspective* (pp. 15-28). Oxon Hill, MD: National Association for Sport and Physical Education.

Mandigo, J.L., & Anderson, A.T. (2003). Using the pedagogical principles in net/wall games to enhance teaching effectiveness. *Teaching Elementary Physical Education, 14* (1), 8-11.

Mandigo, J.L., & Holt, N.L. (2003, October 17). *A practitioners guide to Teaching Games for Understanding*. Oral presentation at the Ontario Physical and Health Education Conference, Orillia, Ontario.

Mandigo, J.L., & Holt, N.L. (2000). The inclusion of optimal challenge in teaching games for understanding. *Physical and Health Education Journal, 66* (3), 14-19.

Mandigo, J.L., & Sheppard, J. (2003, October 25). *Putting the "U" back into games: Pedagogical principles in Teaching Games for Understanding*. Oral presentation at the Canadian Association for Health, Physical Education, Recreation, & Dance Conference, Winnipeg, Manitoba.

Mandigo, J.L., & Sheppard, J. (2003, December 12). *Children's affective experiences in TGfU game environments*. Presentation at the Second International Conference on Teaching Sport and Physical Education for Understanding, Melbourne, Australia.

Sheppard, J., & Mandigo, J. L. (2003, December 11). *Understanding games by playing games: An illustrative example of Canada's Play Sport program*. Presentation at the Second International Conference on Teaching Sport and Physical Education for Understanding, Melbourne, Australia.

16

Scouting Opponents the Right Way

Joe Trinsey

Over the course of a season, volleyball coaches make thousands of decisions about their teams. They instruct players on the fundamental skills, teach strategy, plan practices, and handle administrative duties. At many levels of play, coaches have two other important tasks: scouting opponents and preparing game plans. At its core, a game plan is a simple thing; it's a *statement of what your team needs to do to maximize its chances of defeating an opponent*. Some challenges are involved in scouting and game planning, but a coach must always remember to go back to this basic definition.

WHAT IS A GAME PLAN?

The three main aspects of scouting an opponent and preparing a game plan are gathering the scouting information and building the game plan, presenting the game plan to the team, and executing the game plan in a match. This chapter addresses all of these aspects. It also addresses one of the most important, yet often forgotten, parts of scouting and game planning: analyzing the results of the match and the effectiveness of the game plan. After reading this chapter, coaches who are new to scouting and game plans should have an idea of how to start the process, and coaches who are experienced scouts should have a new idea or two that can help their teams win one more point in the next match.

A good game plan considers both teams involved in the matchup. Some coaches get so caught up in the opponent that they forget to consider what their own team can and cannot do. For sure, things such as gathering statistical information on opposing passers, charting serving and attacking tendencies, analyzing rotations (and all of the other things discussed in this chapter) are very important. Yet all of them go out the window if the team doesn't execute the game plan properly, or if the plan doesn't mesh with the system the team has been playing all year.

A game plan, then, is not just preparation for an opponent, but an expression of what you have worked for and what you value as a coach. The way you prepare for your toughest opponents should reflect the things you value in the game of volleyball as a whole.

BUILDING A GAME PLAN

Putting together game plans can be intimidating for some coaches. As in all things, the best way to improve is through experience. Most coaches who are skilled at putting together game plans have a system that evolves over time, both by specific planning and natural evolution. It's often best to start simple and add to the process over time, adding and subtracting things as you notice what works and what doesn't work. The three foundational tasks for building a game plan are gathering the information, deciding what's important and relevant, and putting it all together into a cohesive plan.

Gathering Information: What's Important and What's Not?

It's a great idea to have a checklist to run down every time you begin to scout an opponent. Splitting this checklist into these four sections is helpful: serve and pass, opponent offense, opponent defense, and lineups and matchups.

Sample Serve and Pass Scouting Checklist

- Who is their overall weakest passer?
- Do any passers have a strong preference to pass float serves with their hands?
- Do any of their passers struggle to pass on their left or right?
- Do they have any rotations with a seam between two weak passers?
- Do any of their outside hitters struggle to pass and hit?
- Do they have any jump spin servers, and what are their tendencies?
- Will any of their servers hit a short serve? Will they do it on their first time up or after they have made a serve?

Sample Opponent Offense Checklist

- What is their general offensive scheme?
  - Do they set quick in the middle? Do they run slides? How much back row do they set? How fast is their tempo to the outside?
- Who is their best hitter, and what is his or her tendency?
- Who are their secondary hitters, and what are their tendencies?
  - Do any hitters like to tip or hit an off-speed shot? In what situations? Do they give it away?

- Does their setter have any tendencies?
  - Will the setter set middle only on perfect passes, or from other locations?
  - Will the setter repeat a set after making an error or getting blocked?
  - Does the setter make the long set backward or forward when running in the other direction?
  - How offensive is the setter in the front row? Does she or he hit or dump the ball?

Sample Opponent Defense Checklist

- What is the best option when our outside hitters have to take a tough swing?
  - Does their line digger cheat up, thereby becoming susceptible to a roll to the deep corner?
  - Does their middle back rotate over, thereby becoming susceptible to the roll to shallow zone 6?
  - Does their line digger play back, or is their off blocker a little lazy on defense, thereby becoming susceptible to tipping short?
  - Are any of their wing blockers susceptible to being tooled on a hard, high swing?
- What do their middle blockers do?
  - Stay neutral and read?
  - Follow the pass or setter?
  - Front the quick hitter?
- Do their wing blockers help in the middle or stay wide and just block the outside attackers?
- Do they have any servers who are weak defenders? Some middles do not play the tip well after serving and can be beat short for an easy point.
- Can this team be beat on a setter tip?

Sample Lineups and Matchups Checklist

- Do they start in the same rotation every time? If so, what is it?
- If they lose a game, will they spin to a new rotation or stick with the same one?
- If they lose a game, will they flip their outsides or middles (or both) to get different matchups?
- What are their most common substitution patterns? Do they substitute only when losing, or will they substitute with a specific goal in mind? (Example: bringing in a defensively minded outside hitter who they will not set as much).
- Based on their trend of rotations they start in, and the rotation I like to start my team in, what will the matchups be for each hitter?

◆ Are any of these matchups especially good or bad? Should we think about spinning our rotation to get better matchups for our hitters or to neutralize an advantage they have?

These sample checklists are by no means exhaustive. At higher levels of play, checklists will be significantly longer and more detailed, and cover a much wider range of situations. On the flip side, a high school or club coach of a young team probably doesn't need to worry about all or even most of that information.

Information Quantity and Quality

When scouting, you need to remember that you have only recorded what happened; there is no guarantee that the pattern will continue. When scouting an opponent, try to find matches in which they are playing teams similar to your own. The best way to do that is to analyze your own match against that opponent! Of course, you may not always have this luxury, so just keep in mind the qualities of the team across the net from the opponent you are scouting. Think about how their skills and system compare to yours. For example, if you are scouting a team that sets its outside over and over, consider whether this is a tendency or a strategy for attacking a short setter or weak blocker on the other side of the net. Also, if you learn of any lineup changes, consider how they might affect your opponent's strategy. A setter who loves to set quick sets may not be so eager to do so after her best middle sprains her ankle and is out of the lineup. Finally, remember that it is better to have no information than wrong information. If you see only two swings by an opposing hitter, don't assume you have that player's tendency figured out. When in doubt, just play your system and be prepared to adjust in-game.

PUTTING IT TOGETHER

After you have watched as many live matches and as much scout video as possible, and gathered as much statistical data as possible, it's time to turn this information into a game plan. You must decide what your team is capable of implementing, and what, if any, changes or deviations you want to make from your base system. The following sections provide a few things to consider.

Skill Level

Many smart coaches have said, "Never attempt tactically what you cannot execute technically." Players may not have the skill level to execute a sophisticated game plan. A rule of thumb is that if you haven't executed something well in practice, don't expect to win any games using it, no matter how good the matchup is.

Training Time

How much training time do you have? How much training time do you want to dedicate to preparing for a specific team? If you think a particular combination play is the key to attacking another team's defense, but you only have one practice before the upcoming match, you might not have enough time to train this play well enough to execute it in competition. Depending on the age of your team and the phase of the season, you might want to ignore any specific preparation and instead focus on strengthening your system.

Preparing for a Game Plan

Preparing for a game plan can be a good teaching tool. For example, if you have an outside hitter who relies solely on his crosscourt shot, telling him that the team you are playing this weekend has a weak right-side blocker who can be attacked down the line can increase his motivation to work on his line shot. These sorts of discussions can also get your players to start thinking about different ways to attack the opponent, raising their volleyball IQ.

When putting your game plan down on paper, start with the most important things. Don't get so caught up in minor details that you forget about more critical parts of the game. Here are the five things that can have the greatest impact:

1. How are we going to win the serve/pass battle?

Sample: Their outside hitter #10 is a weak passer and really struggles when he has to pass with his platform, so all of our servers will target him when possible. When he is having a tough time, they will sometimes move him out of the passing formation and try to pass with two passers. If they do that, our servers will look to serve hard in the seam. They have two good jump spinners who hit across their bodies from zone 1 to our 1/6 seam. Our left-back and middle-back passers will take a step to their right, and the coaching staff will stay on our passers in practice to clarify their seams prior to each serve.

2. How are we going to stop our opponent's best hitter?

Sample: Their best hitter is their middle hitter #7, who plays next to the setter. They set her a slide any chance they can, and she loves to hit it back sharp crosscourt. Our left-side blockers need to stay inside and not drift out with her. Our middles are free to trap (leave early) toward her, especially if the pass is perfect.

3. What does our opponent like to do in each rotation?

Sample: In any rotation in which their outside hitter #8 is in the front row, they will look to set him the ball whenever possible. Middle blockers must be aware of this and work hard to get a double block up.

In rotation 6, they run the middle on a slide but almost never set him; our middle blockers should cheat toward the outside to stop that. In rotation 2, they sometimes like to run an X play; blockers need to make sure to see it happening early and communicate if the hitters are changing zones.

4. Do we have any matchups to exploit on our offensive end?

Sample: Their outside hitter #4 is a small, undisciplined blocker, so we will look to backset the right side or the slide as much as possible when she is front row. Their middles are poor defenders, so our setter is free to dump whenever they serve.

5. Who are their secondary offensive options, and do we need to prepare specifically for them?

Sample: Middle hitter #8 is a good quick hitter, but only when he gets a perfect set. When the pass isn't perfect, we won't worry about him, but we may commit (jump with the quick hitter) on a perfect pass. The opposite (right-side hitter) #11 will tip every set that isn't perfect, so our off blocker will come across to play for tip on him. Their setter almost never dumps.

The final thing to remember when building your game plan is that everything should be linked to an action your team will take on the court. Don't become a journalist, describing the other team without any thought of what your team will do to counter. Determine a few specific things to do, and make sure your team can do them well.

PRESENTING THE GAME PLAN

Once you have gathered all the necessary information and formulated a reasonable game plan, it is time to transfer that game plan into a material scouting report that will help the players when the day of competition comes. Although coaches have a variety of tools at their disposal to accomplish this, the two most common are paper scouting reports and video study meetings.

Two-Part Plan: Part I

Coaches can use a variety of scouting report formats, from a simple one-page outline of the game plan to a more in-depth multipage report. I have found that, for many teams, a simple two-part scouting report can present all of the necessary information without overwhelming players. Part I should be a general description of the game plan, including some or all of the following points. See the special element, Sample Game Plan: Part I, for notes on a game plan.

Serving Target

Will you try to serve one player consistently the whole match, or will it change depending on the game situation, such as serving the front-row outside hitter or into a seam in a specific rotation? This is probably the most important part of your scouting report. See the special element, Sample Game: Part I, for examples of the serving target.

Passing Notes

You may or may not want to include specific notes on their servers for your passers. Remember to focus on the actions you want your passers to take, instead of simply describing the servers.

Hitter Tendencies

It is good to include information about their hitters—specifically, how you want your blockers to line up and any adjustments you want your backcourt defenders to make. If time is limited, just pick their one or two main hitters.

Setter Notes

You may want to include some notes on their setter(s), describing any tendencies they have and how much you want your blockers/defenders to read and respect the setter attack. See Sample Game Plan: Part I for sample scout rotations based on setter locations.

Offensive Game Plan

Although you will discuss this more with your setters than anybody else, you may want to include some notes on how you want to attack this team offensively. Also, it can be good to let your hitters know where they can hit an off-speed shot to when they get in trouble.

Keys to Victory

Although presenting keys to victory can seem cliché, sometimes listing three to five simple keys can help the players focus on what is most important. The best keys are often not opponent specific. They can simply be reminders of the most important parts of your system, so the players have them in mind before they study the specifics of the opponent. See the bulleted list of sample keys in Sample Game Plan: Part I.

Serving Target

- We want to serve #12 as much as possible, especially short.
- If they hide #12, attack the deep seams between two passers.

Passing Notes

- #10 likes to short serve on her second time up.
- #12 hits a hard jump-spin that moves from left to right. Passers communicate early in the seam.

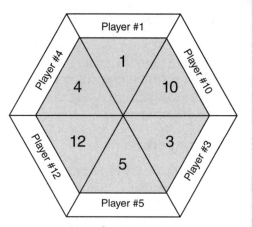

Note: Serving target.

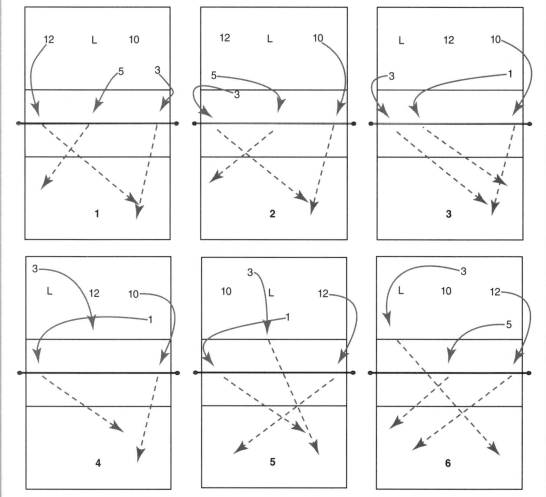

Note: Scout rotation numbers are based on where the setter is located. Indicate where each player will pass and attack for each rotation.

Keys to Victory

- Communicate: Passers communicate in the seams and call out their short serves early.
- Deep Corners: Hitters look to go deep to their corners, especially if we're out-of-system.
- Pursue: Watch the tips and rolls and pursue them relentlessly. Nothing hits!

Two-Part Plan: Part II

Part II should be a rotation-by-rotation breakdown. It can be one or two pages long, depending on how big you want to make the rotation charts. The following sections outline important information to include. See the special element, Sample Game Plan: Part II, for sample hitter tendencies and notes.

Serving Target

Highlight or otherwise emphasize the serving target in each rotation, even if it is the same one. This is so important that you should mention it over and over throughout the scouting report.

Hitter Routes

What plays do they run in each rotation? Do they change, or do they run the same thing in each rotation throughout the game?

Setting Trend

Do they prefer to set one hitter more than the others in a particular rotation?

Blocking and Defensive Adjustments

List any adjustments your blockers and defenders should make for each rotation. For example, against a hitter that likes to tip, you may want to tell your line digger to stay up at the attack line in that rotation.

Scouting Meetings

Somewhere along the line, you probably had a class in which you sat in your chair trying not to fall asleep while the teacher read the lecture notes in a boring, monotone voice. Don't let your scouting meetings be like this! If you remember that the laws of learning still apply even when you're off the court, your scouting meetings will be much more productive. The following sections provide some tips for making your scouting meetings more productive.

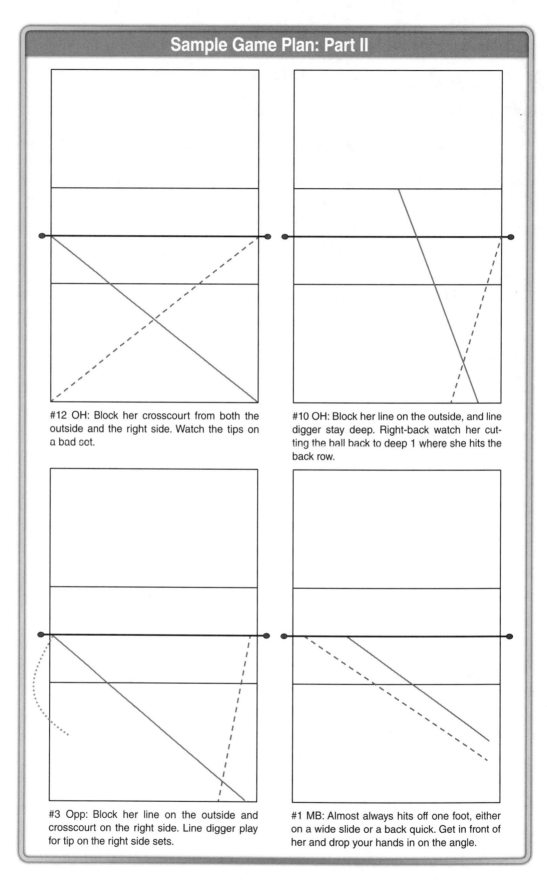

#12 OH: Block her crosscourt from both the outside and the right side. Watch the tips on a bad set.

#10 OH: Block her line on the outside, and line digger stay deep. Right-back watch her cutting the ball back to deep 1 where she hits the back row.

#3 Opp: Block her line on the outside and crosscourt on the right side. Line digger play for tip on the right side sets.

#1 MB: Almost always hits off one foot, either on a wide slide or a back quick. Get in front of her and drop your hands in on the angle.

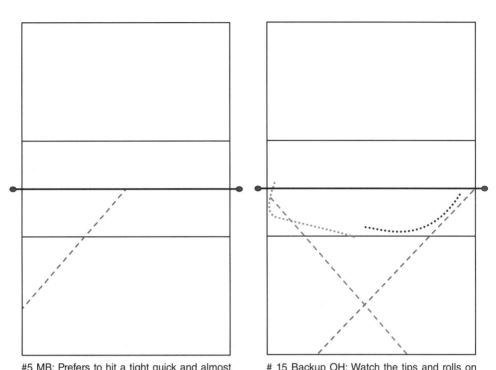

#5 MB: Prefers to hit a tight quick and almost always hits sharp to zone 5. Middle blocker line up with this angle, and left-side blocker help out.

15 Backup OH: Watch the tips and rolls on any set. Off-blockers come across the middle to help out with this.

Note: Dotted lines refer to ball direction. Dots refer to tipped or rolled balls.

General Offensive Plan

- Their setter #4 is a good blocking target to go after. Outsides look to swing high off her hands when you are in trouble.
- Their wing blockers don't help much in the middle, so middle hitters look to get available, especially in transition. You can score on the angles.
- They cover the short tips well, so if we are in trouble, look to roll deep to the corner, rather than tip short.

Setter Notes

- Loves to make the long set, so be ready for her to set back when she is running forward and set forward when she is moving back into zone 2.
- Almost never dumps, so if she is jumping near the set, it is usually to jump-set the quick. Blockers wait on the setter, and then go up on the quick.
- When the game is tight, or after we've scored a couple of points in a row, she will look to go to #10. Make sure we get a double-block up on her.

First and Last

Your players will remember the beginning and end of the scouting report, and probably lose quite a bit of the middle. Make sure you address the most important things first (serving target, how you will stop their best hitter, and what your hitters can do when in trouble), and then finish your report with the same things.

Involve the Players

Ask your players what they remember from the last time they played this team, or whether they've seen this team play. If the opponent has a good jump server, ask your players what you did the last time you faced a server like that, and to consider whether they want to do the same thing or something different this time. Feel free to quiz players, and make it clear that it's ok to be wrong at first, because everyone will work together to learn the game plan. Get any misconceptions cleared up in the meeting so they don't carry them into the match.

Use More Than One Coach

As brilliant and engaging as you may be, listening to anybody talk for an extensive period of time can be difficult. In your scouting meetings, have one coach discuss the offensive strategy and another discuss the defense. Or have one coach go over the general summary, and have another run through the rotations, or have a player read part of the report. The more the scouting report seems like a cooperative effort, the more engaged the players will be.

Keep It Simple

When in doubt, say less. If you cover only two or three things in the scouting meeting, but your players know them inside and out and can execute them at a high level, you will have an excellent chance to win. If you overwhelm your players with too much information, you risk their losing all of it.

Incorporating Video

One of the best ways to engage players and enhance the scouting report is to use video. Collegiate and professional teams use sophisticated scouting software that can tag every contact, which makes it easy to call up anything the coach needs for a scouting meeting. If you have the ability to create video montages of all swings by a particular opposing hitter, or to go through and pull out all of the opponent's side-out opportunities in a particular rotation, then please do so! Hearing or reading about it is one thing, but seeing what the opponent does on video is incredibly helpful to players. If you don't have access to this sort of scouting software, a good replacement is to simply go through the video and find a number of plays to watch. Record the time they took place in the video and write down a note for each play. You can then skip to those plays in the scouting meeting.

IMPLEMENTING THE GAME PLAN

After you have gathered all the important information, developed it into a game plan, and gone over the game plan with your team, it's time to focus on the most important aspect of the game plan: executing it in the game! This is where the rubber meets the road, so remember that even the best game plan will fail if your players do not understand how to execute it properly. If you have done your best to gather the right information and present it in a way that makes sense, then you have given your players the best chance to succeed.

Know What the Keys Are

When teaching your players how to perform fundamental skills, you probably developed a list of keys for how to teach those skills. Keys are short phrases that condense a detailed concept into a few important words. The same idea can be applied when teaching and implementing your game plan. You already know that keeping things simple makes the scouting report easier to read, so stay consistent and keep your verbal coaching simple when the match starts. Remember that keys don't have to be unique to every opponent—something like, "Dig the ball high and off the net" will be a key in almost every match you play. If it's important, feel free to remind your players about it constantly. In this way, the game plan becomes less about creating a new way of playing for every opponent and more a statement of how you want to play, with some adjustments for each match.

In developing your game plan, you will have already defined your keys and presented them in the scouting meeting. Now it's just a matter of reinforcing them during the match. Following are some suggestions to keep in mind.

Pregame Communication

Your scouting meeting could have been hours before the match started, or even at a previous day's practice. Given the distraction of warm-ups, introductions, and nervousness, your players may have forgotten some important things. Use a short pregame huddle to quickly remind them of the important keys. If you have done your homework, you will have a good idea of their starting rotation, so tailor your comments to what will likely happen at the start of the match.

Frontload

Find a player on the bench who is getting ready to enter the game, and remind him of what he needs to execute on the upcoming points. He can also be responsible for carrying information to his teammates. This is much more effective than trying to shout out onto the court, especially in a loud arena!

Know Their Rotation

Know what rotation the opponent is in, and coach for what is coming up. If they have been killing you on the slide, but their setter just rotated into the back row, make a note of it, and come back to it when you are likely to see that play again. If you stay focused on the next play, so will your players.

Reinforce

Use your time-outs to deliver short bursts of information. This is not the time to get into detailed explanations of why you devised a particular strategy (hopefully, you've already done that in practice and your scouting meeting). Now is the time to keep things simple and give players one or two things they can focus on to help them win the next point.

Call and Confirm

The players should constantly remind each other of their responsibilities for the next point. Wing blockers can give a visual 1 or 2 behind their backs to indicate whether they are blocking line or cross, the libero can call out whether the setter is back row or front row, the setter can let the hitters know what shots are open, and so on. Get your players in the habit of confirming with their teammates (e.g., the right-side blocker signals to right back that she is blocking line, and the right back responds with "yes"), and they will stay on the same page throughout the match.

Know When to Adjust

Sometimes your scouting is perfect and the players execute the game plan like a well-oiled machine. You roll through the other team and win the match with ease. Unfortunately, these matches are few and far between. The fact is that coaches often need to adjust the game plan on the fly. You want to remain flexible enough to adapt, while not abandoning your game plan because one play went differently than you expected. Because this is not always easy, you need to have ways of monitoring what is happening during the game so you have some information on which to base your decisions. Following are some good in-game evaluative measures to take.

Statistics

If your team is fortunate enough to have a dedicated statistician during the match, this person can record valuable information. You can track the success of your rotations (and theirs), track which hitters are hitting with the highest efficiency, and see which passers are struggling. However, one thing to keep in mind is that statistics are not valid until you are well into the match; studies have shown that a player's first five passes of the match do not predict how that player will pass the rest of the match. A rule of thumb is to witness at least 10 attempts (whether it's passing, hitting, or serving) before basing decisions off statistics. This may mean that statistics don't come heavily into play until the third set of the match.

Charting From the Bench

A good practice is to have somebody charting the opponent's rotations as the match goes along. This coach (or staff member) can record what plays the opponent is running and what they are setting, based on the quality of the pass. She should have a copy of your rotation game plan from the scouting report and should be comparing the in-game chart to that, to see whether or not your opponent is doing what you expected. She should also be responsible for knowing what rotation the opponent is in during every time-out to keep feedback focused on the upcoming rotations, rather than giving instructions on a situation that won't occur for several points.

Coaching Eye

Statistics are often superior to the human eye for charting long-term trends, but the human eye can be superior at spotting a pattern from a small amount of data. The key is to observe not the result as much as the process behind it. For example, if you scout a team and notice that they don't rely much on their middle attack and they score on two quick sets early in the game, you need to consider a few things before deciding whether to make an adjustment. If both kills were on medium-speed hits that your defenders just mishandled, you might want to keep everything the same and expect your team to just execute better next time. However, if the setter–hitter connection is perfect and their middles thunder the ball to the floor in a way you hadn't seen previously, then maybe they have changed something in their game. You may want to make an adjustment to match it.

Player Feedback

Using player feedback is helpful, but it has to be done carefully and respectfully. Your players should feel empowered to pay attention to the game situations and suggest changes as the match goes on. These adjustments might be best made between sets, when you all have a little more time to discuss them.

As a coach, you will develop your own style regarding when to make changes. Some coaches prefer to base changes on certain statistical criteria, whereas some like to use their eye. Some coaches like to adjust during the match, and some adjust only after losing a set. With each match you will gain more experience and improve in your ability to implement a game plan and adjust it as the match goes on.

ANALYZING THE GAME PLAN: WHAT WORKED AND WHAT WENT WRONG?

After the match, one of the most important things you can do is debrief. Sit down by yourself (or gather your staff) and look at what your team did well and not so well in the match. A great way to do this is to view the match through the eyes of your game plan. To do this, you will need the following information:

- Serve and pass statistics
- Attacking statistics
  - In-system (after good or perfect passes)
  - Out-of-system (after poor passes)
  - Transition
- How the top attackers on each team performed and how the other team defended them
- The lineups each team started with any changes they made and the match-ups they created
- The trends and tendencies in each rotation

You can gather this information from several sources. Hopefully, you have some way to record statistics for your matches. Statistical software programs, ranging from simple to advanced, can help you track stats during a match. However, at many levels, simple statistics recorded on paper can be very effective. Tables 16.1 and 16.2 are examples of ways to tally your results after a game.

TABLE 16.1 Rotation Chart

	In-System			Out-of-System			Transition		
	Kill	**Attempt**	**Error**	**Kill**	**Attempt**	**Error**	**Kill**	**Attempt**	**Error**
Rotation 1	IIII	IIII		卌	III		卌 I	卌 卌	II
Rotation 2	卌	IIII	I	I	IIII		III	卌 I	III
Rotation 3	III	卌		III	III	I	III	卌 I	IIII
Rotation 4	IIII	IIII	I		II	II	III	卌 IIII	II
Rotation 5	II	II		I	IIII	I	IIII	卌	
Rotation 6	卌 I	II	II	II	I		卌 I	卌 I	IIII
Total	卌 卌 卌 卌 IIII	卌 卌 卌 卌 I	IIII	卌 卌 II	卌 卌 卌 II	IIII	卌 卌 卌 卌 卌	卌 卌 卌 卌 卌 卌 卌 卌 II	卌 卌 卌
	24	21	4	12	17	4	25	42	15

TABLE 16.2 Post-Game Percentages

Passing (% In-System)	49/(49 + 34) = 59%
In-System Hitting %	(24-4)/49 = 41%
Out-of-System Hitting %	(12-4)/33 = 24%
Transition Hitting %	(25-15)/82 = 12%

In addition to statistics, you should use your eyes to add qualitative information to the evaluation. You can do this from your memory of the match, but the best way to do this is to use video. Many computer programs allow a coaching staff to code and tag video to record and recall specific events, but even without that, you can still go through and watch the match video and write down observations. Watch some attacks by your opponent's best hitter and see how your team defended them and how well it worked. Just as important, look at how your opponent defended your best attacker. If they were able to slow her down, understand that another team, whether through scouting or just as part of its system, will use the same strategy, so be prepared to deal with that in the future.

After reviewing this information, an important task is to translate this into teachable moments for yourself, your staff, and your players. Usually, the match will fall into one of the following four categories:

1. *The team executed the game plan and played well.* This is always the hope for all coaches! After a match like this, point out what the team did well and emphasize the importance of continuing to do so.

2. *The team did not execute the game plan, but still played well.* This is not a bad result at all, because it means that you are teaching your team enough fundamental skills to win without executing a specific game plan. These types of matches are important for the staff to review to figure out how to improve the game plan. You may need to adjust the way you scout (to give your players more accurate information) or change the way you present the information to players.

3. *The team executed the game plan and played poorly.* After a match like this, decide whether the game plan was incorrect, or whether the problem was with fundamental skills execution.

4. *The team did not execute the game plan and played poorly.* Review the match and decide whether the team would have done better by following the game plan more attentively, or whether the issue was more related to a lack of skill.

CONCLUSION

Many of these teachable moments are just as important for the coaching staff as they are for the players. Keep in mind that the goal of scouting and game planning is to help the players be as successful as they can in the match, not to follow something because it sounds good on paper. Consider what you could have done better as a coach to prepare your players. Did a situation occur in the match that you didn't see coming? Add that to your scouting checklist. Were you able to slow down their best hitter? Write down that note and come back to it the next time you play a similar hitter. Did your players struggle to retain the information in the scouting report? Think about a better way to present the information, or simplify things so you don't overload them. By constantly reviewing your decisions, you can improve your process and continue to get better at scouting and game planning. In time, you will be able to consistently put your players in position to win, even against your toughest opponents.

17

Statistics for More Effective Coaching

Todd Dagenais

I was lousy at math growing up. I could never conceptualize the importance of numbers and how they worked. It's really ironic how important math has become to my career as a volleyball coach and educator.

Sports give us the ultimate opportunity to use statistics to train our teams and shape the environments they compete in. Of course, in many situations the outcome of an athletic battle simply comes down to who has the most talent. However, when the talent level is reasonably close between teams, the understanding of math and statistics can tip the scales in favor of one team. Just look at the baseball phenomenon chronicled in the film *Moneyball*. How could an unheralded team of nobodies possibly contend for the Major League Baseball championship? The answer is simple: math. A tightly contested volleyball game can be decided by 2 points, and I believe that understanding math can be worth at least 5 points.

On the other hand, statistics lie. There, I said it. It's always the elephant in the room when making a presentation about volleyball statistics. No chapter on volleyball statistics would be complete without this disclaimer. Numbers can be manipulated to create any story you are trying to sell. So why use them? The following four sections answer this dilemma.

ASKING BETTER QUESTIONS

All too often, coaches depend on statistics to provide the answers to difficult questions. Statistics can answer simple questions, but they can't always answer the deeper questions involving who, what, and how. Kevin Hambly, head volleyball coach at the University of Illinois, says his main reason for using statistics is not in the answers they provide, but in the questions they force him to ask. Statistics can clearly tell us that we had only five kills in a set and that our attacking game is weak, but *five kills* isn't the answer. Knowing we had only five kills allows us to ask the most important question: Why? Is it our attacking? Is it our setting? Is it poor passing leading to low-quality attacks against a triple block? These are the real questions that need to be answered. An example later in this chapter illustrates how statistics force us to look deeper and ask the right questions.

EVALUATING SKILL LEVELS OBJECTIVELY

Two coaches often see the same event two different ways. Our emotions, prejudices, and subjectivity creep into every evaluation and decision. Statistics can be a valuable check and balance for our subjectivity. They can be used when an athlete comes to you and asks, "What do I need to do to get better?" Statistics are also your best friend when parents pull you aside and want to talk about playing time for their child. There is nothing better than a set of objective statistics to fall back on when you have to explain your decision.

COMPARING PERFORMANCES TO STATISTICAL GOALS

Every team has statistical goals; I like to call ours *performance axioms* (ours are listed at the end of this chapter). Each year we try to take a close and honest look at the makeup of our team. From there, we decide what type of statistical marks we need to hit for maximal performance. We take a look at each of our statistical measurements during drills and competition and then compare them to our performance axioms to determine our team's progressions and regressions. We all know that practice time is very valuable. Smart use of statistics maximizes a team's time in the gym and ensures that players are working on the areas in which they need the most improvement.

SCOUTING OPPONENTS MORE EFFECTIVELY

Teams with higher levels of talent only *start* with the advantage. Volleyball is still a game of strategy and execution. This opens the door for teams with less talent to have an opportunity to win a 25-point set. Having a clear understanding of an opponent's makeup can give a less talented team an ample shot at the upset. Even the most powerful teams have weaknesses on the court, but those weaknesses aren't always evident at first. Statistical trends in specific situations can create an advantage that may not be plainly apparent. For example, even the greatest passers can have a weakness passing high or low or on a certain side of the body. Certain attackers may experience a drop in hitting percentage after passing a serve, even an easy serve. These are some of the things statistics can reveal when scouting opponents. Chapter 16 covers scouting opponents in more depth.

ISSUES WITH USING STATISTICS

Coaches should be coaching; they need to spend as much time as possible in the moment and not with their heads down writing on paper. One of the greatest issues with keeping statistics is that the process of recording them can keep coaches from doing their primary job—coaching. But if the coach isn't recording statistics, who should be? As the head coach on the bench, I have a sheet of paper on which I keep track of only the one or two statistics I believe are important to win the current match. These often change from opponent to opponent. Everything else is delegated to someone else who can quickly give me information as needed.

Statistics are only as valid and reliable as those recording them. It's often a challenge to find a reliable bench player, parent, or team manager who can keep accurate statistics. I love to have the backup setter keeping track of my team's passing and attacking statistics. It keeps her mind in the game, and it helps her understand what is working out there on the court. The same could be said for other players such as backup middles, outsides, and defensive players.

One of the greatest weaknesses of statistics is what many people call paralysis by analysis. A coach could easily make the mistake of taking numbers at face value and not using them to ask deeper questions. Some coaches spend too much time diving into the numbers and ultimately lose their coaching instincts. A coach who makes decisions completely based on numbers is just as susceptible to coaching mistakes as a coach who depends completely on instinct and subjective evaluation. The ideal situation is somewhere in the middle.

Statistical programs can be very expensive, or their complexity can make them very time-consuming. However, the recent development of tablet and iPad applications is making it very easy and inexpensive to track basic statistics. Several current programs include iVolleyStats, Volleyball Ace, and Rotate 123. The devices and applications will continue to change, so pay attention to new developments and use the right one for your program.

TRACKING STATISTICS

It's really easy to say that detailed statistics should be taken during every practice and every competition. At the NCAA Division I level, a full staff and coaches are dedicated exclusively to the Data Volley statistical program. More often than not, recording statistics is the job of an assistant coach, bench player, or parent. I firmly believe that coaches should put coaching as their first priority. Coaches who have difficulty taking statistics and providing real-time feedback to their athletes should delegate the statistics to someone else. Those with limited options for statisticians are better off video-recording the match or practice and recording statistics from the video later.

The summer USA Volleyball High Performance teams often have a limited number of staff members. Obviously, the Olympic pipeline for USA Volleyball is extremely important, so recording quality statistics is as well. Following are some methods that can be used with a pen and paper and a limited staff.

Box Chart

Using a box chart, a coach can record multiple statistics at one time. The following box chart (table 17.1) shows who executed the serve receive, the rating of the pass, and what happened after the pass was set.

We can gather a great deal of information from this chart. First, Jocelyn had 25 total passes for 43 total passing points. That means that her passing efficiency was 1.72 (43 passing points divided by 25 passes). We also know that 6 of her passes resulted in a first-ball kill, 10 passes resulted in a ball kept in play, 4 passes resulted in a first-ball error, and she was aced 5 times. We also can determine that 9 of her 25 passes were perfect (36 percent). This box chart can be used to track multiple stats for several players. The data can also be used to extrapolate areas of strength and weakness in a particular skill.

TABLE 17.1 Serve Receive

Player	First-ball kill	Ball in play	First-ball error	Aced
Jocelyn	3 3 2 3 2 3	2 1 3 3 3 2 2 1 1 1	3 3 1 1	0 0 0 0 0
Luc				
Reece				
Emily				

Stat Line

Using a stat line also works very well when a coach doesn't have enough time to chart events. With this method it's quite simple to keep track of many statistics at once. Following is a stat line chart for attacking, passing, and defense.

Luc: K 3 3 D 0 B A 3 2 D A B K E E

The translation of Luc's stat line would read like this from the first stat entry: kill, three pass, three pass, dig, zero pass, block, attack attempt, three pass, two pass, dig, attack attempt, block, kill, attack error, attack error. From this stat line we can determine the following about Luc's performance:

2 kills + 2 attack errors + 2 other attack attempts = 6 attempts

2 kills out of 6 attempts = 33% (kill percentage)

2 kills – 2 errors out of 6 attempts = .000 (kill efficiency)

5 serve-receive attempts for a total of 11 passing points = 2.20 (passing efficiency)

2 digs and 2 blocks

Most Important Statistics to Track

This subject is up for a great debate. The answer may lie in the type of team you have. If you have a team that scores at a very high level, then you are likely tracking the major offensive statistics. If your team depends on defensive skills to equalize matches, then you should be focusing more on serving, blocking, and defensive strategies. Let's have a quick refresher on the basic statistics in volleyball.

Basic Offensive Statistics

Kill: When an attack attempt leads directly to a point

Attack attempt: When an attack attempt results in neither a kill nor an error

Error: When an attack attempt is blocked for a point, hit in the net, or hit out of bounds. Balls that are blocked are considered forced errors, whereas balls hit in the net or out of bounds are considered unforced errors.

Basic Defensive Statistics

Block: A block is awarded to a player or players who score a point for their team by blocking an opponent attack. As many as three players may receive a block if they are all part of an attempt to block an attack.

Block solo: When a player is the only one blocking a shot

Block assist: When more than one player blocks an attack, all players receive a block assist regardless of whether they were the player who blocked the ball

Block error: When a referee determines that a blocker has made illegal contact with the net

Dig: When a player stops an opponent's attack attempt from being a kill

Cover: When a player digs a teammate's attack after it has been blocked by an opponent

Basic Setting Statistics

Set attempt: When a player attempts to set to a teammate for a kill

Assist: When a player sets to a teammate and the attack is a kill

Ball handling error: When a referee calls a player setting the ball for a lift or double contact

Basic Serving Statistics

Serve attempt: When a player attempts a serve

Ace: When a server's attempt is not passed and directly results in a point

Serve error: When a player's attempt is served in the net or out of bounds, or a player commits a service line fault

Basic Serve-Receive Statistics

Reception: When a player attempts a serve receive

Reception error: When a player's poor serve receive leads to a direct point for the serving team

The following table 17.2 illustrates the two primary measurements of team system success, how those statistical measurements are determined, the best way to track the systems, and some goals your team might try to achieve.

TABLE 17.2 Team System Statistics

Team system	Determined by	Goal	Easiest way to track	Scoring
Side-out percentage (SO%)	Number of side-out points divided by number of opponent serves	Team goal of 62% side-out	Plus and minus system	6 out of 10 = 60% (SO%)
Point-scoring percentage (PS%)	Number of serving points divided by number of team serves	Team goal of 43% point scoring	Plus and minus system	4 out of 10 = 40% (PS%)

SERVE-RECEIVE STATISTICS

One of the most common ways to determine the success of your serve-receive game is to grade each serve reception.

Passing Average (3-Point Scale)

How to most accurately rate this statistic is up for great debate. Many coaches use a traditional 3-point scale ranging from 0 for an ace or overpass to 3 for a perfect pass. Figure 17.1 represents the value of each pass based on where the ball would have landed on the court. The team goal is to achieve a 2.30, or a 60 percent 3 pass.

Passing Average (4-Point Scale)

There is a statistical problem with the 3-point passing scale. Statisticians will tell you that anything with an odd number of data points is not statistically valid or reliable. Therefore, many higher-level programs use a 4-point scale ranging from 0 for an ace or overpass to 4 for a perfect-perfect pass (see figure 17.2). The team goal is to achieve 2.70, or a 60 percent 3 and 4 pass.

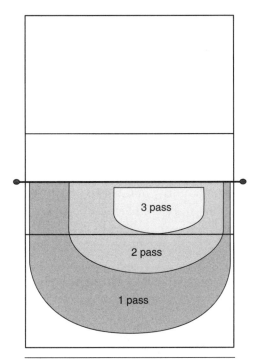

FIGURE 17.1 Passing average, 3-point scale.

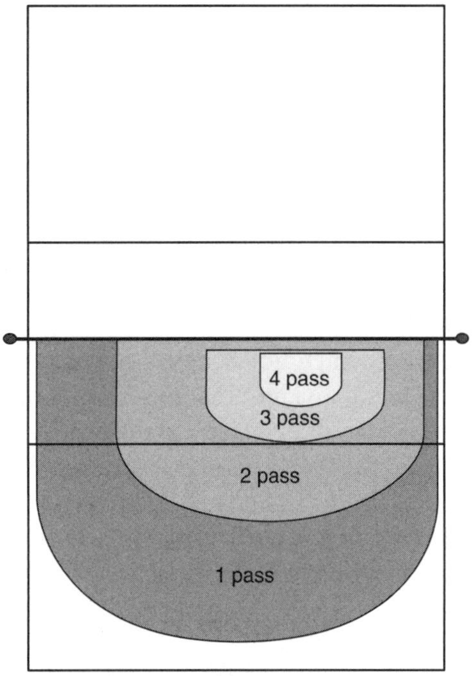

FIGURE 17.2 Passing average, 4-point scale.

Passing Average (Weighted Scale)

Recently, I had a conversation with Jim Dietz, who is the very numbers-savvy head coach for Lincoln Land Community College in Illinois. He has been working with a passing scale that is weighted to include an expected success outcome based on the quality of a pass (see figure 17.3). It's fair to say that a 2 pass is twice as likely to yield a point as a 1 pass. A 5 pass is 5 times as likely to yield a point as a 1 pass. The team goal is to achieve 3.30, or a 60 percent 5 pass.

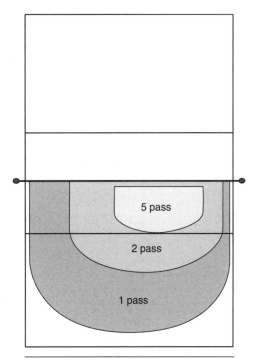

FIGURE 17.3 Passing average, weighted scale.

OFFENSIVE PRODUCTION STATISTICS

There are several simple calculations to quantify and evaluate an attacker's performance. The two most common are calculating kill percentage and kill efficiency. An attacker's errors factor into the kill efficiency making it a more complex, but more accurate, reflection of the attacker's rate of success.

Kill Percentage (K%)

Kill percentage is the simplest statistic for evaluating attacking. This is important because kill efficiency can give the coach an idea about the number of points that are being given to the opponent. Both calculations and a simple method of keeping track of each is listed in the following table 17.3.

TABLE 17.3 Determining Kill Percentage and Kill Efficiency

Team system	Determined by	Goal	Easiest way to track	Scoring
Kill percentage (K%)	Kills divided by total attempts	Team goal of 43%	Plus and minus system	5 kills on 10 attempts = 50% (K%)
Kill efficiency (Effic)	Kills minus errors divided by total attempts	Team goal of 24% + or better	Plus and minus system	5 kills + 2 errors on 10 attempts = 30% (effic)
First-ball side-out percentage (FBSO%)	First-ball kills divided by total number of passes attempted	Team goal of 42% or better	Line tracking system	4 kills on 10 passes = 40% (FBSO%)
Dig to swing percentage (DS%)	Number of transition swings divided by total number of digs	Team goal of 85% or better	Line tracking system	7 swings on 10 digs = 70% (DS%)
Dig to kill percentage (DK%)	Number of transition kills divided by total number of digs	Team goal of 32% or better	Line tracking system	3 kills on 10 digs = 30% (DK%)
Dig opportunity percentage (D%)	Digs divided by total attacks into a player's defensive area	Individual and team goal of 80% or better	Plus and minus system	15 digs on 20 attempts = 75% (D%)

Kill Efficiency (Effic)

Kill efficiency is the most commonly used evaluation of attacking. It takes into account attacking errors and is expressed by a decimal number to the 1/1,000th. An example is 5 kills – 2 errors on 10 attempts = .300

First-Ball Side-Out Percentage (FBSO%)

First-ball side-out percentage means that a ball that is terminated on the first attempt leaves the opponents no opportunity to score. An example is 4 kills on 10 pass attempts = 40% FBSO.

Dig to Swing Percentage (DS%)

A dig is important, but being able to get a quality swing after a dig is even more important. An example is 7 swings on 10 digs= 70% (DS%).

Dig to Kill Percentage (DK%)

After stopping opponents' first-ball kill attempt, a dig to kill is your first opportunity to score. An example is 3 kills on 10 digs= 30% (DK%).

Dig Opportunity Percentage (D%)

Tracking dig opportunities is very simple, but it also has an element of subjectivity. A defensive player has the responsibility to dig each attack that enters her area. We can easily calculate her success rate using the following method.

If 20 attacks are hit into a defensive player's area of responsibility, and the player digs 15 of those attacks, then the dig opportunity percentage is 75%. An example is 15 digs on 20 attacks into a player's area = 75% (D%).

DEFINING TEAM ROTATIONS

Before we can begin to discuss anything involving floor rotations, we need to clarify how rotations are named. When using a traditional five-hitter, one-setter offense (5-1 offense), and the setter is positioned in the right back, the team is considered to be in rotation 1. When the setter is positioned in the middle back, the team is considered to be in rotation 2, and when the setter is positioned in the left back, the team is considered to be in rotation 3. When the setter is positioned in the left front, the team is considered to be in rotation 4, when the setter is positioned in the middle front, the team is considered to be in rotation 5, and when the setter is positioned in the right front, the team is considered to be in rotation 6.

TABLE 17.4 Analyzing Rotations Using the Plus and Minus System

Rotation	Plus and Minus																				Plus	Minus	Overall
1	+	-	-	-	+	-	+	-	-	-	+	+	-	-	+	+	+	-	-	+	+9	-11	-2
2	+	+	-	-	+	-	+	-	+	-	+	+	-	-	+	+	+	+	-	+	+12	-8	+4
3	-	-	-	-	+	-	-	-	-	-	+	+	+	-	+	+	+	+	-	+	+9	-11	-2
4	+	-	-	-	+	-	+	-	-	-	+	-	-	-	-	-	+	-	-	+	+6	-14	-8
5	+	-	-	+	+	-	+	-	-	-	+	+	+	-	+	+	+	-	-	+	+11	-9	+2
6	+	-	-	-	+	-	+	+	-	-	+	+	-	-	+	+	+	-	-	+	+10	-10	+0

Explanation: positive (points scored in a rotation) minus (points given up in a rotation)

The line grid (table 17.4) tells a coach that rotation 4 needs the most work in practice, rotation 2 is the best rotation, and the other rotations are slightly positive or negative. They would warrant attention, but not as much as the weakest rotation.

Determining Plus and Minus in the Serve and Serve-Receive Split

The preceding grid clearly shows that rotation 4 is very weak, but we do not know which phase of the game the team is weak in. We can take our line grid to the next level to determine the issue as shown in table 17.5.

By analyzing rotation 4, we can see that the serve and the serve-receive phases are both –4 in points. All rotations in the serve phase are negative, which is not uncommon. So, we have identified the culprit, but we still don't know why this is happening. Let's add up the point-scoring percentage (PS%) and side-out percentage (SO%) for each rotation.

We have already identified that our goal for side-out percentage (SO%) is 62 percent, and the goal for our point scoring (PS%) is 43 percent. Taking a look at our problem rotation 4, we can see that the serving phase is below our goal, but not enough to cause such a poor performance for the rotation. However, when we compare the serve-receive phase of rotation 4 with all the other serving rotations, we can instantly see our issue. A side-out percentage of 30 percent is significantly lower than our goal of 63 percent. We have our answer: We are struggling in the serve-receive phase of rotation 4. OK, but why? It's time to do a terminal point analysis on the serve-receive phase of rotation 4.

Determining Plus or Minus in Each Rotation Using Terminal Points

Terminal points refer to the skill that was being performed at the time the rally terminated. These skills may be kill (K), service ace (SA), service error (SE), attack error (AE), first-ball kill (FBK), first-ball error (FBE), block (B), or ball-handling

TABLE 17.5 Determining Plus and Minus in the Serve and Serve-Receive Split

Rotation 1	Serve	+ - - - + - + - - -	-4	It's not uncommon to be +0, or slightly minus in Serve Phase
	Receive	+ + + - - + + + - - +	+2	We want to be positive in Serve Receive, but +2 isn't enough
Rotation 2	Serve	+ + - - + - + - + +	+2	
	Receive	+ + - - + + + + - +	+4	We can see that Rotation #2 was a total gain of 6 points
Rotation 3	Serve	- - - - + - - - - +	-6	Our Rotation #3 Serve is killing us, find out why later.
	Receive	+ + + - + + + + - +	+6	Our Rotation #3 Serve Receive is great , helping make-up for Serve
Rotation 4	Serve	+ - - - + - + - - -	-4	
	Receive	+ - - - - - + + - -	-4	A total of -8 for Rotation #4 could cost us the match
Rotation 5	Serve	+ - - + + - + - - -	-2	A normal average for the Serve phase
	Receive	+ + - - + + + + - +	+4	A normal average for the Serve Receive phase
Rotation 6	Serve	+ - + - + - + - - -	-2	
	Receive	+ + - + + - + - - +	+2	We can see Rotation #6 was a net gain of ZERO overall

error (BHE). The following table 17.6 is the same as the preceding, but the plus and minus points are on different lines, and the terminal point is recorded instead of a plus or a minus.

TABLE 17.6 Determining Plus or Minus in Each Rotation Using Terminal Points

Rotation 4	+: FBK SE K
Serve-receive phase	–: AE SA SA AE SA SA SA AE

Our statistics are helping us to ask the right questions. The answers to those questions are now becoming a bit clearer. Of the eight points we are losing in the serve-receive phase of rotation 4, five of them are service aces. Our rotation 4 passing is terrible! Now we must go to work in practice to determine whether it's the result of a receiving footwork issue, a body position issue, or a passing platform issue. Most important, we have to determine which players are causing the issue. We can use the same plus and minus grid for individual players.

Tracking Player Pluses and Minuses

Explanation: positive (points scored by a player) minus (points given up by a player)

Teigan: + + + – – + + + – +

The preceding stat line tells us that Teigan scored 7 points and conceded 3 points to her opponents. Therefore, Teigan is +4.

The following table 17.7 tracks Betty's terminal points. As you can see here, Betty is basically a neutral player in the serving phase; however, she is a major liability in the serve-receive phase. She had 7 errors in this phase alone, and given that she was aced 3 times, you can bet we will be working on serve receive in the next practice!

TABLE 17.7 Tracking Player Pluses and Minuses Using Terminal Points

Serve phase	+) K B –) SE
Serve-receive phase	+) FBK K B –) SA SA SA FBE FBE AE AE

Earlier, we discussed our goals for side-out percentage (62 percent) and point scoring (43 percent). If you add these two percentages together and the total is over 100 percent, you will *never* lose. If you have a weak serving, blocking, and defense team, then you had better be above average in the serve-receive, setting, and first-ball kill game. I can tell you that it is much easier to increase the percentage of the serving phase than it is to increase the combined percentages of the serve-receive phase. However, it's important to accept the identity of the team you coach. Accentuate the positives and continue to work on the negatives.

STATISTICS WITHOUT A DIRECT CORRELATION TO WINNING AND LOSING

Coaches have done many statistical studies at all levels of volleyball. The common consensus is that some stats correlate very little to winning or losing. It's highly likely the best attacking team is near the top of the conference standings, but the best blocking team, the team with the most service aces, and the team with the most digs could be the last-place team. I'm not saying these three statistics are not important in the game of volleyball, but it would be unwise to use an overabundance of practice time in these areas.

WHO DO YOU WANT AS YOUR STARTER?

We have already determined that statistics are important for determining the most deserving players. Be cautious, however; statistics may not be as dependable as you think. Consider Reece and Emily, who are two outside hitters competing for the final starting position on your team. Let's say that you have decided they are equal in passing and defense. Therefore, you are going to give the position to the best attacker. Reece is hitting .200 kill efficiency. Emily is hitting .100 kill efficiency. Easy decision, right? Reece is the best hitter . . . or is she? Let's look deeper.

Reece's stat line: 7 kills + 5 errors + 10 attempts = .200 kill efficiency

Emily's stat line: 1 kill + 0 errors + 10 attempts = .100 kill efficiency

You need to ask yourself whether errors matter. Some teams can overcome the errors of a player with a 70 percent kill percentage, whereas others may need to use the player with only a 10 percent kill percentage, but an extremely low error rate. Are all .200s the same? Let's look. Kenadie is hitting .200 kill efficiency, and Teigan is hitting .200 kill efficiency. On paper they are the same hitter, but are they really?

Kenadie's stat line: 6 kills + 4 errors + 10 attempts = .200 kill efficiency

Teigan's stat line: 2 kills + 0 errors + 10 attempts = .200 kill efficiency

Once again, does your team need the kills to get to 25 points, or do your players need to make sure it's not too easy for the other team to get to 25 points? Jocelyn and Luc are each passing a respectable 2.20, but we need to look into the details.

Jocelyn: 3 3 1 0 0 3 3 3 3 3

10 passes / 22 pass points / 2.20 / 70% perfect / 20% error

Luc: 2 3 2 3 2 3 1 1 3 2

10 passes / 22 pass points / 2.20 / 40% perfect / 0% error

Jocelyn is passing over the team goal for perfect passes, but 1 out of every 5 passes scores a point for the opposing team. It's a bit harder to run your offense from Luc's passes, but he isn't giving any points directly to the opponents.

AXIOMS

This section presents our team's statistical goals, or axioms, in each phase of the game. These numbers are based on studying hundreds of matches, asking advice from coaches at all levels, and examining the number marks achieved by teams that win at all levels. You may adjust these numbers up or down based on the level of competition you play.

Serve-Receive Phase

Side-out percentage (SO%)	62%
Passing efficiency	2.30 (3-point pass scale)
Perfect pass percentage (PP%)	55% or more
Medium pass percentage (2P%)	30% or less
Poor pass percentage (1P%)	12% or less
Aced or overpass percentage (0P%)	3% or less
Kill percentage on a 3 pass	53%
Kill percentage on a 2 pass	38%
Kill percentage on a 1 pass	25%

Serve Phase

Point-scoring percentage (PS%)	43%
Opponent's pass efficiency	2.00 or less
Opponent's perfect pass percentage	45% or less

Our aces per game	1.50
Opponent's first-ball kill percentage	35% or less
Blocks per game	2.6

Transition Phase

Dig to kill percentage	32%
Dig opportunity percentage	80% or better
Transition attacking error percentage	12% or less
Transition kill percentage	35% or better
Transition kill efficiency	22% or better

General Offense

Team attacking efficiency	24% or better
Middle blockers	33% or better
Outside hitters	23% or better
Right-side hitters	28% or better
Team kill percentage	42% or better
Team attack error percentage	12% or less
Kills per game	15 kills
First-ball kills	9 kills
Transition kills	6 kills

General Defense

Team digs per game	17 digs
Opponent kill percentage	33% or less
Opponent kill efficiency	20% or less

Other Guiding Axioms

Free-ball or down-ball kill percentage	85%
Unforced errors per game	6 errors (ball handling, attacking, serving)
Consecutive side-outs	7 side-outs in a row
Runs of 3 points	3 per set
Opponent runs of 3 points	1 or fewer per set
End of the set	0 unforced errors after 20 points
Serving	Never have 2 serving errors in a row

STATISTICAL CORRELATION TO VICTORY (2004 OLYMPICS STUDY)

To offer a final visual of the importance of some statistics over others, table 17.8 presents the results of a study that was done on the women's volleyball tournament at the 2004 Summer Olympics in Athens, Greece. The results of the 2004 Olympic statistics can help guide a coach toward the most important statistics to consider when evaluating their team's performance. These results illustrate what coaches should be considering when evaluating their teams' statistics.

TABLE 17.8 2004 Olympic Statistical Rankings (12 Teams Participating)

Finish	Team	Attack efficiency	Opponent attack efficiency	Kill %	Opponent's kill %	Passing average	Opponent's passing average	Perfect pass %	First-ball kill %
1	China	1	2	2	3	2	1	2	2
2	Russia	4	8	4	8	3	9	3	4
3	Cuba	5	9	5	9	9	4	9	3
4	Brazil	3	6	1	2	1	7	1	1
5	USA	7	4	8	6	11	3	11	7
5	Japan	8	10	7	7	4	6	7	8
5	Korea	9	5	11	5	7	12	5	6
5	Italy	2	1	3	1	5	8	6	5

First, it's easy to see why China won the gold medal. They were in the top three of each important category. How was Cuba able to overcome the fact they were poor passers and defenders? The answer is offense—more specifically, first-ball kill in serve receive. Despite not being very strong in serve receive, they were able to get a first-ball kill on 42 percent of their passes. Opposing teams had few opportunities to score in transition on them. Russia was in a similar situation, but they were able to overcome poor defense with a lethal offense. Although it's not shown on the graph, Japan and Korea made it to the quarterfinals because they are very low-error teams that simply forced their opponents to score all of their own points.

CONCLUSION

Understanding and using statistics will likely make you a better coach. However, it is important to remember that players should stay focused on playing the game while you worry about the statistics. While there are numerous areas in volleyball that can be statistically quantified, analyzed, and ranked, it's always important to keep statistics as simple and meaningful as possible. Coaches should only track and calculate those statistics they actually intend on using to determine team weaknesses, team progressions, and for individuals earning playing time.

18

Offensive Tactics

Bill Neville

Every volleyball team should have an offensive philosophy and a system of organization that reflects it. Further, it must be organized by rotation because each rotation is a new situation. There are important elements to be considered. An offensive philosophy should consider the following items:

* Players
* Ability to control the first contact (free, down, attacked balls, and serves)
* Rules
* Training time
* What is required to beat an opponent

PLAYERS

Regardless of the offensive system a team uses, it must have the personnel to run it. Coaches will always try to take advantage of rules. In the United States, where rules allow anywhere from 12 to unlimited substitutions and several game entries, coaches can specialize to maximize individual players' strengths and hide their weaknesses. Volleyball was originally designed to develop athletes to play the whole game, which requires a high level of competency in each skill (this is still the case at the international level). In the United States, beginning at a young age, players specialize based on presumed physical attributes. Descriptions permeate coaches' discussions of players (e.g., Is she a 3 rotation player or a 6 rotation player?).

Coaches must determine the philosophy that drives their system decisions. Many traditional assumptions influence systems design. Following are two of the most common:

* It is preferable to have three front-row hitters.
* Setters are often small, can't hit, and are weak blockers.

But what are the trade-offs? Do you really use three front-row hitters or do they get in the way of each other reducing the potential of a good approach and swing? The assumption is that a short setter is a liability as a blocker. How often is the setter really exploited as a blocker? Do offenses function with two setters in a 6-2 system? If setters were given a choice, would they rather play in a 5-1 or a 6-2? Does having three front-row hitters outweigh the premise that setters require constant involvement to maintain a rhythm, considering that they will always have one of the three contacts in a play sequence? Is it possible that in every rotation there can be five hitters, considering the back-row potential? A majority of setters would want to stay on the court for all six rotations if given the choice. Other than the obvious selfish reasons, most setters likely feel that they lose their rhythm and end up setting the ball less consistently and less accurately when they play half the time. Also, the setter is often the leader, or at least one of the leaders, of a team. It is tough to lead from the bench.

Shorter setters are often assumed to be liabilities as blockers. Therefore, the United States' extravagant, liberal substitution rules allow coaches to sub a big right-side hitter/blocker in for a small setter and bring in another setter in the back row. This does seem logical. The question is, how much of a liability is the small front-row setter? Does that liability outweigh the consistency and leadership the setter brings to the court? Does a rotational analysis of how points are scored show that the three rotations with the setter in the front row lose points over how many points are gained? Analyze your six rotations. In a 5-1 scheme, the setter is in the back row in rotations 1, 2, and 3, with three attackers at the net. The setter is at the net in rotations 4, 5, and 6, with two attackers. Comparing the first three rotations with the last three, which ones score the most and which yield the most points? And how often does the opponent take advantage of the small setter? Finally, are there blocking schemes that can hide the setter?

When the Japanese men's national team reigned supreme in the early 1970s, its setter was Katsutoshi Nekoda. He was short (5 feet, 9 inches) and had difficulty jumping over a painted line. But, oh my, could he set! It can be argued that he was the greatest setter ever to play the game. However, he was a pathetic blocker in a relatively pathetic blocking team. The Japanese decided that having Nekoda on court all the time was more advantageous than sitting him. Therefore, they created blocking schemes that moved him around so that the opponents had to focus their attack on seeking him out, which took them away from their normal attack.

ABILITY TO CONTROL THE FIRST CONTACT

The ball comes over the net from the opponent in four ways: as a free ball, a down ball, an attacked ball, or a serve. Even though there are various types of serves, the movement of the served ball is the most predictable because it begins play and all passers are in position. At younger ages, the serve generally dominates the receiving team because (1) the server is in control of the event and can dictate the terms of engagement and (2) it is easier for players to master the serve than the more complex serve receive. As players mature and play more, their serve-receive abilities begin to catch up, although at the highest levels of play, players still find it a challenge.

Free Balls

A free ball usually is the easiest of the first-ball contacts—or at least it should be. It is usually a saving play because the opponent is merely trying to keep the ball in play. The ball often comes over in a rainbow arc. In Japan, a free ball is translated as an "opportunity ball" because it is a ball that should be easy to control, and the receiving team should be able to counterattack with a full complement of weapons. This ball should be controlled overhead to maximize the speed of the counterattack. However, many coaches prefer that players always pass with their forearms.

Down Balls

A down ball is often described as a ball that goes down. Actually, the term refers to a down block. The ball comes across in a flat trajectory with some heat and often with topspin. It is often sent across the net from deep in the court or hit from a standing position. The block determines whether it is not hit hard enough or is hit from too great a distance to block. Therefore, the blockers yell "down!" because the flat trajectory of the down ball is usually handled with a forearm pass.

Attacked Balls

An attacked ball has a number of personalities. The one consistency is that the attacker gets an approach and jumps. There are a variety of approaches as well, but generally they lead the hitter to jump. Attacks range from a tip (the softest of contacts) to an all-out swing. Moreover, attackers hit a mix of angles and spots. In general, approximately 80% of attacks are hit in the direction of the approach angle. The better the attacker, the wider range the attacker can hit. Much like a good pitcher in baseball, the volleyball attacker can vary the velocity and locations. An attacker who is very consistent with her velocity and angles is easy to defend. However, the attacker with a good mix of velocities and angles is difficult.

Serves

The serve is the most common first ball. It is arguably the toughest of the first-ball opportunities because the server (if good) has complete control. Even though it seems that the hard-hit attack is the toughest, it doesn't happen as often as the serve. Statistics show that the winner of the serve-and-receive game often wins the match.

RULES

The U.S. substitution rules are different from those used in the majority of other countries. International rules restrict each team to six substitutions per set with only two entries per player. The United States has several rule adaptations; the most significant has to do with substitutions. (*Note:* The FIVB, the governing body of international volleyball, is considering some changes in the substitution rules: six free subs, allowing players to go in for any other players, and expanding to eight substitutions per set.) The U.S. substitution rules range from 12 to 18 per set with no limit on entries per player.

A historical perspective is in order here. When the FIVB adopted rally scoring and soon followed with the libero rule, the six-substitutions-per-set rule remained. With the side-out game history and rally scoring in play, the use of six substitutions plus the libero opened up the game to increased specialization without completely compromising the original intent of volleyball (i.e., to discourage specialization and encourage all players to master all the skills). The rally-scoring game was intended to make the sets and matches more predictable in terms of time, mostly to attract television viewers (it hasn't quite worked out as predicted).

The United States traditionally plays by its own rules. Applying 12 to 18 substitutions in a 25-point rally-scoring set means that a coach conceivably can formula-substitute without worrying about running out of substitutions. This leads to specialization as well as discontent among parents who wonder, "If you have all those subs, why isn't my child playing more?" On paper it appears that a coach can put in big hitters in the front row and smaller ball handlers in the back row. The liberos most often replace the middles in the back row. Much of this decision making is based on assumptions such as these: middles can't play back-row defense; short(er) players can't play effective front row; setters can be double-subbed so that a bigger hitter/blocker can replace the setters in the front row because (as you know) setters are short, usually can't jump, and are not good blockers, especially against the opponent's left-side hitters.

Are these assumptions proven by reality? Does having setters, middles, and opposites play half the time benefit the ultimate set and match outcomes? Does the reduction of rhythm caused by having a basic unit on the floor cause a team to play inconsistently? Does the shuffling of players in and out stifle the hot-handed hitter or knock a setter out of a groove? Are there players who need to be on the floor because of the force of their personalities, players who, just by their presence on the floor, elevate the play of those around them? Just because rules allow virtually unlimited changes doesn't mean that a coach should use them.

Another U.S. volleyball consideration is that players are being specialized at young ages. Without saying it out loud, we are implying that they can't perform particular skills. By taking a middle hitter out of the back row, we send the message that the player is not good enough to play in the back row. Sadly, at far too young an age, players begin to believe these messages. This leads to recent common queries from recruiters, such as, "Is she a 3 or a 6 rotation player?" Ideally, the answer should be, "She is a volleyball player!"

OFFENSIVE SYSTEM DESIGN BY PRINCIPLES

The more complex an offensive system is, the more training time is required. The age and abilities of the players are also significant. What do your players need to do to win? It can be argued that the level of your competition determines the systems you use. However, it is critical that your system not exceed your players' ability to play. Otherwise your win–loss record will be on paper only.

Prior to designing an offensive system, you need to list important considerations (as noted earlier). The next step is to establish a set of guiding principles to follow. Here are some examples:

- Simple is better.
- Attempt tactically only what you can execute technically.
- Go only as fast as you can control.
- Make sure the offensive system accommodates each rotation.
- Expose your strengths.

After choosing your guiding principles, design the rotational organization. Most people refer to offensive systems as 4-2, 6-2, 5-1, and so on. Actually, these are rotational organizations because teams play defense in these organizations as well. Generally, people think in offensive terms. When organizing an offensive system, this thinking makes sense. However, volleyball is the consummate transition game: once the ball is put into play, there will be a conclusion resulting in a point. Coaches must consider the rapid transition from offense to defense and vice versa when designing systems. When the opponent attacks, can the players recover to play good defense? If the opponent uses a certain type of defense, can the players get into a counterattack quickly?

Charting Offensive Schemes

As offensive systems are charted, terms and symbols need to be defined. Also, each scheme must be reflected in each rotation. Different programs use different descriptions for routes, set positions, tempos, and combinations. Jargon, audibles, and system names are ultimately at the coach's discretion. The basic organization outlined in this section is based on one that the late Jim Coleman developed. Dr. Coleman was one of the greatest innovators in volleyball. To simplify the offensive designs he created the following:

- Since the court is 9 meters wide, he divided it into 9 equal zones, numbering them from left to right beginning with 1 and continuing through 9.
- He also identified the height of a set by number approximating the height of a set at its apex estimated from the top of the net. Therefore a 4 set would be approximately 4 feet at its apex above the top of the net.
- Then he combined the two numbers to specify location, height, and speed of the net. Therefore a 14 would be a set 4 feet above the net at its apex

located in the 1 zone. The first number always designates the zone and the second number is the height.

♦ The speed of the set is determined by the height. (The lower the set, the faster it is.) An example of a relatively fast combination of potential sets to three front-row players would be: 13–51–93.

The numbering system is excellent at describing sets and locations but is cumbersome for audibles by the attacker or setter. Therefore, nicknames emerged over time for quick communication. Most of the audible nicknames are hard, one-syllable words, easily said and easily understood. The following list contains the most prominent definitions of these nicknames.

Definitions

BIC: A back-row quick attack behind the front-row middle attacker (how quick depends on the coach and the players' abilities).

Pipe: Coined by 1984 men's USA Olympic team captain, Chris Marlowe, a back-row attack slower than a BIC but hit right down the middle.

Gap: A quick–set between the outside set and the middle; also called a 31 (3-zone, one foot above the net).

Push: A variant of the middle quick (51) that the setter sets just beyond the opposing middle blocker's right hand. A 51 is vertical, but a push is angled toward the 4 zone.

Fade: Similar to the push, although a little wider and a little slower.

Back slide: An approach in which the spiker begins in front of the setter and slides to the back of the setter; most often, a one-foot takeoff much like a basketball player shooting a layup is used.

Front slide: The opposite of the back slide. The spiker begins the approach from behind the setter and goes in front. It is most comfortable for left-handers.

Front quick: Also known as 1, quick, or 51, a hit directly in front of the setter (noted above). The hitter is either above the setter as the ball is in the setter's hands (quick quick) or in the final step (slow quick)

Back quick: A quick set hit directly behind the setter; also known as back.

Double quick: Two players up for quick sets in any combination of inside locations (e.g., front gap and back 1, front 1 and gap).

Slow quick: A quick hit in which the hitter is in the last step of the approach.

Quick quick: A quick hit in which the hitter is in the air above the setter with the ball in the hands.

Naked quick: A quick hit in which the hitter faces no outside hitting threat.

Hut: Set to the left side and about 2 1/2 to 3 feet inside the antennae and 4 to 6 feet at its apex above the net.

Go: Usually, an audible calling for a fast left-side set; actually, an audible modifier for any set to go faster.

Red: A set on the right side; named after the favorite set of 1984 men's gold medalist, Steve Timmons, who has red hair and was nicknamed Red.

Left inside: A left-side hit in which the hitter approaches inside the gap hitter and hits a slow quick.

X series: Any combination in which one player crosses another's approach path.

Audibles: Voice signals indicating where a hitter is going and at what tempo. Audibles should be one-syllable, hard-sounding words that are easily uttered and easily heard. An audible can be given by the setter or hitter.

Series: Several plays organized to feed off the options in a preconceived attack plan.

Pattern: The organization of the plays within a series including routes and tempos.

Option: The individual attacker's role in the pattern.

Tempo: The speed of the attack; also referred to as step tempo to indicate the step the attacker is in when the setter touches the ball.

Attack Zones

In this section Jim Coleman's symmetrical zone system is used to illustrate series, patterns, and options. Certainly, other systems are used including the U.S. women's national team system, which identifies with letters the attack zones in front of and behind the setter.

In Coleman's system the front-row zones are designated with numbers 1 through 9, reading left to right, each a meter wide. The back row is divided equally in four "corridors" and designated with the letters A, B, C, D, reading left to right. See figure 18.1 for a representation of attack zones.

Attack Series and Patterns

Series and patterns are not art forms. They each have the purpose of pressuring the opponent's defense to wear it down and create scoring opportunities. The diagrams depicted here are not necessarily found in one team's arsenal, but rather, constitute a menu from which to choose. Coaches must decide what series and patterns best fit their teams, their players, and their offensive philosophies.

Following are explanations of how the numbers and symbols are used in the charts:

- ◆ **Numbers** refer to the set location and relative tempo based on the height of the set at its apex above the net. For example, 14 is attacked in the 1 zone and is 4 feet at its apex. The common audible is "Hut."

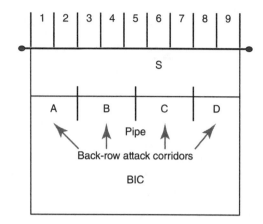

Set Lexicon: the first number is the zone the set is attacked.
The second number is the height of the set at its apex above the net.
Each set has a one syllable nickname and corresponding hand signal.

Number	Nickname	Hand signal	Comment
13/14	Hut	Closed fist	"GO!" modifies the speed.
32	Lob	3 fingers	Modification to 31
31	Rip/Gap	3 fingers	Is called or audible.
51	Quick	Index finger	
53	Two	Index and middle in V	Index and middle in V.
43	× (2)	Index and middle tight	2 feet at its apex above net.
71	Back	Index finger laid on back of hand	Play-set crossing behind 51.
92/93	Red	Little finger	Off one or two feet.
95	Five	Five fingers	95

FIGURE 18.1 Attack zones and examples of sets and signals.

- **Number sequences** designate which hitter has what set. For example, 14-51-43 (D) reads from left to right to back row. The left-front (LF) hitter gets a 14; the middle hitter (MF) gets a 51; and the right-front hitter (RF) gets a 43 (even though the RF hits in the 4 zone; this would signify an X route). The designated back-row hitter would hit out of the D corridor.

- **Lowercase letters** refer to the blockers: rb = right-front blocker; mb = middle blocker; lb = left-front blocker.

- **Abbreviations** for hitters in designated roles are as follows: R = release hitter, designated as a hitter expected to hit an out-of-system set when other options are not available; PS = play-set hitter, usually assigned to the second tempo of a play; QH = quick hitter, usually the middle hitter; BRH = back-row hitter; SW = swing hitter used in a swing offensive system. In most standard systems the left-side hitter is designated as the outside hitter (OH).

Not all options are included in the following charts. For example, although several back-row attack options are included, the BIC is not. The BIC is seen primarily in international men's volleyball, where big, high-, and long-jumping human beings can launch from behind the 3-meter line and hit at the net. If you have a 13-year-old girl who can execute such a play, please include it in your offensive package. The push and fade are not included either. They would be adjustments within any of the quick options based on the unfolding situation.

Key

1st #	Left-side hitter
2nd #	Middle hitter
3rd #	Right-side hitter
BR	Back-row hitter
BSW	Back-row swing hitter
PS	Play-set hitter
JS	Jump setter
QH	Quick hitter (middle)
R	Release hitter (left)
SW	Swing hitter
LB	Left-side blocker
MB	Middle blocker
RB	Right-side blocker
■	Opposing blocker

X Series

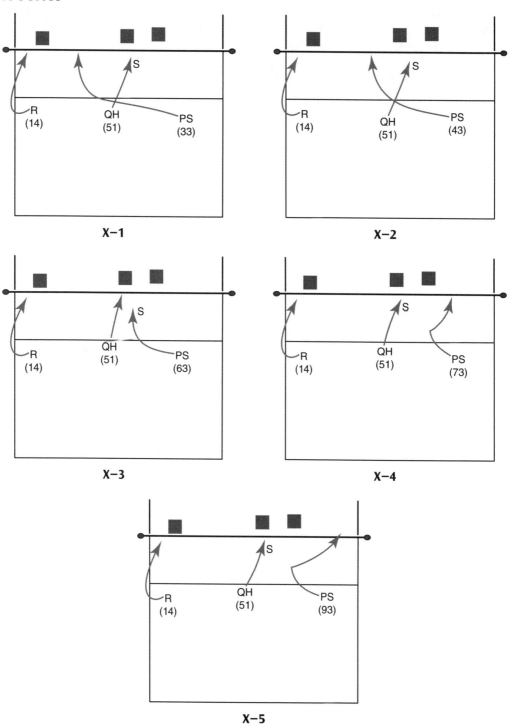

X–1

X–2

X–3

X–4

X–5

X Series Notes

Tactical goal	Pattern	Tactical goal	Play	Tactical goal
Create piston effect; bunch blockers in middle; attacking reading and/or small middle blocker	14-51-33 (X-1)	Isolate on right-side blocker; force mb to take a step and reach away from the middle; pick lb on mb	14	Line shot
			51	Seam between mb and lb/rb
			33	Seams straight to middle back
	14-51-43 (X-2)	Pressure rb to pin in (opening up 14); catch mb indecisive and flat-footed; screen lb on mb	14	Line shot; cross-court seam
			51	Cut back
			43	Both angles; seams between lb/rb
	14-51-63 (X-3) or tandem	concentrate attack on mb (small mb, poor blocker); force lb and rb to pinch in opening spread plays later	14	Line shot; cross court seam
			51	Cut back
			63	Flat trajectory either angle
	14-51-73 (X-4) or fake X	Mirror image of X-2; best after establishing X-1and X-2; needs good jab step fake; will force lb to jump to their left opening seam between lb and mb	14	Line shot; cross court seam
			51	Seam between mb and lb
			73	Line or seam between mb; faking lb
	14-51-93 (X-5) or flare out	Best after establishing X-1 and X-2; with good deal fake lb will fade trying to catch up with ps; 51 is one on one; 14 should be one on one with rb	14	Line shot; cross court seam
			51	Seam between mb and lb
			93	Line and off lb; sharp cut back

Spread Series

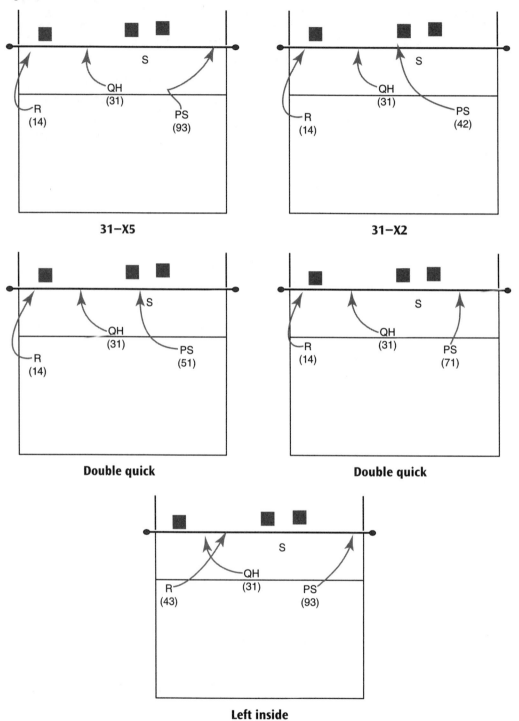

31–X5

31–X2

Double quick

Double quick

Left inside

Spread Series Notes

Tactical goal	Pattern	Tactical goal	Play	Tactical goal
After bunching block inside spread patterns will force blocker to chase ball outside; also good against big, slow mb	14-31-93 (31-X5)	Primarily opens up X5; with QH going away from the mb more away from X5 set; set selection should to primarily to X5	14	Line is best shot
			31	Primarily angle toward opponent position 5
			93	Either angle or line (off fooled blocker)
	14-31-42 (31-X2)	Best after 31 - X5; PS fakes to X5 taking lb out; then PS comes back into 42; mb with QH and 31; best option is PS hitting 42	14	Line
			31	Angle toward position 5
			42	Straight ahead toward position 1
	14-31-51 (double quick)	Blocking reduced to guesswork if pattern is run correctly; 1 on 1 is guaranteed on each option; opens up 14 for big hit	14	Angle toward 31 with split block
			31	Angle to position 5
			51	Angle to position 1
	14-31-71 (double quick)	Same as above; 71 is suited for left hander; spread out even more	14	Angle toward 31 with split block
			31	Angle to position 5
			71	Angle to position 1
	43-31-93 (left inside)	Misdirection play; based on establishing others first; primary set is to 43 hit by R; good against commit block	43	Straight ahead toward position 6
			31	Angle to position 5
			93	Line

RX Slide Series

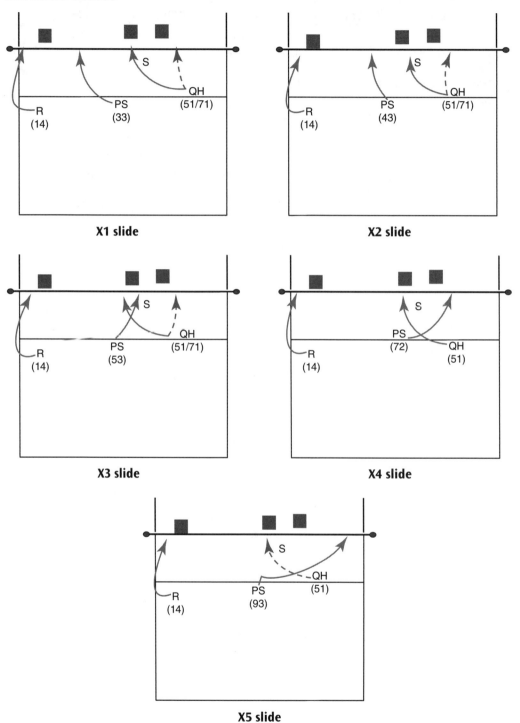

X1 slide

X2 slide

X3 slide

X4 slide

X5 slide

RX Slide Series Notes

Tactical goal	Pattern	Tactical goal	Play	Tactical goal
Will hesitate before going if QH is lined up on right and PS is in the middle; gives mb a different look with QH coming from different angles	14-33-51/71 (X1 slide)	Forces lb to block quick	14	Line or angle (reverse quick from right side)
			33	Shot to position 1 corner or cut
			51/71	Straight to position 1 past lb
	14-43-51/71 (X2 slide)	Should open up PS if mb chooses to go after QH; if timed right, piston effect is on	14	Line or angle based on rb position
			43	Shot to position 1 corner
			51/71	51 hit either angle; 71 hit angle to position 1
	14-53-51/71 (X3 slide)	Puts pressure on mb and lb; piston effect; it does not work if set is too high	14	Line or angle based on rb position
			53	Angle to position 1
			51/71	Cut back to position 5
	14-72-51 (X4 slide)	Scissor pattern picks mb on lb; good after X1 or X2; if used as a change up it can open up 1 or 0 blockers	14	Line or angle based on rb position
			72	Position 5 corner
			51	Angle to position 1
	14-93-51/71 (X5 slide)	A wider version of X4 slide; a good opener of series; lb goes with sliding QH; picks mb; PS open	14	Line or angle based on rb position
			93	Down line to position 5
			51/71	Either angle

Double Quick Swing Series

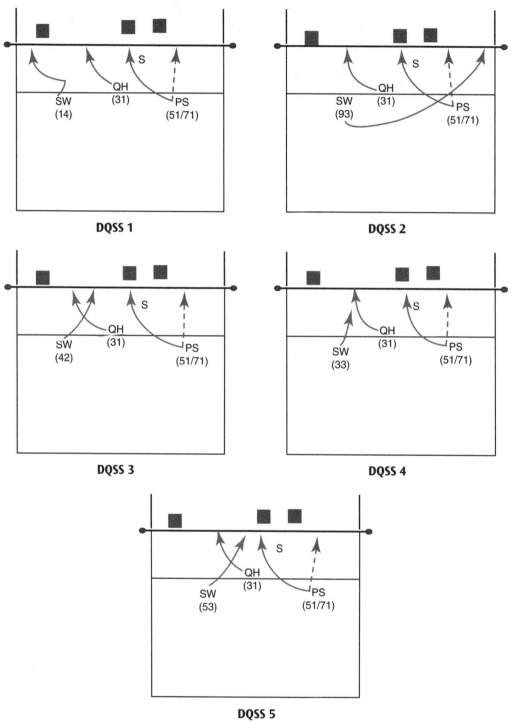

DQSS 1

DQSS 2

DQSS 3

DQSS 4

DQSS 5

Double Quick Swing Series (Setter Back Row) Notes

Tactical goal	Pattern	Tactical goal	Play	Tactical goal
To isolate either outside blockers; to split rb and mb with simultaneous quicks	14-31-51/71	Open up quick 1 on 1; isolate SW on weakest blocker; this pattern and next one are main options with others to mix it up	14	Line off fooled blocker
			31	Either angle, but best to positon 5
			51/71	Either angle, but best to positon 5
	93-31-51/71	Disappear-reappear behind quicks; same as above, good swing movement important	93	Line off fooled blocker
			31	Either angle
			51/71	Best angle to position 1
	42-31-51/71	Best used after above has been established; then come inside	42	Straight to position 5
			31	Hit to corner in position 5
			51/71	Best to go to 71; opens up 42 hit
	33-31-51/71	Intended to overload blocker taking 31; great play if they are a slow blocker	33	Either angle
			31	Either angle
			51/71	Either angle
	53-31-51	Same except focus is on blocker going after 51	53	Either angle
			31	Either angle
			51/71	Either angle

Back-Row (BSW) Swing Series

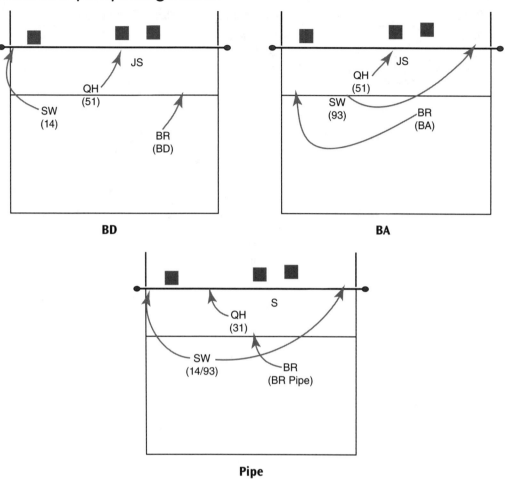

BD

BA

Pipe

Back-Row Swing Series (Setter at the Net) Notes

Tactical goal	Pattern	Tactical goal	Play	Tactical goal
Threatens with 4 attackers (QH, SW, BR, setter); spread blockers forcing them to move inside to outside; open up seams inside and forces block to reach or fade outside	14-51-JS BD	It is critical to success for SW to go inside before swinging back out to hit 14; rb must follow inside and then choose; BR goes B or opposite of SW; having all the attackers moving is the key	14	Line or different angle if rb fades
			51	Either angle
			JS	Dump behind block; lefty hit position 5
			BD	Line to position 5 corner or deep position 1 angle
	93-51-JS BA	Fake is to 14 then swing right to 93; goal is to force blocker inside then chase SW outside; lb/rb pull away from mb opening up quick; best option is to get blocker to chase SW hitters outside opening middle	93	Line or angle if block fades
			51	Either angle
			JS	Dump behind block; lefty hit position 1
			BA	Line position 1 corner
	14/93-31-JS Pipe	Swing hitter going wide to either side will occupy mb and open up middle for BR	14/93	Line or angle if block fades
			31	Either angle
			JS	Dump straight over
			B Pipe	Position 1 or 5

CONCLUSION

Offenses can be very complex or very simple and anything in between. It is up to the coach to determine what the team's personnel can effectively execute and what is needed to be successful at their level. As indicated earlier offensive systems are not art forms but rather tools to give a team the best chance to win.

CHAPTER

19

Serving Strategically

Shelton Collier

Perhaps the best thing a coach can do to increase a team's ability to score 25 points and ultimately win matches is to develop a strong tactical serving team. The serve is the most immediate and direct way to score a point as well as a great way to put the opponent at a disadvantage. Very significant is the fact that a team with less experience, less height, less athletic ability, and yes, even less experienced coaching can be competitive in a game in which they seem to be overmatched. This is possible with a successfully implemented tactical serving plan. In the case of evenly matched teams, serving is often a key factor in determining the winner.

Developing an excellent serving team occurs in three phases: (1) formulating a serving philosophy that is clearly understood by every coach and player in the program; (2) creating practice drills and practice environments in which players can rehearse the application of the serving philosophy; and (3) teaching the team how to gain an advantage by executing tactical serves.

FORMULATING A SERVING PHILOSOPHY

Formulating a serving philosophy is an essential first step in creating a great serving team. It should be a philosophy the players can understand and apply in both practices and matches.

What rules will you have with regard to not missing a serve? Will you have a conservative approach or an aggressive approach? Will you be signaling zones from the bench areas where to serve to, or will the players be on their own to choose a serving target? Will you allow some players to use higher-risk serves such as jump serves or serves from deeper behind the end line? Will the rules for these players be different? How will you enforce your philosophy in practices and matches?

A key concept to address in a sophisticated serving philosophy is that of a good miss and a bad miss. For example, missing a serve just long or slightly out of bounds on the sideline is preferred to serving it in the net. Why? Because the passers may attempt to pass a serve that is over the net and out of bounds past the end line, and such a serve will certainly create some indecision and pressure on the opponents. A serve in the net does none of this. Therefore, a good miss must be openly accepted, and a bad miss should draw some criticism.

Some coaches consider a 1:1 ratio of aces to errors to be a reasonable goal. Recently, however, more coaches have evolved to accepting a higher error ratio because more difficult serves are necessary to put the receiving team at an immediate disadvantage and to get them out of system (i.e., unable to run a good team offense). The scoring rate per serve (e.g., 40 to 50 percent) seems to be a better reflection of a server's impact than an ace-to-error ratio.

COMMUNICATING YOUR PHILOSOPHY

One of the most common errors or limiting factors when developing a serving team is giving players a mixed message. In the pregame pep talk, the coach may indicate that "serving tough" and "serving aggressive" are crucial in the match. Then, when players miss serves, the coach may react negatively with facial expressions, body posture, or verbally. In the postgame meeting, the coach may then indicate that a reason for the loss was missing too many serves. Then, in the match the following week, players on the court and from the bench are saying, "Just get it in" as the servers prepare to serve, because they do not want to be the reason for negative feedback from the coach. Coaches must understand that mixed messages keep teams from developing into top-notch serving units.

Another problem is the mixed message sent by a coach who stresses the importance of getting every serve in the court. This coach has a conservative serving philosophy. After a loss, this coach might say, "They outserved us" or "They got more aces than we did—that was the difference." A coach with this philosophy must communicate to the players that they should improve their passing, blocking, or defense to win. This is because the serving philosophy stresses keeping the ball in play; this team is not about outserving the opponent. It is doubtful that the coaches' desired response from the postgame talk is for the players to attempt to serve more aces in the next game, thus risking the inevitable result of more missed serves. Consistency in applying and reinforcing a serving philosophy is critical.

Determining Players' Abilities

Can all or some of your players control their serves well enough to be an asset in carrying out a game plan? Do certain players have difficulty with some serves, and should those serves not be used even if a game situation lends itself to them? Suppose the opponent's weak passer is in the left-back position, but your server is not comfortable serving down the line. In some cases, allowing a player to serve her best serve anywhere on her own will result in more points per serve than if you directed her to serve a specific zone each time. Evaluation and analysis are needed to make these determinations.

Scouting Report

Scouting reports can range from a detailed video analysis of previous matches to watching a team play once and taking notes to walking by a court on which the team is playing and making a mental note or two. All versions provide some information to work with.

One of the best ways to raise the confidence level of your team is to provide some information about an upcoming opponent's weaknesses. Some teams have an assistant coach or manager keep a rotation-by-rotation chart of the opponent and monitor the types of serves that are effective and which players are passing poorly in each rotation. Some coaches can notice specific players having difficulty passing or structural weaknesses in certain formations. That can be taken advantage of as well.

A common method of tactical serving is for the coach to signal the zone in which she wants the ball served. Figure 19.1 indicates the serving zones.

The coach simply holds up the number of fingers (often hidden behind a clipboard) that corresponds to the appropriate zone. A fist is used to designate zone 6, the serve directly down the middle. An advanced method is to flash two zones to indicate a ball served in the seam between the two zones signaled. For example, flashing three fingers and then four fingers indicates that the player should serve a short ball directly between the opponent's left front (zone 4) and middle front (zone 3).

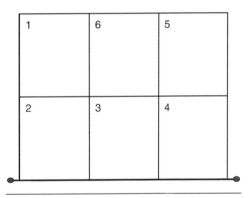

FIGURE 19.1   Serving zones.

HANDLING CRITICISM

When using an aggressive serving plan, one of the most difficult issues is the reactions of fans and parents following a serving error. A coach can dedicate weeks to developing a tough serving team in practice and invest a large percentage of practice time to serving each day. Then, as the team is executing the plan in a critical match and upsetting a longtime rival, some parents are yelling "Just get it in" before every serve or some football players in attendance are yelling "No more missed serves." After the match, these people may approach the coach and say, "Coach, you really need to work at not missing so many serves."

It is extremely important to educate fans and parents about the risk–reward continuum of an excellent serving team. This helps them understand the importance of accepting a certain error ratio and keeps them from intruding on the team's focus as players perform challenging serves. Players can help by explaining the serving philosophy to their parents and friends. A helpful analogy is that a good tennis player will never beat another good tennis player simply by serving easy in the court every time. With such an explanation, the crowd may be more supportive of your teams' point-scoring effort, and your players will feel more at ease about serving aggressively for points.

CREATING PRACTICE DRILLS

Once a philosophy has been established and communicated, it is time to create practice drills to teach and reinforce the appropriate serving behaviors. Obviously, it is important to first deal with technique. Without question, the main reason for service errors and inaccuracy is a poor toss. As you initially evaluate your players' serving abilities, emphasize the importance of a consistent and efficient toss or placement of the ball. Coaches often chastise a player for missing a serve when a simple adjustment of the toss would solve the problem. Tossing the ball directly in front of and in line with the serving shoulder is key, as is having the height at an ideal location for consistent contact. "Step to target" and "palm to target" are good reminders.

The degree to which you implement and enforce your serving philosophy in practice will directly correlate to your team's ability to follow through with it in matches. Don't expect your team to serve great under pressure or pick apart an opponent's weaknesses if the extent of their serving in practice is standing on either end line and serve back and forth for 5 to 10 minutes.

When designing drills for any skill or situation, creativity is important. Clarify the outcome you desire, score what you value, and create a drill to enhance the likelihood of this happening. Following are examples:

- **To develop the server's ability to hit specific areas with a serve:** Have creative contests (with winners and losers) in which players must serve to specific zones or targets.

- **To develop the ability to serve under pressure:** Create pressure! Have players who miss serves do sprints or push-ups. Instruct the whole team to watch or make noise when a player is serving. Mandate that servers get a certain number of serves in the court in a row without a miss to avoid consequences.

- **To develop tougher serves in games:** In a scrimmage, award two points instead of one point for an ace.

- **To develop consistency in serving:** Give the opponent a side-out plus a bonus point if a serve is missed.

- **To help players get a feel for their limits**: Have players serve at 60 percent, then 80 percent, then 100 percent so they begin to sense the percentage at which they are most effective.
- **To enforce your serving rules**: Take a point away from a team that breaks a serving rule in a scrimmage in practice.

There are endless creative ideas that can enhance a player's ability to serve. As with any skill, the return that you see in matches corresponds to the specificity of effort devoted in practice.

SERVING STRATEGIES

Coaches should have extensive lists of serving strategies to help their teams win. Developing a group of players who can control the accuracy of their serves is obviously step one, but the critical second step is identifying weaknesses in the opponent's reception patterns that can be exploited. Following are several tactical possibilities.

Directing a serve to an area near the player you believe is the weakest passer. This is an excellent strategy and can serve the dual purpose of putting the opponent at a disadvantage while creating confidence in your team. The key, however, is to make the weak passer move and pass a tough serve, rather than merely serving an easy ball to this player.

Serving tough to primary hitters who are exposed in the passing formation. Front-row attackers are becoming increasingly responsible for more area as serve receivers. The primary hitter has a harder time passing a tough serve than approaching to attack. Serves directed at this passer can be short, deep, directly at the passer, or to the side opposite the direction in which the passer intends to approach.

Serving short around the middle hitter who is preparing to hit a quick set or slide attack. This is an extremely effective serve because it can take that middle hitter out of his offensive rhythm or causes confusion among the primary passers.

Serving down the line. This is one of the most difficult serves to pass accurately to the setter position.

Serving to the right-front position (zone 2). This forces the setter to receive the ball over her shoulder as opposed to straight on, limiting her ability to get set up and survey the offensive options.

The short–deep combination. A server with a good one-two punch is extremely valuable. This is a "take what they give you" strategy. If the receivers are deep, a short serve can cause great difficulty. When the passers adjust and move in closer to guard against the short serve, a deep serve is then even more effective.

Serving to force passers to receive the ball on their right side. Volleyball serve reception is traditionally left to right in orientation. Passers generally pass much better from the left side than from the right side.

Immediately serving again to a player who has just been aced. After being aced, a player's confidence is reduced, and a server's confidence is boosted. This favors the server in a major way and should be immediately taken advantage of. This should be enforced in practice as well for two important reasons. First, servers need to rehearse this important strategy, and second, passers who have just been aced need to be aware that well-coached teams will go right back after them. They must learn how to respond with good passes.

Look for the cover-up. A particularly good passer may adjust his court position to cover up for a passer who is struggling. Sometimes, the good passer will stray too far from his own court responsibility and leave an area vulnerable or unprotected.

Serving in a Critical Fifth-Set Situation

In the fifth set, it is critical that the team understand the coach's philosophy. Is it the same as in a normal game? Is it considerably more conservative because a missed serve seems to carry more weight in the shortened game? Whatever strategy you choose, it is crucial that your players understand it and embrace it. This will provide the confidence they need to serve and play well. Because players are more nervous in a fifth set to begin with, any uncertainty about their serving strategy and assignment will compound their anxiety.

I suggest against the "just get it in" approach in a fifth set. There is no better way to break open a final game than to run a string of unanswered points. This can create tremendous momentum and allow a team to build what could be an insurmountable lead. A well-coached, disciplined group of servers can have a tremendous advantage in a fifth-set situation.

Serving Recipes

Developing a serving recipe is similar to, and as important as, developing a recipe for a meal. First, you must assess exactly what ingredients you have to work with; then organize them for the best results. Competing coaches, like cooks, can have similar ingredients to work with, but making the best use of the ingredients yields the better product.

After assessing the abilities of your starting six servers, you can begin to plan accordingly. Following are some serving recipes:

- ◆ Three tactical zone servers (to be given signals by the coach) and three players serving their most comfortable serves

- Two players serving from deep behind the end line, two players serving the short–deep combination, and two players serving a standard low, hard, flat serve
- Three players serving conservatively to get all serves in, two players serving to areas signaled by the coach, and one player using a high-risk jump serve
- Six players serving to areas signaled in by the coach on every serve

Obviously, many combinations are possible. The key is to determine the strengths, weaknesses, and abilities of your players. After your players have done some strategic serving, consider distributing a questionnaire in which they rate their favorite serves and list any serves they felt particularly uncomfortable using. Ideally, a high-level server will be able to serve several influential serves that can affect point scoring and pressure opponents. You may want to have each server have one signature serve that he masters, practices every day, and feels a special pride in executing. This will give your servers ownership of specific serves and increase their confidence when they are serving under pressure in matches.

SERVING RULES

At critical times in a match, it is important not to miss a serve. Serving rules must be clearly communicated and enforced in matches as well as in practice. Following are some times when it is important to get the serve in:

After the teammate who served before you misses. This is important because you don't want to throw away two consecutive opportunities to score on your opponent.

After the opponent has just missed a serve. Following an opponent miss, the momentum shifts to your team. Perhaps their coach, their team, and their fans are a little uneasy at this point. The worst thing you can do is immediately return the favor.

After an opponent time-out. You have forced the opponent into a stressful time-out situation. You likely have the momentum in the game. To maintain the momentum, force the opponent under pressure to play the ball as opposed to being let off the hook with a missed serve.

At the beginning of a set. All players are keyed up at the beginning of a set. Missing the first serve can be extremely deflating to the serving team and allow the receiving team to get off to a fast start.

After the opponents have scored several points in succession. It is important not to miss at this point because your serve-receive unit has just struggled and finally earned the right to serve. You need to give your point-scoring unit an opportunity to break the opponent's string of points.

After your team wins a long, inspired rally. It is often said that after winning a long rally with a lot of great defensive plays, a team has earned not only that particular point, but several more immediately following because of the momentum factor. It is important not to lose this opportunity for an inspired string of points with a missed serve.

CONCLUSION

Volleyball is a complex, multiskilled game. Developing proficiency in all skills in all players is at times an insurmountable challenge. However, it is quite possible to develop a high-level serving team with a commitment of time and focus. An excellent serving team may be able to score 25 points against an opponent even if overmatched in every other skill area. There is a difference between coaching a team to simply play volleyball and coaching a team to win points. Investing time in serving and developing a sophisticated serving strategy can be a key element in helping your team win matches.

20

On-Court Decision Making

Jennifer Petrie

On-court decision making—exactly what does that mean? As coaches, we know how arduous it can be to address every detail before every match. It starts with the details that only a coach can control, such as the starting lineup, time-outs, substitutions, and matchups with the rotation order. Some of those decisions are made prematch, and others are game-time changes. During game time our focus is on time-outs, rotational matchups, substitutions, and midgame strategic adjustments. Those adjustments could be as minor as implementing the back-row attack or as major as changing the offensive or defensive system. The team should be prepared to make adjustments in serve-receive patterns and defensive base positioning, and possibly switches in blocking assignments.

Although table 20.1 does not cover every situation that may occur in a volleyball match, it should give you a start in thinking about decisions you may need to make quickly during a match. Spend some time thinking through game scenarios and come up with decisions, patterns, and players you will use to make adjustments. Making changes is much easier when you have them in your notebook ready to refer to when your team needs help to win the next point.

TIME-OUTS

Aside from venting frustration for losing or for the team's lack of focus, the information disseminated during a time-out should be the same regardless of whether the team is winning or losing. The strategic information must continue to be communicated. The team should always be clear on the game plan, and they need to feel the trust and belief of the coaching staff. One of the important decisions during a match is when to call a time-out. Should it be used early in a game to spark change, or saved until the end of a set to focus on crucial point-scoring opportunities?

Use the flow of the game to determine when to call a time-out. You can identify both lethargy and focus in your team by the level of communication on the court. Communication breeds confidence, and the more constructive information that is shared between the players on the court, the better their performance will be. In

TABLE 20.1 Possible On-Court Decisions

On-court adjustment	Purpose
Time-out	• Relay a strategic change in offensive or defensive system. • Interrupt the momentum of the opponent. • Refocus as a team; increase intensity. • Disrupt the rhythm of a strong opposing server.
Substitutions	• Address poor performance. • Create a better matchup. • Review the game plan. • Rest players when you are ahead. • Give experience to young players who may need game time at the end of the season. • Out of time-outs. • Routine substitution such as a defensive specialist for a front-row hitter.
Matchup or rotation order change	• Create a better matchup between your offense and their defense, or vice versa. • Start in a rotation with your best point-scoring attacker in left front during a fifth set. • Start a set in the rotation in which you successfully finished the last game.
Serve-receive pattern change	• Address poor individual passing performance. • Stack or spread your offense for better production. • Allow your libero to make more first contacts.
Offensive system change	• Use audible play calls versus set offensive plays. • Focus on the hot hitter. • Use the back-row attack.
Defensive system change	• Change to rotation defense. • Create a perimeter defense. • Counter the rotation defense. • Change the base positioning. • Change block matchups.

the best-case scenario, your team came ready to play and a motivational time-out is not needed early on. You may need an early time-out, however, if the game plan in place does not match the opponent's current strategy.

Time-outs can be used strategically toward the end of a well-played set when you need to slow down the opponent, change defensive positioning, or run a particular offensive play. The team needs to know exactly what rotation the opponent is in and the corresponding defensive response. Setters need to know where the offense has been successful and what may be open as a late-game option.

Who speaks during the time-out depends greatly on the reason for calling it. If the team is not performing well because of a lack of effort, concentration, or chemistry, then the leaders of the team should have an opportunity to encourage, demand, and inspire their teammates. Most of the information relayed during a time-out should relate to game-time adjustments—what is working for the team and what changes need to be made.

Certainly, a time-out can help to change the momentum of a game. A coach deserves a pat on the back when the opponents miss a serve after a time-out. Sometimes, a team just needs a chance to refocus and concentrate on the game plan. Other times, a time-out can be used to increase the intensity on the court and encourage maximal defensive effort. Perhaps coverage is the focus, giving multiple opportunities to attack. Patience is a big key during a match, and in particular during a long rally. A time-out should allow a team to respond as a unit, putting into action the new game plan, an increased intensity, and the determination to win the match.

SUBSTITUTIONS

Important game-time decision making most certainly includes substitutions. The question, ultimately, is whether a player on the bench will positively affect the outcome of the match if given the opportunity to perform. The reasons for the change can be poor performance by a starter, different player-for-player matchups, or the development of backup players on the bench.

I am not known for substituting much during a match, perhaps to a fault. Over the course of a week in practice I gain trust in a lineup, its chemistry, and the production of players. Playing time is earned outside of competition. However, every coach has a limit to the depths of a slump. Plenty of players on the bench deserve an opportunity to make a change in the game. I believe that not making quick substitutions allows players to relax and play without the stress of being taken out. Psychologically, I want confident players who know that their coaches believe in them. When a substitution is made, the player must understand that her teammate is there to help win the match.

MATCHUPS AND ROTATION ORDER

The best matchup scenario depends greatly on the opponent. Do they have a weakness in their block, a short setter, or a slow-closing middle? Perhaps they have an all-American outside or a middle who runs only slides. Determine the matchup based on how you think you can beat your opponent, or better yet, on how you think they might beat you.

On our team, if the opponent has one player who we believe merits our primary focus, we try to match our best blocker against that player. When our offense is strong, their blockers are less important than running our plays well. At times we want to attack certain zones on the court depending on where their blockers line up or what type of blocking system they are running. If they are pinched in for their blocking base, we run our offense wide to the pins. Often, you can hold a blocker in the middle by running one attacker as a decoy right at her, and then set over her. If the opposing team is spread in its blocking base, the middle of the court is freed up to run quick attack or combination sets.

Matchups can change as the game progresses. Keep your eye on the opposing team's most current point scorer and the plays it is running most often in each rotation. Both the player and the system will help you determine your best blocking matchup.

ROTATION ORDER CHANGES BETWEEN SETS

At times, the matchup of blockers versus attackers will dictate whether to rotate your lineup between sets. For us, most of the time, our comfort level starting in a particular rotation is the most important factor. The starting rotation in the fifth set is a crucial decision. Some coaches like to have their biggest point scorer start in the left front to get the team off to a fast start. Again, the option of lining up your strongest defense against their best attacker is a consideration going into the final set. Either way, a pattern is established during the flow of the match, and you need to identify where your team is strongest in the rotation order.

To determine your strongest rotation, keep track of the points your team scores and the points scored against you in each rotation. Those statistics will not only help you during the match, but also give you a focus in practice. It is good to know which rotations need extra work in practice; on the other hand, perhaps new offensive patterns are needed for players to be more effective in siding out.

SERVE-RECEIVE PATTERN CHANGES

The libero plays a very important role in the smooth function of the team's serve receive. Hopefully, the team trusts the libero to shift the serve receive based on what is best in the current situation. There are several reasons to change a serve-receive pattern. The first is the most obvious: one passer is out of sync and the opponent has broken her down. Short of a time-out, it works well to drop that passer out or push her up toward the net depending on whether she is in the front or back row. Because passing is all about the player's current confidence level, in practice passers should get used to stepping in and out of serve receive when a weakness has been exposed.

The second reason for changing a serve-receive pattern is to stack the offense on the right or left side of the court for a better attack. The block may be weaker on the left than on the right, and flexibility is important in positioning your attackers for the best offense. Another reason to make a change in the serve-receive pattern is to give the opposing server something to think about and hopefully disrupt her serving routine.

On most teams, the libero is the strongest passer on the squad. This player should be allowed to position herself to receive the highest number of serves. If the opponent is consistently serving to a certain area of the court, the libero should pinch a passer toward the sideline to take more area. The libero needs to be extremely vocal and confident in serve reception.

Whatever terminology you choose as a coach, your team needs to know exactly what you are requesting in an instant. At any point you should be able to tell the passers to push up, push out, pinch, stack, or spread, thus changing the look of your serve-receive pattern.

OFFENSIVE SYSTEMS

Some teams are extremely predictable in their offensive patterns. At times, those teams have had great success. An effective, yet limited, offensive system allows teams to perfect the plays that they run. The key to a limited offense is making sure to set each of the players in the system somewhat equally. If your pattern is a hut-1-5, but you set only the hut, then the opponent will begin to release their middle on your outside hitter. But if your setter can diversify the offense by reversing the flow of the pass, setting pin to pin, or jump setting to hold a blocker, then a simple offensive system can be very successful.

With a veteran team, a more varied offensive system can be difficult to defend against. If you have a team with good ball control that remains in system most of the time, then diversifying the offense is easier. When running many patterns and plays, the hitters must know when to call out of a pattern by simply running a release set (i.e., a safe set). In addition, the setter must always have a release set in the back of her mind. No matter how advanced or complicated the pattern is, the setter should know that, when in trouble, a set option is always available.

Setting the Hot Hitter

Any attacker on your team can be the hot hitter as opposed to a go-to player who has established herself over time by consistently putting balls away at crucial points in the game. During a time-out, you can privately relay to the setter the attack percentages over the last several points. If the setter does not already know who the point scorer is at a particular time, this information will guide her in her on-court decision making. Our setter will go to a hot hitter during a match, setting her several times over a course of points as long as she continues her streak of scoring. When a team needs a side-out or to score the last point in a tight match, in most cases the go-to hitter is used.

Using the Back-Row Attack

The back-row attack should always be a set play or option in your offensive system. The setter should provide the call to the back-row attacker in serve-receive, but it should be an audible call from the back-row players in transition. It is very important that the passers pay attention to the pattern being run, so they do not step into the approach lane of the back-row attacker.

When the pass is pushed to the left side of the court, and the opponent's blockers are releasing to the outside hitter, this is a good time to drop off the pipe (set to middle back) behind the setter. This option is important to hold the blockers when the passing is not accurate.

In transition, the back row should consistently call for the set and be available for the attack. When the setter is front row, she needs to be able to hear the audible call from her middle and use the appropriate back-row player in conjunction. For example, if the middle hitter is running a slide, then the pipe hitter would be an option. If the middle hitter is running in front of the setter, then the D (right back) hitter is an option.

DEFENSIVE SYSTEMS

There are many defensive systems, and it can be advantageous to use a couple of them during a match. The basic systems are rotation, counterrotation, and perimeter.

Rotation Defense

To use the rotation defensive system, release your right-back defender up for tips and deflections and pull your off blocker to the 10-foot line to defend sharp cross while the left back digs the hard angle; the middle back plays high seam to the line (see figure 20.1). This defense works best for teams that tip a lot from their outside attacker. It allows the setter to be quick to the net in transition, and she can start her base defense up for the dump.

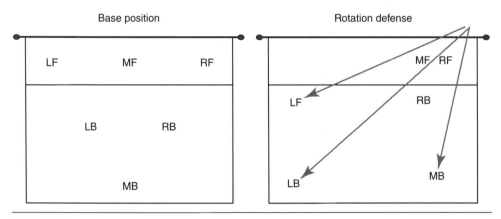

FIGURE 20.1   Base position and rotation defense versus a left-side attack.

Counter Rotation Defense

With the counter rotation defensive system, instead of releasing the right-back defender for tips and deflections, your team rotates in the other direction placing

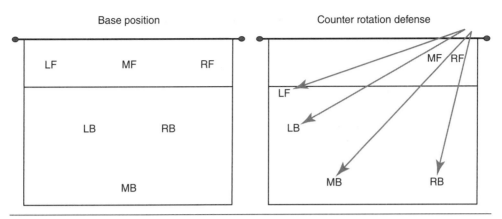

FIGURE 20.2   Base position and counter rotation defense versus a left-side attack.

the off blocker into the court and making her responsible for all tips and deflections (see figure 20.2). The right-back defender plays deep on the line, while the left back has all attacks in the angle and the middle back has high seam through the block. If your team has a strong block, then you will force the opponent into tips and deflections from hard-driven shots. Counter rotation allows your outside hitter, with good ball control, to make the first contact allowing your setter to run the offense on the second contact. Counter rotation, in opposition to rotation, frees up the setter to run the offense if the ball is tipped.

Perimeter Defense

The perimeter defense system positions all of your defenders on their respective lines (perimeter of the court) for the attack. When playing against a team that does not hit shots or tip well, it is best to defend deeper in the court (see figure 20.3). If your team is good at reacting to the ball and to the deflection, then a perimeter defense may serve you well.

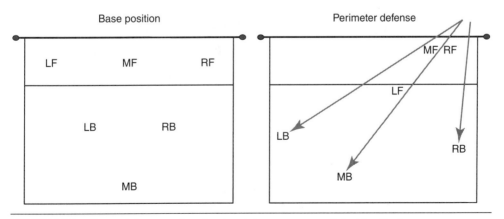

FIGURE 20.3   Base defense and perimeter defense versus a left-side attack.

In addition to defensive systems, the base positioning of the defenders in a match will vary with the given opponent. If the opponent's setter attacks the second ball often, then you may want to designate a defender to start her base in that attack zone. When the opponent has three attackers in the front row, with a back-row setter, the base defense can be deeper for the entire defense. Where the ball is passed along the net will also dictate the position of the base defense. If the pass is pushed closer to the defender, then her base will move with the pass. These decisions made by the defense must become instinctual.

AUDIBLE VERSUS SET PLAYS AND FREE-BALL PLAYS

Determining what type of offense to run depends heavily on the experience of the setter. With an experienced setter, the offense can run audibly, meaning that the hitters can call their attacks when the ball crosses to their side of the net. If the setter is comfortable making quick decisions during a rally, then it is possible to run audibles. If the setter is unfamiliar with the team or the offense, she may want to have a set play in place during the rally. Consistency in the offense makes it much easier for a setter to make the best decisions during the rally. It is possible to start a match with an audible offense, and then finish with only set plays. As a coaching staff, if you like the predictability of a set offense, knowing who and where the ball will be set, then a set offense at the end of the match is a good choice. In an audible offense, the setter's on-court decision making is crucial. She needs to be able to read and process the defense during the rally to best isolate her hitters.

Establish set patterns in serve receive and play short scoring games in practice so that those patterns are run during crucial points in the game. Be sure that either the setter is organizing in-system plays or the players are comfortable running audible plays. It is very important for hitters to identify out-of-system passes quickly, and to know what sets to run in a release situation. You don't want to eliminate attackers because the pass is not accurate.

ON-COURT DECISIONS MADE BY THE COACHING STAFF

Each coaching staff functions in its own unique way. The information gathered and disseminated is determined by the head coach. A large staff can divide the game into sections. For example, one coach can focus solely on the opponent's offense to create valuable strategic changes for your defense. Another coach could concentrate on the patterns your own setter is running. This information is crucial so that the setter knows which player is scoring well and out of which zone the offense is strongest. If your staff is limited, it can be very difficult to focus on what is most important at a particular moment.

CONCLUSION

Remember that the role of the coach is to keep the team unified in its strategy, be it offensive system, defensive system, or blocking schemes. A successful team plays under control and with confidence. Limit the confusion by communicating all systems prior to the match, during time-outs, between sets and then again after the match. The best decisions and adjustments come to light after the match has concluded. There is a lot to be learned by examining those decisions together as a staff and then sharing them with the team.

About the AVCA

The **American Volleyball Coaches Association (AVCA)** is dedicated to the advancement of the sport of volleyball with AVCA coaches at the epicenter of leadership, advocacy, and professional development. With a membership of over 6,400 and counting, the AVCA provides a professional network for those individuals and companies dedicated to enhancing and promoting the sport. Members include collegiate, high school, club, youth, and Olympic coaches as well as volleyball club directors. The AVCA provides education to volleyball coaches, recognition of elite players and coaches, promotion of volleyball competitions throughout the world, and networking opportunities for volleyball products and service providers.

About the Editor

Cecile Reynaud, PhD was the head coach of the Florida State University (FSU) volleyball team from 1976 until her retirement from coaching in 2001, compiling an impressive 635 wins in her 26 years at the helm. After her coaching career, Reynaud was a research associate professor at Florida State University, where she taught both graduate and undergraduate classes in the sport management department.

During her illustrious coaching career, she won seven conference championships and was twice named Atlantic Coast Conference Coach of the Year (1992, 2000). She was inducted into the FSU Athletic Hall of Fame (2009) and the USA Volleyball Florida Region Hall of Fame (2011). She is a member of the USA Volleyball Board of Directors and the AVCA Board of Directors. Reynaud is also a USA Volleyball CAP clinician. Reynaud has served as color analyst for collegiate volleyball matches on various networks. She earned her doctorate degree in athletic administration from FSU in 1998. She is a 1975 graduate of Southwest Missouri State University (SMSU), where she enjoyed an exceptional volleyball career and was twice named among the Outstanding College Athletes in America. In 1983, she was inducted into the SMSU Women's Athletics Hall of Fame. She has filmed numerous volleyball DVD's for Coaches Choice and published several books with Human Kinetics: *The Volleyball Coaching Bible, Vol. I, She Can Coach!*, and *Coaching Volleyball: Techniques and Tactics.*

About the Contributors

Ben Bodipo-Memba enters his fourth season as assistant coach with the California volleyball team and his 19th season overall as an NCAA Division I coach. For seven seasons, Bodipo-Memba served on the Georgia Tech coaching staff as both assistant and associate head coach. During his time in Atlanta, Bodipo-Memba helped guide the Yellow Jackets to three NCAA Tournament appearances, two Atlantic Coast Conference regular season title wins, an ACC tournament championship, and two top-10 national hitting percentage rankings. In 2008, he was an assistant for the U.S. Women's National A2 team that captured gold at the U.S. Open Championship, and in 2005 he assisted the U.S. National Team joining head coach Jenny "Lang" Ping's staff for the Pan-American Cup and helped the team qualify for the 2006 World Grand Prix. Bodipo-Memba played at San Diego State and earned a silver medal at the 1990 U.S. Olympic Festival. Bodipo-Memba also played professionally in Finland for Raison Loimu in 1996 and has served as a mentor in the AVCA Coaches Mentoring program for the past four years. He spent six years representing the ACC on the AVCA Assistant Coaches Committee and is also a member of the AVCA Education and Publication Committee, representing all assistant volleyball coaches.

Chris Catanach has been the head coach for the University of Tampa volleyball team for 31 seasons. In that time, he has led his teams to 24 Sunshine State Conference titles, 29 NCAA appearances, 17 trips to the NCAA Elite Eight, four national runner-up finishes, and the 2006 and 2014 NCAA Division II national championships. He currently has a career record of 972-167, averaging 31.3 victories per season while ranking among the all-time leaders in both victories and winning percentage. Nationally, Catanach's .853 career winning percentage ranks third among the winningest active NCAA II coaches while his 972 total victories rank second among active NCAA II coaches.

Shelton Collier has a long history of proven success at the NCAA collegiate level as well as with the USA national team program. He has posted a career winning percentage of .788 with three universities in over a 30-year career. Collier started his head coaching career in 1981 at Pittsburgh, securing 296 wins in nine seasons. From there he was named assistant coach for the USA women's national team. He then accepted the head coaching position at Georgia Tech, building the team from scratch into a top 20 program. As the head coach at Wingate University, he was named 2013 NCAA Division II National Coach of the Year, and amassed over 400 wins and a .840 winning percentage. He is also active as a top coach in the USA High Performance program, and was the head coach of the USA youth and junior national teams from 2002 to present.

Danalee Bragado-Corso was hired by Florida State in 2012 to begin a premier collegiate sand volleyball program and has since produced seven All-American honorees, advanced to three consecutive AVCA National Championship Final Fours, and collected a 46-3 mark in regular season dual match competition. Corso is a graduate of Loyola Marymount University, Los Angeles, where she majored in business and played indoor volleyball from 1989-92. After graduating, she went straight to the women's pro-beach tour for one year prior to 13 seasons excelling in several professional double tours. In 1989, Corso played professional court volleyball in Paris for Racing Club de Villibeon. In 2004, Corso received a Brazilian Pro-Beach Coaching Accreditation and helped coach the United States National Beach Volleyball Team from 2004-07 with team members Rachel Wacholder and Tyra Turner. She has also coached 2008 Summer Games Olympian, Nicole Branagh, as well as top professionals Makare Wilson, Michelle More, and Suzanne Stonebarger. She won the 1995 Motherlode Open in Aspen. Corso and her family moved to Tallahassee after she spent 20 years in Los Angeles. Her husband, Brian Corso, has a master's degree in sports science and coaches with her as the assistant coach of the FSU sand volleyball team. They have two children, Camryn and Asher.

Dr. Gylton B. Da Matta is an adjunct professor of education, sports management, and sports pedagogy at Colorado State University. Currently collaborating with the USA Volleyball coaching education program, Dr. Da Matta owns a center for excellence in volleyball, YOSA, The Youth Sports Academy in Fort Collins, CO. In 2013, during the Men's U23 World Championship and in 2014, during the Senior Men's World Championship in Poland, Dr. Da Matta worked as a technical evaluator and as a member of the control committee. Since 1986 he has coached volleyball at all levels. In 2005, he earned the USA women's volleyball national championship title at the Open Division. Dr. Da Matta has several publications on skill development in volleyball, the impact of rule change in practice, and the role of technology and visual feedback in motor skills acquisition, as well as best practices across the spectrum of expertise. He has presented at dozens of volleyball clinics, camps, exchanges, and workshops across the United States and internationally.

Todd Dagenais enters his eighth season in 2015 as head coach of the UCF women's volleyball team. He has amassed a 127-95 record and has been named the American Athletic Conference Coach of the Year. In 2014, he led the Knights to an American Athletic Conference title and the program's first NCAA Division I Tournament appearance since 2003. Dagenais has coached five American Volleyball Coaches Association All-Americans and seven AVCA All-Region selections. He coached the U.S.  Women's Junior A2 programs in 2011 and 2012 and was the head coach of the 2007 USA White Selection National Team that won the silver medal at the USA Volleyball High Performance Championships. Dagenais has served as a member of the staff for the U.S. Women's National Team Open Tryout and was a part of the U.S. volleyball women's national team coaching delegation to the 2004 Olympic Games in Athens.

Randy Dagostino has always been an athlete. As a high school student, he competed in three different sports and played baseball at the collegiate level for the University of Illinois, Chicago. After college, Randy became a coach in Chicago for baseball, golf, and basketball. To escape the harsh winters, Randy moved to Florida and became the head girls' volleyball coach for Berkeley Preparatory School in Tampa. Since then, his girls'  volleyball teams have won 15 state championships and boasted a postseason record of 96-10 making 17 FHSAA Finals appearances. He won the Gatorade Coach of the Year honors 4 times, and his career coaching record of 829-161 helped him receive the Coach of the Year honors from the state of Florida seven times, an induction into the FHSAA Hall of Fame in 2008, and the main court in the Straz Family Field House was named in his honor. Randy started the first club volleyball program in 1984 and served as a member of the FHSAA's Volleyball Advisory Committee. Presently, he and his wife, Lauri, run large-scale volleyball tournaments up and down the East Coast of the United States. Not surprisingly, both of their children play collegiate volleyball, daughter Mackenzie, for the University of Florida and son, Kyle, for Stanford University.

It took ninth-year USC men's volleyball head coach **Bill Ferguson** just a short time to put the Trojans back on the volleyball map. He has a 140-96 career record at USC, with three trips to the NCAA Championships, two MPSF regular season crowns, and an MPSF tournament title. He has gone  11-6 against crosstown rival UCLA, has twice been named AVCA National Men's Coach of the Year in 2009 and 2012, and in 2011 was the MPSF Coach of the Year.

John Kessel has been playing or coaching volleyball for over half a century and is an AVCA Hall of Fame coach. As an FIVB International and USAV CAP instructor, he has taught coaches and players in over 50 nations and all 50 states in the United States. Starting in 1984, he has worked every Summer Olympics and Paralympics except one. In over 25 years with USA Volleyball he has directed the grassroots, beach, coaching education, Paralympic, and now sport development departments. Since 1995 he has also been involved in the Paralympic side of volleyball, currently serving as the World ParaVolley director of development. He also has been secretary of NORCECA's and the FIVB Technical, Coaches, and Development Commissions for over 25 years.

Wayne Kreklow, the 2013 Southeastern Conference Coach of the Year and 2013 Southeast Region Coach of the Year has built the Mizzou volleyball program into a national power over the past 15 years. Wayne and his wife, Susan (2000 Big 12 Coach of the Year), took over a historically downtrodden Mizzou program in 2000 and led the Tigers to eight consecutive NCAA Division I Tournament appearances and 11 total NCAA Tournament appearances in the past 15 seasons, advancing to the second round four times, the Sweet 16 in 2010, and Elite 8 in 2005. The 2013 season saw the Tigers finish 34-0, winning the school's first ever SEC Championship, and leading the nation in team hitting percentage, kills per set, assists per set, wins, and points per set. Kreklow has also been involved with the USA High Performance Programs, including being selected to serve as one of the head coaches for the 2012 A2 College National Team that competed in Columbus, Ohio. Prior to taking over the Mizzou program in 2000, Wayne and his wife, Susan, won two consecutive NAIA National Championships in 1998 and 1999, and they were also both named NAIA National Coach of the Year in 1998 and 1999.

The University of Texas Rio Grande Valley (UTRGV) department of intercollegiate athletics recently hired **Todd Lowery**, who won two national championships as the head coach of the University of Texas at Brownsville (UTB) volleyball team, as the new head coach of the UTRGV volleyball team. He holds a career record of 416-36 to go with four NAIA national championships. In 2014, Lowery led University of Texas at Brownsville to a 34-5 record and the No. 2 ranking in the nation after reaching the national championship match. His student-athletes have included 31 NAIA All-Americans, three NAIA National Players of the Year, six Region III MVPs, and six Red River Athletic Conference (RRAC) MVPs. Lowery has racked up the personal accolades as well, earning the 2006 NAIA National Coach of the Year award, two NAIA National Tournament Coach of the Year awards, six

RRAC Coach of the Year awards (2009-14), and one South Dakota Associate Press Coach of the Year award (2002). Lowery earned his master's degree in education administration in 2002 from Chadron State. He completed his bachelor's degree in physical education with minors in athletic coaching, chemistry, and health and wellness at Black Hills State in 2000.

Erin Mellinger finished her third season as head coach at Blinn College with an overall record of 106-11. The Buccaneers won back to back NJCAA Division I National Championships in 2013 and 2014, appeared in three Region 14 tournaments and won two consecutively. Mellinger was named the AVCA Two Year College National Coach of the Year in 2014. She was also named the NJCAA Division I District K Coach of the Year and AVCA Two Year College Southwest Region Coach of the Year two times. She has coached a NJCAA "Betty Jo Graber" Female Athlete of the Year and seven NJCAA/AVCA All-Americans. Prior to Blinn, Mellinger was an assistant coach at the College of Southern Idaho (2007-2011), where she helped guide the Golden Eagles to the 2009 national championship. Prior to her stint at CSI, Mellinger spent two seasons as head coach at Lewis-Clark State College (2005-2006), an NAIA Division I program. She was also the head coach at Independence (Kansas) Community College (2003-2004), where she led the NJCAA Division I/II program to a 62-21 record and was named NJCAA Division II District K coach of the year.

Jamie Morrison is entering his 10th season working with the USA men's and women's national teams. While serving as both a technical coordinator and assistant coach, Morrison helped lead the Men's Olympic Team to a gold medal at the 2008 Olympic Games, as well as helped the 2012 Women's Olympic Team to a silver medal at the 2012 games in London. Morrison has served as an assistant coach with the UC Irvine women's volleyball coach for the past two seasons, in addition to serving as director of training at Newport Beach, CA. based Prime Volleyball Club. Prior to UC Irvine, Morrison was part of the U.S. Men's staff as technical coordinator from 2005-2008 and assistant coach/technical coordinator for the U.S. Women from 2009-2012. In 2010-2011, Morrison was the head coach of SVS Post Volleyball Club in Vienna, Austria. The professional club, which had six Americans including 2012 Olympians Courtney Thompson and Tama Miyashiro, won the Austrian Championship and the silver medal in the Middle European League. Morrison spent one season as an assistant coach at the University of Southern California working with both the men's and women's volleyball programs immediately before his tenure with the U.S. Men's National Team. He assisted the Women of Troy to the semifinal round of the NCAA Division I Volleyball Championship in 2004.

Bill Neville is one of the most experienced and knowledgeable volleyball coaches in the world. He was the assistant coach for the 1984 USA Men's Olympic gold medal team and has served as an assistant coach or head coach for many other successful teams for USA Volleyball. He was the head coach at the University of Washington for ten years and now owns Nevillizms Volleyball Coaching Gym in Bellevue, Washington. He is also  the USA Volleyball National Commissioner for Coaching Education. In 2012, he was inducted into the AVCA Hall of Fame and was named a USA Volleyball All Time Great Coach. He has published various books and videos throughout his stellar career.

Jennifer Petrie has done an outstanding job directing the fortunes of San Diego volleyball since taking over as the Toreros head coach in 1999. Petrie has guided the Toreros to the NCAA Division I Tournament in 13 of her 15 years at the helm, including taking the team to the Sweet 16 in the 2004, 2006, and 2013 seasons. In 2013, Petrie helped lead USD to perhaps its best season in program history when USD defeated four top-25 teams. USD then shot up to No. 2 in the national polls, mark-  ing the highest ranking of any team at USD in the Division I era. USD went on to win the WCC championship for a second consecutive season, and reached the Sweet 16 in the NCAA Tournament. For her efforts in 2013, Petrie was selected as the AVCA Pacific South Region Coach of the Year. Petrie has led the Toreros to a total of seven WCC championships, and has produced 12 AVCA All-Americans, five WCC Players of the Year, three WCC Defenders of the Year, three WCC Freshman of the Year, and 34 All-WCC first-team selections. Coach Petrie has also been recognized as the WCC Coach of the Year four times.

Former Penn State All-American, **Salima Rockwell**, re-joined the Penn State sideline in 2014. Widely regarded as one of the nation's top assistant coaches, Rockwell returned to Penn State as an associate head coach for the Nittany Lions after spending five seasons at the University of Texas as an associate head coach. In her first season back, Rockwell helped guide the 2014 Nittany Lions to their seventh NCAA Division I national  championship title in program history and sixth in the last eight years. She also mentored 2014 AVCA National Player of the Year, Micha Hancock, and Penn State's starting setter and multi-year All-American, Alisha Glass. While with the Texas Longhorns, Rockwell helped guide Texas to three NCAA Division I national semifinal appearances, including a national championship in

2012. Rockwell was the recipient of the 2013 AVCA National Assistant Coach of the Year Award. During her collegiate career at Penn State, Rockwell was a three-time All-American from 1991-94, picking up four All-Big Ten honors, including three first team selections and Big Ten Player of the Year honors in 1993. She also earned back-to-back NCAA Tournament All-Tournament team honors at the 1993 and 1994 national finals. She played for the U.S. National team from 1995-99 and was an alternate for the Olympic Games in 1996. Rockwell and her husband, Jeff, have two sons, Logan and Rylan.

Becky Schmidt made her mark on Hope volleyball as a student-athlete and now is doing the same as a head coach. Schmidt guided the 2014 Flying Dutch to their first national championship with a 6-0 run during the NCAA Division III Tournament. Schmidt's 11-season Hope record is 302-73 (.805), which ranks her among the nation's elite. In November 2008, she was elected the NCAA Division III representative to the board of directors of the American Volleyball Coaches Association (AVCA) and has published articles in "Coaching Volleyball." She regularly presents at coaching and player clinics across the country. A 1999 Hope graduate and kinesiology major, Schmidt played middle blocker and ranked among the NCAA leaders in several statistical categories. She was voted the most valuable player in the Michigan Intercollegiate Athletic Association (MIAA) as both a junior and senior. As a senior, she became the first Hope volleyball player to receive NCAA Division III All-American honors. She was also awarded an NCAA postgraduate scholarship. After graduating from Hope, she was a graduate assistant volleyball coach at Miami University of Ohio while completing her master's degree in sport behavior and performance. Becky is married to David Fleece, the announcer at Hope volleyball matches for several years.

Charlie Sullivan will enter his 17th season as head coach of the men's volleyball team and assistant professor of physical education at Springfield College. In 16 previous years at the helm, Springfield has established a pedigree of championship success, producing eight national titles, including three-straight NCAA Division III Championships. One of the most recognizable names in men's volleyball, Sullivan was chosen to receive USA Volleyball's All-Time Great Coach award in the Donald S. Shondell Contemporary Division for 2015. In addition to his role as the men's volleyball coach at Springfield, Sullivan has also had several stints with the U.S. national team, including the summer of 2014, when he guided the U.S. men's Pan-American Team to the silver medal of the IX Men's Pan-American Cup.

Erik Sullivan just marked his fourth year on head coach Jerritt Elliott's Texas Volleyball staff. Sullivan joined the Texas staff after making two previous Big 12 coaching stops at Nebraska and Colorado. On the Forty Acres, Sullivan works with the Horns' liberos and outside hitters, while developing Texas' team defensive systems and scouting reports. Sullivan, a two-time U.S. Olympian, brings a wealth of playing experience into the Texas program, including eight years with the U.S. national team. He started for Team USA as a libero at the 2004 Summer Olympic Games and served as co-captain of Team USA at the 2000 Olympics in Sydney, Australia. Sullivan's playing experience has also stretched to the professional ranks in Europe, playing five seasons abroad. A two-time All-American at UCLA, Sullivan led the Bruins to a pair of national titles during his four-year playing career (1992-95). He graduated from UCLA with a bachelor's degree in physiological science in the spring of 1995.

Joe Trinsey was hired as the technical coordinator for the U.S. Women's National Volleyball Team in spring of 2013 and helped the program to a 25-6 record in his first season. Recently, he was part of the staff of the 2014 World Championship team that captured gold in Milan, Italy- the first Women's World Championship title in USA volleyball history. Trinsey is responsible for match video analysis and statistics for the squad and implements the data into training session plans and match-time decisions. Trinsey served as a coach with the Brandywine Volleyball Club in Wilmington, DE from 2009-2012 where he worked with athletes from 8-18 years old. His teams qualified for the Girl's Junior National Championship all three years. Trinsey also served as the second assistant coach during the 2013 FIVB Women's U23 World Championship Team that was led by Karch Kiraly and volunteer assistant coach with the Loyola Marymount University women's volleyball program in 2012.